Lapidary for Beginners

Lapidary for Beginners

The Complete Book of Pebble, Rock and Gem Polishing

Edward Fletcher

BLANDFORD PRESS
POOLE · DORSET

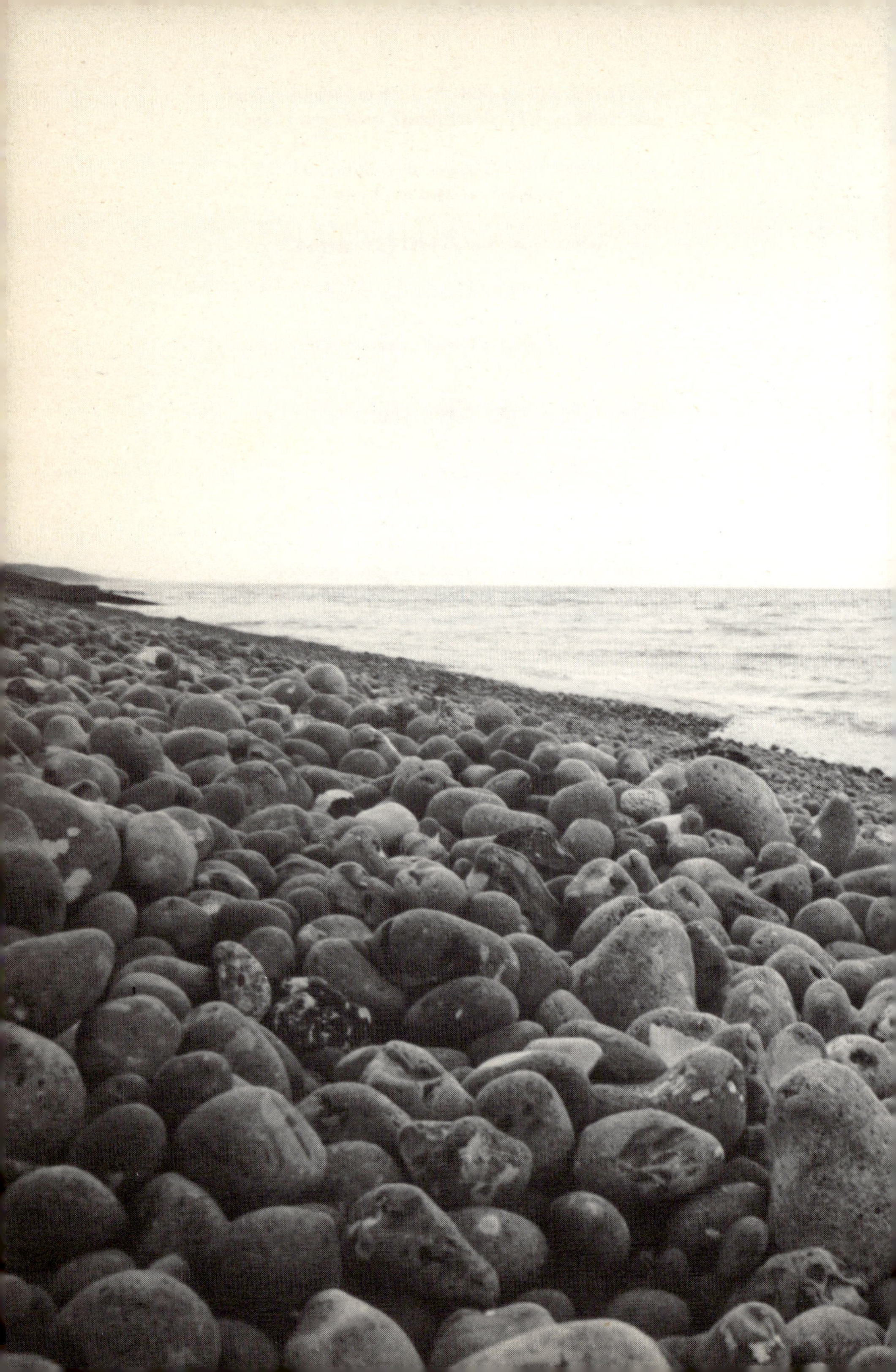

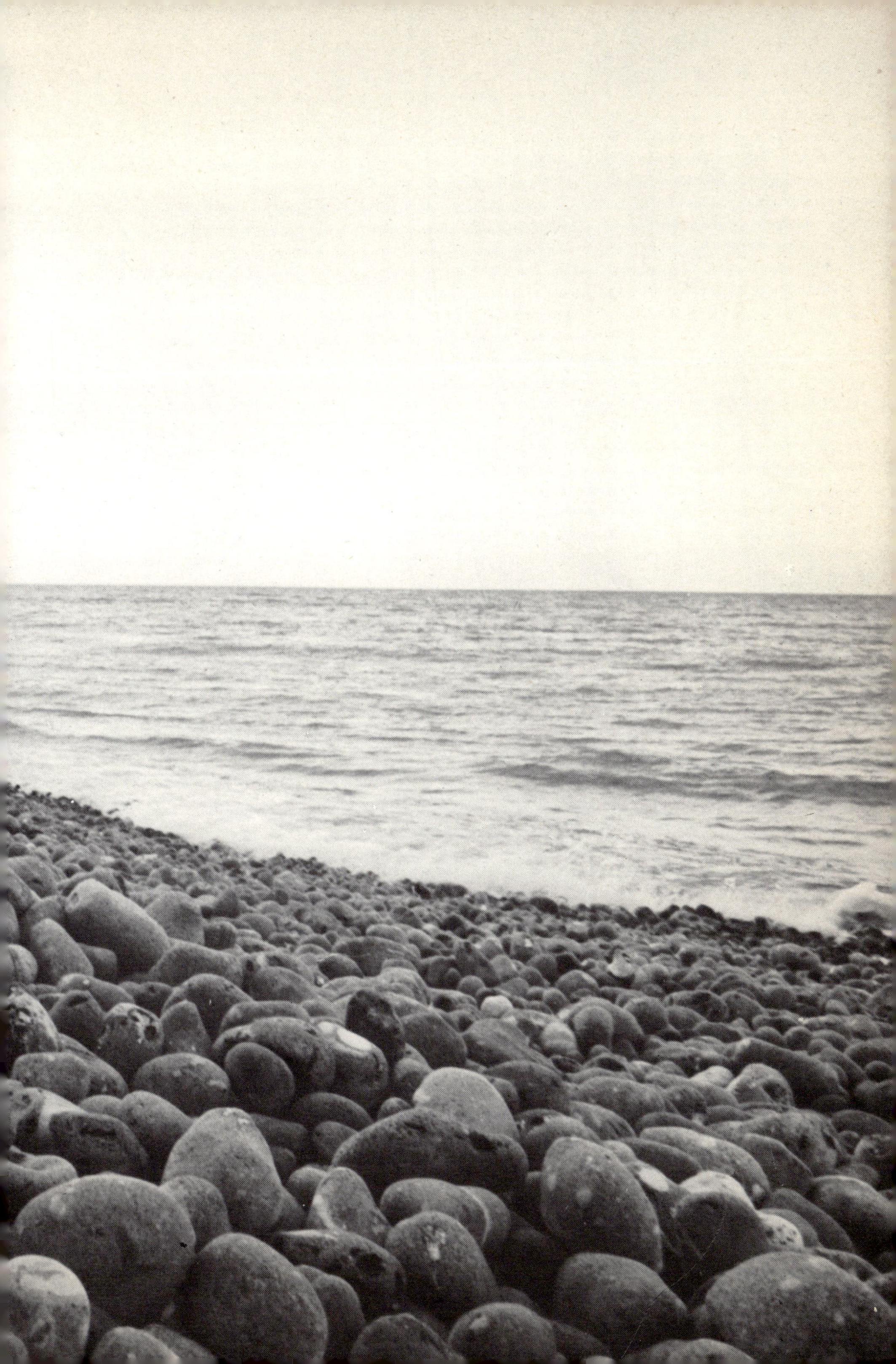

Pebble Polishing

A guide to collecting, tumble polishing and making baroque jewellery

Pebble Polishing

A guide to collecting, tumble polishing and making baroque jewellery

by
Edward Fletcher

Blandford Press
Poole   Dorset

First published 1972
© 1972 Blandford Press Ltd,
Link House, West Street,
Poole, Dorset BH15 1LL

Second impression 1972
Third impression 1974
Revised 1977

ISBN 0 7137 0566 3

All rights reserved. No part of this book may be reproduced or transmitted in any form or by any means, electronic or mechanical, including photocopying, recording or by any information storage and retrieval system, without permission in writing from the publishers.

Text set in 11 on 13 Bembo and
printed in Great Britain by
Unwin Brothers Limited
Old Woking, Surrey

List of Contents

Introduction — 7

Chapter 1: Where to find the pebbles — 9
    The best areas—Longshore drift—Equipment—Safety

Chapter 2: Selecting your pebbles — 14
    The basic rules—Grouping the pebbles—Hard pebbles—Soft pebbles—A closer look at what is left

Chapter 3: Tumble-polishing machines — 40
    How they work—Choosing the right machine—Advantages and disadvantages of different models—Home-made and more advanced machines

Chapter 4: Perfect polishing — 52
    Grits and polish—Last minute checks—Loading your barrels—A grinding and polishing chart—The first grind—Quality control—The second grind—The third grind—The final polish—The last wash—Fault finding

Chapter 5: Jewellery making — 74
    Basic equipment—Fittings—Making the jewellery

Chapter 6: Exotic stones from foreign lands — 87
    Grouping—Lapidary shops—Descriptions and tumbling hints

Chapter 7: More advanced machines — 94
    Diamond saws—Grinding wheels—Polishing discs—Cast iron laps—cabochon cutting—Faceting—Machines on the market

Chapter 8: Rules and regulations — 99
    Purchase Tax—Income Tax—Import Duty—Local authorities

Selective list of lapidary suppliers — 100

Maps showing the locations of pebbles — 101

Index — 106

Acknowledgements

The author and publishers are grateful to the following who have helped to produce this book:

Michael Allman, F.I.I.P., F.R.P.S., who took the colour and most of the black-and-white photographs for the book;

John Wood, who drew the illustrations;

Gemrocks Ltd, Holborn, London E.C.1, stockists of tumble-polishing machines and foreign stones illustrated, who devoted a great deal of time and care to checking the manuscript and setting up many of the black-and-white photographs;

M. L. Beach (Products) Ltd, Church Street, Twickenham, manufacturers of tumble-polishing and other lapidary machines, who supplied Figs. 42(a), 43, 44 and 45.

Roland Phelps, then employed at Gemrocks Ltd, who supplied the pebbles for Plates 1, 2 and 3 and the fossil for Fig. 11;

British Travel Authority for Figs. 1, 2, 4 and the endpapers;

Institute of Geological Sciences (Crown Copyright) for Fig. 8;

B. T. Batsford Ltd, whose publication *Collecting and Polishing Stones* by Herbert Scarfe (1971) supplied references for Figs. 5(a)–(d), 7(a)–(c), 10, 19(a) and 34.

Introduction

Pebble-collecting, which was well known in our grandparents' day as a casual pastime for those infrequent one-day visits to the seaside, has come back into fashion lately in a big way. At the same time it has developed into a creative, absorbing occupation for the hobbyist, offering tremendous personal pleasure and satisfaction.

Mass production of cheap costume jewellery has enjoyed a boom in recent years. Millions of pounds are spent annually on rings, bracelets, pendants, baubles and beads manufactured from coloured glass and plastics and sold in chain stores up and down the country. The discerning woman, anxious to acquire something different, something unique in costume jewellery, finds little to satisfy her tastes in a market where 90 per cent of the goods are of a very low standard.

It is to fill this gap that thousands of women (and not a few men) have seized on pebble-collecting and tumble-polishing as a means of making their own unique and beautiful jewellery. Unlike their grandmothers, who relied on skilled lapidaries to transform their finds to gems, todays' collectors can polish and mount their pebbles easily, quickly and at little expense. This has been made possible thanks to the recent introduction of tumble-polishing machines, epoxy resin and inexpensive jewellery fittings, all of which are extremely simple to use. To work efficiently, a tumble-polisher requires nothing more than connection to the household electricity supply, some pebbles, a suitable abrasive grit or polish and ordinary tap water. It will transform humble beach pebbles into highly polished gems with the minimum of care and attention. Epoxy resin is simply strong, permanent glue and modern jewellery fittings come in a wide variety of shapes and sizes, catering for every taste. With a little patience and artistic flair anyone can make jewellery of the highest quality.

Of course, the other great attraction of the hobby is that it combines out-door fun with indoor pleasure. Collecting the pebbles is as exciting as making the jewellery. Britain's beaches abound with beautiful stones; amethysts, cornelians, jaspers, agates, milky quartz and serpentine can all be found quite readily at a hundred and one different holiday locations. Whole summers can be spent in happy and successful hunting—perhaps on a Cornish beach seeking pairs of matched serpentine pebbles for earrings; at Whitby searching the beach for jet; in Suffolk where cornelians and amber (known to the ancients as the tears of the Sun God, Apollo) can be found; or more likely simply collecting some of the countless millions of more humble yet just as colourful pebbles which attract the eye on almost every beach in Britain.

Detailed knowledge of geology is not essential to make pebble-collecting and polishing worthwhile. Knowing a few simple rules—and what *not* to collect—is all that is required. Collecting the pebbles will almost certainly stimulate a desire for a greater knowledge and it will not be long before a newcomer to the hobby begins to recognize most of his finds. With this knowledge will come deep appreciation of this truly fascinating subject and its possibilities.

The purpose of this book is to take the beginner step by step through every stage in baroque jewellery-making: where to find the pebbles, which ones to collect, buying a tumbler, achieving first-class results when polishing, and how to mount the polished stones on the fittings. For those who do find that they want to study the subject in more depth, I have included a brief chapter on foreign stones and one on more advanced equipment. The time will come when you will want to polish some of the exotic stones which are now imported into Britain from all over the world, for example Tiger's eye, Malachite, Rose quartz or Snowflake obsidian; or try your hand at grinding, cutting or even faceting stones. Finally, there is a list of the main lapidary suppliers situated throughout the country, where the latest machines and equipment are available.

1 Where to find the pebbles

No matter where you live in Britain you can drive to a shingle beach in a couple of hours, and as every stretch of shingle will present you with a million pebbles it might seem a little superfluous to begin this book by telling you where to go. Almost anywhere is good, but there are certain coasts which can rightly claim to be better than others. My aim here is to give you a gentle push in the direction of those better beaches.

Most of us like variety and that is just what the best beaches have—a wide variety of colourful and beautiful semi-precious pebbles which are yours for the taking. Luckily these special areas are very fairly distributed—four in England and Wales and three in Scotland—and while any reader lucky enough to live in one of these seven areas is to be envied, the rest of us can hardly grumble. Nature has shared her prizes so well that anyone should be able to reach at least one really outstanding area and return home with all the pebbles he or she can carry within a day. Even more fortunately, these seven extra-special areas happen to be on coasts with popular seaside resorts.

Fig. 1 The fishing fleet and pebble beach at Hastings, Sussex

The best areas

You can, if you wish, take a pebble-hunting holiday without forfeiting good hotels, food or entertainment.

The seven best pebble areas are:

1. *The West coast of Cornwall*, recommended to readers living west of the Isle of Wight.
2. *The Anglesey area of North Wales*, recommended to readers living in the Birmingham–Liverpool areas.
3. *The Ayrshire coast*, recommended to readers living around Glasgow.
4. *The coasts of Northern Scotland*, recommended to all holiday-makers in Scotland.
5. *The Fifeshire coast*, recommended to readers living in Eastern Scotland.
6. *The East Yorkshire Coast*, recommended to all North of England readers.
7. *The Norfolk and Suffolk coasts*, recommended to readers living in Eastern and South-Eastern England.

Do not let this list of seven best sites deter you in any way from your own local beach or particular beauty spot on the coast. Good pebbles are to be found anywhere. Even the semi-precious pebbles which make the above areas worth visiting *can* be found on other beaches. The pheno-

Fig. 2 Red Wharf Bay, Anglesey

menon known as longshore drift is forever at work in your favour, feeding other beaches with a never-ending supply of new and interesting pebbles.

Longshore drift

If you have ever thrown a handful of currants into a basin of flour and stirred vigorously you will understand longshore drift. The currants are swept along in the direction of your spoon until they are evenly distributed throughout your pudding mixture. On the coast a similar movement goes on. From the tip of Cornwall pebbles are swept eastward along the coast towards the Isle of Wight; from North Wales pebbles move up the coast towards Cumberland; Ayrshire pebbles also travel northward, but once we round the far north of Scotland the direction of drift is southward. Down the coast comes all that is best in Scottish pebbles. Those from Aberdeenshire can be found on the Yorkshire coast, and the wonderful semi-precious pebbles to be found in Yorkshire are in their turn swept southward to join those of Norfolk and Suffolk.

Thus a never-ending movement goes on, providing an inexhaustible supply of pebbles for every stretch of shingle around Britain's 7,000 miles of coastline. The sea is always at work, moving and depositing the shingle which, on most beaches, rests on a shelf of permanent rock. If this rock is on an exposed part of the coast, particularly a long, straight coast, the rate of movement is quite considerable. Whole beds of shingle can vanish in a single violent storm in such places; while shingle beds on beaches protected by headlands and coves are moved rather less. But whatever your favourite collecting spot, it is certain that the pebbles you cast your eyes over on one visit are not the ones you will pick up and choose from next time.

Equipment

There cannot be many hobbies which require so little outlay on equipment as pebble-collecting. True, you need a tumble-polishing machine if you are going to polish your finds when you get them home, but the basic raw materials —pebbles—are yours for the taking. You can get by with a pocket handkerchief or a brown paper bag if you find yourself with half an hour to spare on an unexpected visit to the coast. However, several basic items—all of which are certain to be lying around at home—are well worth taking on any expedition. They are:

> three small plastic bags (the ones you buy potatoes in are ideal) to put your pebbles in
> a penknife with a strong blade
> a small steel file.

For most people collecting pebbles is a family activity, with Dad, Mum, the children and even the family dog joining in, so three bags are not so unmanageable as they sound. In the next chapter I will explain how you can group your pebbles in a way which will help you achieve the best results when you go on to polishing. As this grouping can be done during collecting with the aid of your penknife and file, and as you will be placing your pebbles into one of three groups, you can complete the job on the beach by putting each pebble into one of your three bags.

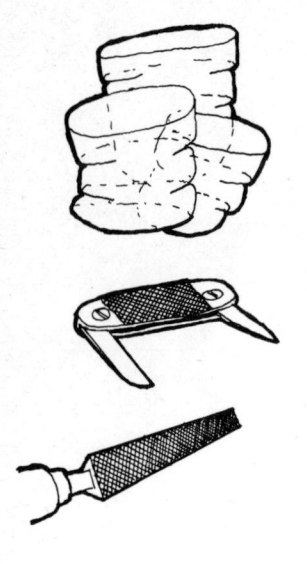

Fig. 3 Basic equipment

Fig. 4 Cadgwith, Cornwall

Or if you go on your own, you can make do with one large bag and carry out the grouping at home.

The best part of the beach to search for pebbles of a suitable size for your tumbler is down by the water's edge, so it is wise to wear an old pair of sandals or plimsolls. And do not forget to take a warm sweater or jumper, even in summertime. You might spend a couple of hours combing the shingle for the pebbles you need and sea breezes can be quite cold no matter how blue the sky.

Safety

There is nothing dangerous about pebble-collecting. The only possible risk arises from the fact that looking for pebbles is such an absorbing pastime that you might forget that tides come in as often as they go out. On some coasts the tide can sweep in with treacherous speed, so do keep an eye on the sea—especially on any beach backed by cliffs. If there is no way out of an interesting cove up the cliffside, make certain that you give yourself ample time to walk to safety before the tide comes in. The local coastguard is only a telephone call away and can give you reliable information about how long you can safely spend on such beaches.

Remember, too, that steep cliffs can hold other dangers. Confine your searching to the shingle on the beach, well away from the cliff face where rock falls could lead to disaster.

2 Selecting your pebbles

Happily, it is quite unnecessary to possess a detailed knowledge of geology to collect pebbles that will polish well and make up into beautiful jewellery. Nevertheless, the question on every beginner's lips is, 'How do I know which pebbles to collect?' The practical answer is to learn half a dozen basic rules which will help you to eliminate pebbles quite useless for tumble-polishing and to collect suitable ones which attract or please your eye. You *will* make mistakes and your first attempts at polishing are unlikely to be first-class. But you will learn far more by this trial and error method than any reference book could ever teach you.

To the perfectionist this may sound like side-stepping the question. For those who would like to go further into it, I recommend a course in geology and gemmology and the books in the bibliography. In a couple of years you will have learnt a great deal about the subject and no doubt have your own views on tumbling. Meanwhile, readers who follow my simpler method of identification will find that their final results are just as good as the results of those who decide to study the subject scientifically.

The basic rules

Size. Always collect small pebbles. Larger ones make excellent door-stops, paperweights and ballast but they do not tumble. Look for pebbles between the size of your smallest fingernail and the top joint of your thumb. One or two slightly larger ones may be included if they are particularly worth having, but bear in mind that your ultimate aim is to make jewellery. You require pebbles suitably sized for earrings, bracelets, necklaces and rings.

Do not make the mistake of collecting pebbles of uniform size. Aim at a good selection between the smallest and largest. Tumblers work more efficiently when loaded with pebbles of different sizes and you will need different sizes when making up your jewellery.

Shape. Beginners usually make the mistake of collecting either all near-perfectly round pebbles or only those which look like the work of an adventurous modern sculptor.

A happy compromise is what you should aim at. Collect a variety of shapes, but consider their usability as you do so. Weird and wonderful shapes have only a limited use in jewellery-making; whereas ovoids, flat discs, spheres and other uniform shapes are all worth collecting.

Amount. The temptation to collect too many pebbles is often hard to resist—especially when you are on a stretch of shingle with an abundant supply of colourful material—but you must learn to discipline yourself. Bear in mind the capacity of your tumbler barrels, the number of jewellery fittings you plan to buy, the length of time until your next visit to the coast and the problems of storage at home.

The removal of large quantities of shingle from beaches is frowned upon by local authorities. Shingle forms a natural barrier against erosion by wave action and its removal is strictly controlled. No one will prevent you from taking away a few pounds of pretty pebbles, but if every visitor to Brighton went home with a couple of hundredweights there would be a big hole in the ground!

What to leave behind. There are far more pebbles on an average beach that will polish than there are pebbles that will not. If you can recognize the ones that will not, you will automatically know the ones that will. Pebbles that will not polish well can all be recognized by their surface appearance and their feel to your fingers. These are the *porous*, the *granular*, the *flaky* and the *veined;* all of them are very soft. Very soft pebbles will not polish in a tumbler. The abrasive power of the grits used in the process is too great; they disintegrate and upset the grinding and polishing sequence in the barrel. (See p. 22.)

(a) *The porous.* These can be quickly spotted. They are the pebbles which stay wet too long. You will often find them well above the waterline and still moist when other pebbles nearby are quite dry. The worst ones will crumble under your fingernail; others will feel very coarse to your touch. They are usually sandstone and probably brown or yellow.

(b) *The granular.* These also stay wet too long, and are

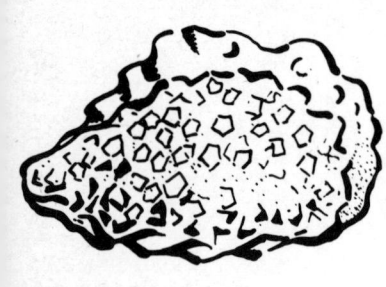

Fig. 5(a) Coarse-grained sandstone

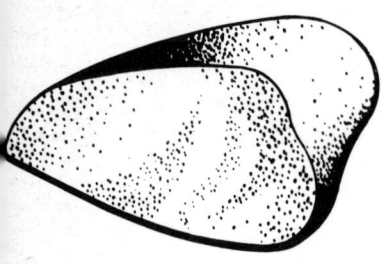

Fig. 5(b) Fine-grained sandstone

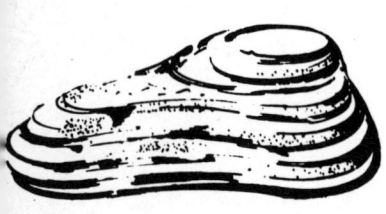

Fig. 5(c) Schist

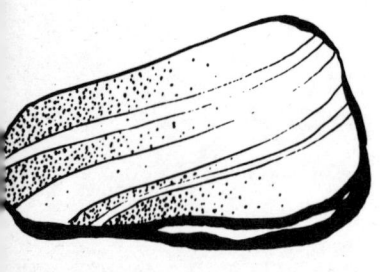

Fig. 5(d) Quartz veins in slate

usually sandstone. They *can* be finely textured but you will probably be able to see the minute grains of sand from which they are formed. They are often collected by beginners because they can be colourful—greens, reds, yellows and browns—but this is simply mineral oxide staining.

(c) *The flaky.* The parallel layers of material which make up these pebbles are usually readily visible to the naked eye. In certain varieties, known as *slates*, each layer represents a single stage in a long process of formation—the laying down and compressing of clay over millions of years. These layers can be flaked off with the point of a knife.

Others, known as *mudstone*, have even closer parallel layers which have been formed from fine mud and these layers can be difficult to see. A knife blade will scratch such pebbles easily. A third and very large group, the *schists*, have the same characteristic layers but often tempt collectors because they contain other mineral particles which impart pretty colours or attractive sparkle.

(d) *The veined.* These cause much trouble to old hands at the game as well as to beginners. They can be extremely beautiful and the temptation to drop one or two into one of your collecting bags is great. Pale pink, deep red, yellow, white and translucent are the colours found, usually as a swirling tracery of veins in finely textured sandstone pebbles. Examine one closely and you will see that the veins stand proud of the general surface. This is because they are composed of much harder material—quartz, feldspar, or jasper—and have resisted erosion far better than the sandstone in the main body of the pebble.

There is another very common type of pebble which you should not collect. This is the badly pitted or cracked specimen of *any* variety. A pebble with a deeply pitted surface will take a long time to grind smooth in your tumbler. Other pebbles will be ready for the next stage in the process long before a pitted one has been worn to smoothness and you will almost certainly have to reject it at some stage. A rare or particularly beautiful pebble which has surface blemishes *can* be saved at the expense of size. This is done either by hand-polishing (a long and slow process) or by putting it through a very prolonged first tumbling phase. The pebble is extracted from the load after a barrel is emptied at the end of the first stage and returned to stock to await the next batch of pebbles going into the barrel for the first time. By doing this three or four times it is possible to wear down the pebble to a point where all surface pitting is removed. It will, however, be greatly reduced in size—a point worth bearing in mind if you are planning to make a piece of jewellery requiring a large pebble. Any badly cracked pebble is likely to fracture during the rugged first stage of tumbling and its sharp edges will not wear down quickly enough to be ready for second-stage grinding at the end of the first run.

The last item on the 'leave-it-behind' list is man-made material. There is a surprising amount on most beaches and you should learn to recognize it. Five man-made materials can be confused with pebbles: brick, concrete, earthenware, china and glass. The ceaseless pounding of the waves and the grinding action of sand can wear fragments of these materials to pebble-shape in a very short time. Corners are knocked off, surfaces smoothed, colours bleached, and a deceptive coating given to the finished shape. Even geologists can be confused. But do not despair: the seeker after pebbles for tumble-polishing is unlikely to be bothered by four of these intruders.

A pebble of brick will be either red or yellow, and when you have examined it closely you will recognize it as brick or else take it for jasper (*see* pp. 23 & 25) or sandstone. Scratch it with a knife. If it scrapes easily, it is not jasper. You already know that sandstone is unsuitable for polishing and should be rejected. Thus brick pebbles should present no problem. Pebbles of concrete should also be thrown away.

Earthenware and china are also likely to be taken for sandstone, in which case the above test applies. You might confuse them with shale or mudstone but, once again, you are not interested in collecting either of these.

This leaves us with glass pebbles which, unfortunately, do not look at all like the bottle glass from which they were formed. Whether clear or coloured, they will be dramatically changed. All glassiness will have disappeared and they will have a frosted, crystalline appearance—very much like pure quartz or some colourful semi-precious pebbles almost unfindable in Britain. The coloured ones are almost certain to be glass, but if you feel lucky break off a tiny fragment with your file. If an obvious glassiness is seen where the fragment has been removed, then glass it is. The colourless pebble could be pure quartz as such pebbles are to be found occasionally on some British beaches. You will be unable to break off a fragment with knifeblade or file if it is quartz. In this case take it home and in a dark room strike it with the blade of your knife. If it sparks and emits a burning vegetable smell you have a valuable quartz pebble.

Incidentally, glass pebbles *will* polish in a tumbler if the barrel is filled entirely with such pebbles.

> *Summary of unsuitable pebbles*
> 1 Porous sandstone
> 2 Granular sandstone
> 3 Flaky shale, slate, mudstone or schist
> 4 Veined sandstone
> 5 Pitted or cracked pebbles
> 6 Brick, concrete, earthenware or china
> 7 Glass pebbles, unless you load your tumbler with nothing else but these
> 8 Finally, remember not to collect overlarge pebbles or pebbles completely regular in size and shape

Grouping the pebbles

Now that you know the pebbles to avoid when collecting we can give some consideration to the pebbles which might end up in one of your bags. Most beginners are attracted to a pebble by its colour and this is a fine way to start. It is unnecessary to arrive at a positive identification of each pebble. You need only know its approximate hardness. Bear in mind, however, that pebbles of the same colour do not necessarily have the same hardness and the first thing you must do when picking up specimens is to determine its approximate hardness. This is a simple operation. Take your penknife and scrape the pebble's surface. You may find that it has a coating—a crust of whitish lime or red, black or even green oxide. Remove some of this crust until the true surface appears. Now attempt to scratch this exposed area with your blade. If you cannot scratch it you have a relatively hard pebble which will probably take a good polish. Try marking it with your hard steel file and if this leaves no mark put it in your 'hard' bag.

Fig. 6 Scratching your pebble with a penknife to determine its hardness

If your knifeblade does scratch the surface you have a pebble which is softer than steel. Check once again that it is not sandstone, shale, mudstone, schist or a man-made material. If not, put it in your 'soft' bag. It will polish under the right conditions.

If your pebble is not marked by your penknife blade but you *can* scratch it with your file you have a borderline pebble which should go into your third bag for closer study at home.

This dividing of pebbles into groups of approximately equal hardness is most important in tumble-polishing. Indeed it might be said to be the key to success. Almost all disappointing results can be traced to insufficient attention to the hardness question, so do make quite sure that you carry out the simple tests described above.

There is a scale of hardness known as Moh's Scale which is often quoted in books on geology, mineralogy and gemmology. It provides a convenient means of indicating the relative hardness of one mineral when compared to another, placing diamond at the top of the scale (10) and talc at the bottom (1). Most British beach pebbles worth polishing lie somewhere in the middle of this scale, and your penknife blade (hardness $5\frac{1}{2}$) and your steel file (hardness $6\frac{1}{2}$) provide two very convenient known hardnesses to enable you to group your finds.

Let us assume you have collected a few pounds of pebbles in your 'hard' bag and you now have them spread out on your kitchen table and ready for grinding and

A closer look at your hard pebbles

polishing. Before you put them into the barrel examine each one closely. Many will probably belong to the quartz family and now is a good time to get to know this family more intimately. Half an hour spent identifying and grouping your finds now will repay great dividends in the future, for you will begin to recognize pebbles and be able to name them more readily. However, it is not essential to know any more about your pebbles at this stage than that they are harder than your steel file. If you wish to skip this next section you may do so and your pebbles will still polish well. I include it for those who wish to improve their recognition skills.

Pebbles having *quartz* as their dominant constituent are found on almost every beach in Britain. As you have already demonstrated for yourself, such pebbles are extremely hard. Their differences in colour and appearance are due to varying amounts of other minerals in each pebble and also to the way in which the quartz has formed.

Quartz is solid silica and if it did not crystallize when it solidified it is known as *flint*—a pebble which most readers will readily identify. You will surely have some in your collection. Pick them all out now and notice the variations possible in this humble pebble; grey, brown or black in colour, often appearing translucent yet not being so when held up to strong light. Everyone knows that two flint pebbles struck against each other will produce a spark, but it is not generally known that all quartz pebbles will do the same and often produce bigger and better sparks.

You will probably confuse chert with flint initially because it can look very similar and differs only slightly in composition. The lighter greys and any smoky-yellow specimens in your flints are likely to be chert. (*See* p. 22.)

Quartzite pebbles are also very likely to be included in your collection. They consist of tiny grains of quartz bonded together in solid silica and usually display a very attractive network of patterns. Unlike the sandstone you have rejected, quartzite is extremely hard. This is because the sand grains in quartzite have been subjected to great pressure and heat at some time in the past and have melted and recrystallized and are now held together in a cement of pure silica. Quartzite pebbles are opaque and colour variations include white, yellow and brown, often with mineral tints of blue and purple.

Quartz breccia was formed in a similar way to quartzite but you should have no difficulty in identifying pebbles of breccia. They consist of angular fragments of rock bonded together in a silica cement. These angular fragments are large enough to see easily and you should rely for identification on this distinctive characteristic since colour variations can be wide. The other pebble which is often confused with breccia is the *conglomerate* (see page 28), but a close look at the rock fragments which make up the pebble will decide the issue. The fragments in a conglomerate will be rounded (like tiny pebbles themselves) and not angular as in breccia.

Milky quartz pebbles should not be difficult to distinguish from flint and chert because they are much lighter in colour (white, creamy yellow) and often translucent or nearly so. They are more likely to be confused with *banded crystalline quartz* which can be white to light brown. Look for multi-coloured patterns and bands. Milky quartz does not have them, banded crystalline quartz does.

If you have been lucky enough to find *agate* pebbles (see p. 23.) you will recognize them by their characteristic and very defined banding and their wide colour range—pink, red, yellow, white, brown and blue. Your file test will have already shown that agates are very hard over their entire surface, unlike veined pebbles which are softer between the veins; you will be delighted with any you polish. Disappointment might come later when you try to decide which of the varieties of agate you have found. They are grouped according to colour and banding but there is a certain overlapping of groups which can be confusing. For determined readers bent on positive identification the main groups are:

Banded agate: bands of colour which are parallel to the outer surface

Fig. 7(a) Banded agate

Plate 1 Pebbles which do not polish well
Quartzite   Fine-grained sandstones   Quartz vein in quartzite
Torridonian sandstone   Garnets in mica schist

Plate 2 Flint and chert in a variety of forms

Plate 3 Good polishing pebbles

White quartz Citrine Brown jasper
Brown beach agate Green and Yellow jasper Whitby jet
Granite Granite Rock crystal

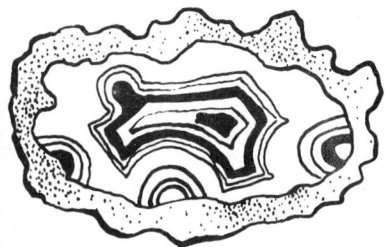

Fig. 7(b) Fortification agate

Fig. 7(c) Eyed agate

Fig. 8 Quartz crystals from Cornwall, magnified × 1½

Eyed agate: bands in concentric rings
Fortification agate: angular bands
Onyx: straight, alternating bands of colour and white
Sardonyx: bands of white and red or brown

If any pebbles suspected of being glass which you have picked up pass your hardness test they may be *clear quartz* (rock crystal). Test them further by striking two pieces together in darkness. They should produce an orange spark and a smell of burning. Perfect quartz crystals are six-sided with a six-sided pyramid at each end, but your chances of finding such specimens on a British beach are remote. Content yourself with very small, frosted pebbles which will reveal their true beauty when tumbled.

Coloured varieties of rock crystal are to be found occasionally on certain beaches. The best-known varieties are:

Amethyst: transparent to semi-transparent; purple to pale pink, with some white banding (*see* p. 26)
Citrine: transparent to semi-transparent; golden yellow (*see* p. 23)
Smoky quartz: transparent to semi-transparent; deep yellow to brown

A variety of quartz which did not form large crystals when it cooled is known as *chalcedony*. It has a waxy lustre, is translucent, and has a milky-white, blue, grey or pale brown colour. It might be confused with milky quartz, but its waxiness should easily distinguish it if the two are compared when dry. The red variety, *cornelian*, is extremely beautiful when polished. These pebbles seem to glow with warm fire when held up to the light and soon catch the eye on a sunny day near the water's edge. Colours vary from pale to deep red and some impure varieties may be speckled and not wholly translucent. Sometimes iron-stained quartz pebbles are mistaken for cornelian but they lack the characteristic waxy feel and translucent warmth.

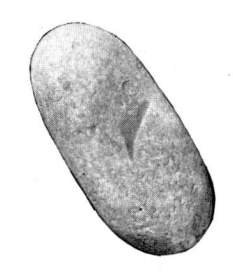

Fig. 9 *Left* a six-sided piece of clear quartz, *centre* a similar piece which has been sea-worn for about 10,000 years, *right* what a tumble-polisher can do in three weeks

You must be very careful of the beginner's mistake of assuming that all pebbles can be neatly allocated to a particular group or variety; that each will display one set of characteristics (as set out above) which will allow you to say, 'this is X, Y, or Z' with certainty. Nature did not make her pebbles for the benefit of the collector or tumble-polisher, and many of your quartz pebbles will resist all your efforts to positively identify them. Content yourself with the knowledge that they qualify as 'hard' and will polish well.

The previous paragraph serves as a good introduction to four pebbles requiring special attention: jaspers, conglomerates, porphyritic pebbles and granites. All four will probably find their way into your 'hard' bag at some time during your collecting expeditions and they have much in common.

You are nearly certain to have *jasper* pebbles in your 'hard' bag because they are to be found on almost every

Plate 4 Rough British pebbles

Green quartz Serpentine Yellow quartz
Obsidian Amethyst Red jasper
Cornelian

Plate 5 The polished versions

Green quartz Serpentine Yellow quartz
Obsidian Amethyst Red jasper
　　　　　Cornelian

beach in Britain. Jasper consists of tiny quartz grains intermingled with clay which has become coloured by iron salts. Although a very ordinary pebble, it can look beautiful when polished and makes up into charming jewellery. By far the most common single-colour variation is a deep red, and you should always suspect any deep red, opaque pebble of being jasper. Less common colours are yellow and green, sometimes with ribbons of clear quartz running through the pebble. Many jaspers will possess a combination of all three colours and they can be confused with conglomerates. However, jasper pebbles do not usually have the multi-colouring of conglomerates. (*See* pp. 23, 26 & 27.)

Because it is a very common pebble, jasper is one of the first which beginners recognize readily and the temptation to drop all jasper pebbles into the 'hard' bag is difficult to resist, particularly on days when you are in a hurry or the weather is unfriendly. This can lead to problems when tumble-polishing because jasper can fluctuate in hardness. If you have a high percentage of very hard quartz pebbles in the tumbling mixture the softer jasper might break down and upset the process.

The same can be said of *conglomerates*. These pebbles are made up of rounded fragments of a variety of rocks (some of which may be quartz) cemented together in a finely-textured matrix. They are usually quite beautiful and

Summary of hard pebbles

Name	Characteristics
Flint	Opaque to semi-translucent; grey, brown or black
Chert	Opaque to semi-translucent; light grey to smoky-yellow
Quartzite	Opaque. White, yellow, brown, often with a network of patterns and tints of blue or purple. Minute quartz grains in a hard matrix
Quartz breccia	Opaque. Wide colour variations. Angular rock fragments bounded together in a silica matrix

multi-coloured but fluctuations in hardness are possible.

Porphyritic pebbles are also formed from a variety of rocks but unlike conglomerates, which have rounded fragments, and quartz breccias, which have angular fragments, these pebbles consist of perfect crystals of quartz and feldspar bounded together in a hard matrix. Once again, different hardnesses are possible.

Finally *granite*. These pebbles are so widespread that you must come across them when collecting. They are composed of three minerals—quartz, feldspar and mica—and vary in colour from grey to pink. The sparkle in granite is caused by particles of mica, while the pink tints are imparted to the pebble by its feldspar content. Variations in hardness are common. (*See* p. 23.)

How then can you decide what to do with these four difficult pebbles? There are three possibilities:

1 Reject them all and stick to pure quartz—an unhappy decision because some of the most beautiful beach pebbles belong to this group.
2 Check each pebble very carefully by trying to scratch its surface in different spots—a better solution, especially if you have only a few specimens.
3 Tumble jaspers, conglomerates, porphyritic pebbles and granite together and keep the purer quartz pebbles apart—the best solution, particularly if you have a tumbler with more than one barrel.

Sometimes confused with	*Tumble with*
Chert	Other quartz pebbles
Flint, limestone	Other quartz pebbles
Conglomerates of similar hardness; jasper, quartz breccia	Other quartz pebbles
Quartzite, conglomerates of similar hardness, jasper porphyritic pebbles, grit	Other quartz pebbles

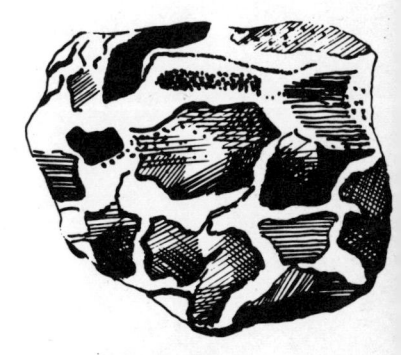

Fig. 10 Quartz breccia

29

Name	Characteristics
Milky quartz	Translucent or semi-translucent. White to creamy yellow
Banded crystalline quartz	Opaque to semi-translucent. White to light brown with coloured patterns or bands
Agate	Characterized by strong banding and wide colour range
Clear quartz	Transparent. Pure silica. Colour variations: amethyst, citrine, smoky quartz
Chalcedony	Translucent and waxy. Milky white, blue, grey, pale brown
Cornelian	Translucent and waxy. Pale to deep red
Jasper	Opaque. Deep red, yellow, green, combinations of these—sometimes with ribbons of clear quartz.
Conglomerates	Opaque and multi-coloured. Consists of rounded fragments of rock cemented together
Porphyritic pebbles	Opaque. Crystals of quartz and feldspar bounded together in hard matrix
Granite	Opaque. Grey to pink with a sparkle caused by mica particles

Sometimes confused with	Tumble with
Banded crystalline quartz, limestone	Other quartz pebbles
Milky quartz	Other quartz pebbles
Any veined pebble	Other quartz pebbles
Glass	Other quartz pebbles
Milky quartz	Other quartz pebbles
Iron-stained quartz pebbles	Other quartz pebbles
Conglomerates, brick, quartzite, quartz breccia, serpentine	Ideally with other jaspers, but can be tumbled satisfactorily with conglomerates, pophyritics, and harder granites. Very hard specimens with other quartz pebbles
Jasper, quartzite, quartz breccia, serpentine	Ideally with other conglomerates, but can be tumbled with jasper, porphyritics, and harder granites. Very hard specimens with other quartz pebbles
Quartz breccia	Ideally with other porphyritics, but can be tumbled with jasper, conglomerates, and harder granites. Very hard specimens with other quartz pebbles
	With other granites unless *very* hard and then best with softer jasper, conglomerates and porphyritics

A closer look at your soft pebbles

A few hours spent hunting pebbles on most British beaches reveals that the vast majority of pebbles fall into two categories—very hard, or too soft. Nevertheless, there is a small but important category somewhere between these two extremes which includes some beautiful specimens. They are soft—but not too soft. With care they can be tumble-polished successfully and the results more than justify their special treatment. One or two in this group are confined to short stretches of coast and this fact can help greatly when you are trying to identify them. But do bear in mind that all pebbles wander far from their birthplace.

One of the best known of the soft pebbles is *serpentine*. It is probably best identified by its feel to your fingers—a soapy, almost lubricated surface which immediately suggests softness. It is an opaque pebble and its main colour variations are pale to dark green and dark red to brown, all with a mottled appearance and sometimes white veins. These might be confused with conglomerates or jasper on appearance but their feel is unique and they are, of course, much softer. (*See* pp. 26 & 27.)

The best location for pebbles of serpentine is The Lizard area of Cornwall, but pebbles can be found on many beaches. If you are collecting in an abundant area such as The Lizard it is a good plan to collect sufficient pebbles to load one of your barrels entirely with serpentine, especially if you are able to find a wide colour range. If you can find only a few pebbles of serpentine they *will* polish with limestone and marble.

Limestone found in Britain is often formed from the skeletons of plants, shells and sea urchins which inhabited these islands millions of years ago and you will often find limestone pebbles which, when polished, will reveal tiny fossils of these organisms. Unfortunately limestone varies greatly in hardness; chalk (a kind of limestone) is too soft for tumble-polishing, but some crystalline limestone can be polished in this way. Best results are probably achieved by polishing limestone pebbles from a limited area together, but the pebbles *will* polish with marble and serpentine. Limestone pebbles are opaque and can be dull white to yellow, sometimes with colourful staining. They can be confused with milky quartz and chert but are much softer than quartz and will effervesce when a weak acid such as vinegar is applied to their surface.

Marble is limestone which has been subjected to great pressure and heat. It is opaque and has a granular appearance, a crystalline sparkle and a wide colour range. Although soft it is compact and polishes well. Again, best results are achieved by loading the barrel entirely with marble, but it will polish with other soft pebbles.

Incidentally, it is worth remembering that fairly round pebbles of limestone and marble are likely to be harder (and therefore more suitable for polishing) than flattened pebbles which were easily worn by wave action.

Jet is very localized in its distribution, the only good collecting area being the coast around the Yorkshire holiday resort of Whitby. A few pebbles have drifted southward as far as Suffolk but finds are rare. Even around Whitby fair-sized jet pebbles are difficult to find nowadays, but a diligent search should still reveal a few specimens.

Jet is not a stone, but is in fact fossilized wood, similar to, but much tougher than, coal. It is opaque, intense black in colour and very light in weight. If you find a pebble you think is jet, test its weight against a piece of glass of similar size. Your jet pebble should be much lighter. If it is, you may still be confusing jet with a water-worn piece of coal. Sea-coal, as it is known locally, is collected from beaches as fuel only a few miles north of Whitby on the Durham coast and many coal pebbles have drifted south to Yorkshire. Once you have compared a jet pebble with a coal pebble you will easily recognize jet's superior glassiness and greater hardness, but caution is necessary until you have become familiar with it. (*See* p. 23.)

There are certain destructive tests for jet which include setting fire to a specimen. Jet will burn with a greenish flame and a pleasant, tarry aroma, but I do not recommend such tests. Sea-coal has a similar smell when burning and I have seen green flames in a fire made with sea-coal. It is better to rely on appearance for identification and risk mistakes than to see a valuable piece of semi-precious jet go up in smoke. Jet is becoming rare and it will take many days to collect sufficient pebbles to load even a small barrel, but if you are lucky and find enough pebbles their beauty when polished will repay all your efforts.

Amber, like jet, is of a vegetable origin and, again like jet, is very localized in distribution. The coasts of Norfolk and Suffolk are most likely to yield amber, though it has been found on Yorkshire and Essex beaches. It is fossilized tree resin which has been carried to the east coast of England by tides and currents from the Baltic. It is very light in weight and will float in a strong saline solution. Opaque to semi-translucent, amber varies in colour from dark red to pale yellow. Occasionally pieces are found containing fossilized insects. Tests for amber include rubbing a suspected piece vigorously on your sleeve and holding the pebble over small scraps of paper. The scraps will fly upwards towards the pebble, attracted by static electricity. Amber is also very soft, and when scraped with a knife blade will powder readily. It can be confused with similar coloured glass, but is of course much softer. Some plastics, not likely to be found on beaches, are very similar in appearance to amber.

Your chances of finding sufficient amber to load a barrel are almost nil, but it can be polished with jet.

It is worth mentioning that *fossils* are often found when

Summary of soft pebbles

Name	Characteristics
Serpentine	Opaque. Soapy, lubricated feel. Pale to dark green, and dark red to brown—all with a mottled appearance and occasionally white veining
Limestone	Opaque. Dull white to yellow, sometimes with colourful staining. In the harder, crystalline limestones a sparkle is characteristic. The softer limestones often reveal fossil remains. Effervesces with a weak acid.

Fig. 11 Fossils in limestone. The fossils are likely to be found as small pieces on a beach, especially on the East Coast

collecting beach pebbles. Indeed, some pebbles are composed entirely of fossils (*see* limestone). Their hardness depends on the mineral which has replaced the animal or plant. If it was silica the fossil might be seen as a pattern in hard flint or chert pebbles; if limestone, then the pebbles will be softer, though equally beautiful. Fossils could, therefore, find their way into any of your three collecting bags.

Sometimes confused with	*Tumble with*
Conglomerates and jasper	Ideally with other serpentine but can be tumbled successfully with limestone and marble.
Milky quartz, chert	Ideally with limestone pebbles from the same area. Can be tumbled with serpentine and marble

Name	Characteristics
Marble	Limestone which has been subjected to pressure and heat. Opaque granular, with a crystalline sparkle and wide colour range
Jet	Opaque. Intense glossy black Confined almost exclusively to the Whitby area of Yorkshire
Amber	Opaque. Semi-translucent. Pale yellow to dark red
Fossils	See text

A closer look at what is left

No two pebbles are exactly alike. There are always minute differences in hardness and mineral content which make every pebble unique. This is particularly true of the pebbles we are about to examine. Because they are very common pebbles and you are certain to find them they are worthy of some attention in spite of the fact that they are not particularly colourful.

I dismissed sandstone earlier because sandstone pebbles are too soft for tumble-polishing. But pebbles of *grit* are a type of sandstone, yet they are very hard. The grains of sand in pebbles of grit are coarse and angular. A well-known example is *Millstone grit*, once very popular as grinding stones for windmills. The pebbles of this rock differ widely in hardness but you should be able to identify them by looking closely for the coarse, angular grains of which they are composed. Colours are usually dull grey or brown. They might be confused with quartz breccia.

Dolerite is another common pebble and, like grit, it is

Name	Characteristics
Grit	Opaque. Coarse, angular grains Dull grey or brown

Sometimes confused with	Tumble with
	Other marble pebbles or limestone
Sea-coal, glass	Probably better to polish by hand
Coloured glass, plastic	Jet, but probably better to polish by hand
	Probably better to polish by hand

dull brown, sometimes with a greenish tinge. It too is composed of grains but they are much finer than those of grit. Tiny crystals of feldspar can also be seen in the pebbles when examined closely. Dolerite is of volcanic origin and is quite hard.

A pebble very similar in origin to dolerite is *whinstone*. It too has crystals of feldspar, but differs in colour, being dark grey to dark blue.

Gabbro is similar to dolerite but has somewhat coarser grains.

Basalt pebbles are pieces of solidified lava which cooled quickly to form dark, iron-black rock.

Finally, *gneiss*—a highly crystalline rock which derives it name from a German word meaning 'to sparkle'. It is composed of bands of quartz, feldspar, and mica—but in spite of its banded appearance (like schist) it can be very hard.

Sometimes confused with	Tumble with
Quartz breccia	Varies in hardness so much that it is probably best not to polish it with other pebbles

Name	Characteristics
Dolerite	Opaque. Fine grained with tiny crystals of feldspar. Dull brown, sometimes with a green tinge
Gabbro	Very similar to dolerite but coarser grained
Basalt	Opaque. Compact, solidified lava. Black
Gneiss	Opaque. Highly crystalline pebbles of banded quartz, feldspar, and mica

Note: There are other pebbles to be found on British beaches which have not been mentioned in this chapter. They are either quite rare or foreign pebbles transported to these shores during the Ice Age or as ballast in ships' holds. If you find one, apply the hardness tests and act accordingly.

Sometimes confused with	*Tumble with*
Gabbro	Your hard pebbles, if it passes the file test
Dolerite	Varies in hardness. Probably best alone
Black glass	Your hard pebbles, if it passes the file test
Schist	Your hard pebbles, if it passes the file test

3 Tumble-polishing machines

Although you may not yet have seen a man-made tumbling machine, you have certainly seen Nature's tumbler at work if you have stood on a beach and watched the rhythmical forces which are constantly at work near the water's edge. Waves breaking on the shoreline cascade their energies up onto the sloping sands. With each wave fragments of rock are rolled up the beach and down again as the energy of each wave is spent, to be caught by the succeeding wave and rolled up once more in a never-ending cycle which carries them up, down and along the beach in a series of gentle arcs. Gradually, relentlessly, these rock fragments are transformed to smooth, round pebbles by the abrasive action of the countless grains of sand over which they roll. A single pebble may be many years in the making, but the sea never stops and the grains of sand are always there and slowly, certainly, each pebble is formed. A thousand years from now those same rhythmical forces which produced it will have reduced it to sand grains.

How they work

It is this very same wearing-down-to-smoothness process which a tumble-polishing machine is designed to reproduce and speed up. Instead of the irresistible force of breaking waves, its energy derives from a small electric motor which turns rollers on which a barrel containing pebbles is placed. Inside the barrel silicon carbide grits take the place of sands on the beach. As the barrel revolves these grits wear down the roughened surfaces on each pebble to perfect smoothness. That which Nature takes years to achieve with waves and sand, the tumbling machine can produce in a matter of days. And unlike the sand on a beach, the grits in the tumbler can be carefully graded from very coarse to exceedingly fine. This means that the wearing down process can be controlled and the smoothing process carried to a degree of perfection quite impossible to achieve with sand grains.

Even the gleaming beauty of a sea-washed pebble can be improved upon by the machine. Polishing agents, introduced into the barrel during the final stages of the process, impart a mirror-finish to each pebble which makes wet beach pebbles look quite dull by comparison. And unlike wet beach pebbles, which lose their shine as soon as they dry out, correctly tumble-polished pebbles retain their gleaming beauty forever.

The right machine

The first step on the road to perfect tumble-polishing is to acquire an efficient and reliable tumbling machine. The machines come in a wide variety of shapes and sizes; making the right choice at the outset can be tricky without some knowledge of the way in which the machine works and the job which each component in the machine must do.

A typical tumble-polisher consists of an electric motor which drives a pulley connected via a belt or some other method of drive to one of two parallel rollers. On these rollers a barrel containing the stones to be polished and a suitable abrasive or polish is made to revolve at a pre-determined speed for a number of days. During this period the abrasives in the barrel are changed at regular intervals, each change being to a finer abrasive, until the polishing stage is reached and the pebbles are ready for making into jewellery.

The whole process takes several days and during that time the electric motor must run continuously. A twenty-day cycle, for example, requires 480 hours non-stop running on the part of the motor. It is of the utmost importance, therefore, that the motor is reliable.

Fig. 12 The working parts of a tumble-polisher

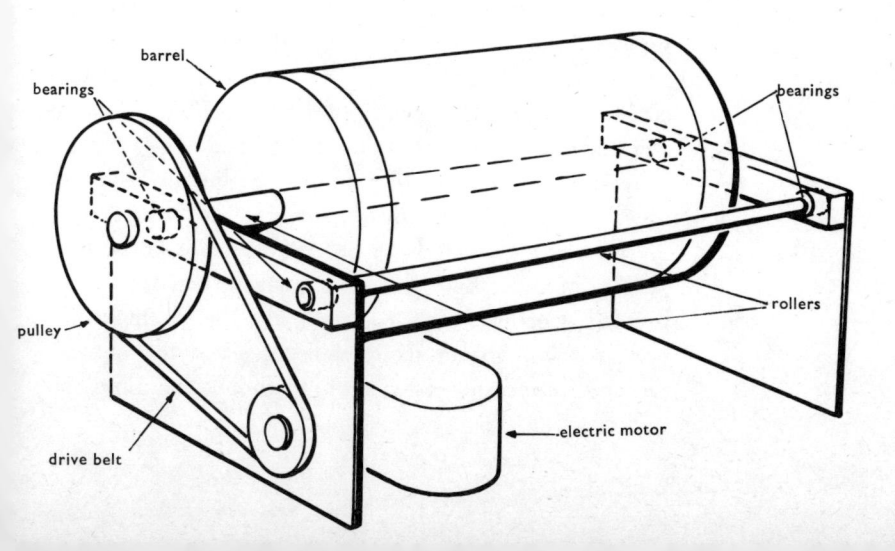

The pulley and belt which transfer the driving power from the motor to the rollers must also be designed to withstand continuous running. A barrel of stones is a heavy load and the job of turning it must be within the capabilities of these components. If other methods of transferring the power of the motor to the rollers are employed, they must be reliable and guarantee positive turning of the rollers at all times during operation.

Rollers and the bearings in which they run must also be designed and built to withstand the toughest wear. The rollers must be capable of withstanding all the friction of a continuously turning barrel of stones and must be of a material which does not allow the barrel to slip as it turns. At the same time they must not in any way prevent free rotation. Bearings are of the utmost importance whatever type or size of machine is considered. They must be tough enough to take long periods of hard work and be designed to allow free roller action. Lubrication must be a simple and straightforward job and must not require dismantling of the machine in order to carry out this essential maintenance.

Finally, we must consider the barrel which probably does more hard work than all the other components put together. A barrel constructed from inferior or non-hardwearing materials will never stand up to the rigours of stone-polishing. It might just be possible to get away with second best on other components but if the barrel has the slightest defect it will certainly be revealed very quickly in use. As will be explained later, water must always be present during the tumbling process and if the barrel is not watertight trouble will soon develop. A leak will certainly impair the efficiency of the rollers if they become wet, and there is a danger of an electrical fault if any leaking water finds its way to the motor. The lid of the barrel must also be wide enough to allow easy entry and exit of the pebbles and your hand because you will be putting pebbles in and taking them out many times during the barrels's working life. You will also be cleaning the barrel regularly so it must be designed in a way that eliminates corners and angles difficult to reach when washing out used abrasives. If even a few grains of a coarse abrasive are allowed to remain in the barrel during any subsequent stage in the polishing sequence the result will be an inferior finish to the final polish. Easy-to-clean, therefore, should be high on your list of points to look for when making your choice.

To summarize: A good tumble-polishing machine must

1. have a reliable motor
2. have a strong pulley and drive belt, or other driving method
3. have tough, hard-wearing rollers
4. have efficient bearings
5. be easy to lubricate and maintain
6. have a strong, leak-proof, easy-to-clean barrel.

In spite of the rigorous specifications outlined above, it does not follow that a good tumbler must be built like a battleship. Good design and the choice of lightweight but durable materials can greatly reduce cost, weight and wear. If a manufacturer has achieved low cost and light weight and is prepared to guarantee his machine against defects for any reasonable length of time, he is likely to be marketing a sound product.

There are many makes, types and sizes of machine on the market and the best advice I can offer you before buying is to keep the above points in mind and buy from a reliable supplier. Such a supplier will *always* guarantee his machine against any of the faults outlined above and give you the benefit of his experience if you call at his premises.

Many readers will be buying their machines by post and it is advisable to write to three or four suppliers initially asking for catalogues and price lists. The less expensive tumblers will not necessarily be the best, but you should be able to check on most of the points already mentioned by comparing catalogues. Incidentally, no reader should worry greatly about ordering by post. The vast majority of mail order firms in the lapidary business are very reliable and most sell on a refund-if-not-delighted basis.

Barrel size: The size of the barrel or barrels on your tumbling machine predetermines a surprising number of things about the pebbles you can put into it. For a start, it determines the amount of pebbles you can polish at once. It is physically impossible to put ten pounds of pebbles into a barrel with a capacity of three pounds.

Secondly, it determines the size of pebbles you can polish in the barrel. A small barrel will not polish large pebbles.

Thirdly, it determines the amount of abrasive grits and polishing powder you need to carry out the process. A very large barrel needs more grits and polish than does a very small barrel.

Fourthly, because the barrel—whatever its size—must be filled to a predetermined level with pebbles, the amount of pebbles you must *collect* before you can start the operation has also been decided once you choose a particular size of barrel.

Fig. 13 A small tumbler with a single 1½-lb barrel

Let us now look at five typical tumble-polishing machines with barrels of different sizes and consider their relative merits:

1. *A small tumbler with a single one-and-a-half pound barrel:* This little machine will be quite inexpensive and will do a lot of work. Its barrel will hold approximately 100 pebbles ranging in size from equal to your little fingernail up to the size of the top joint of your thumb. It will be very economical on grits and polish and you should have no difficulty in finding enough pebbles to fill it during an hour's stroll along a good shingle beach.

Its disadvantages are:

(a) if you have collected both hard and soft pebbles and filled the barrel with the hard ones you will have to wait approximately three weeks before you can make a start on the soft ones;
(b) you will not be able to polish pebbles larger than the sizes mentioned above;
(c) if you have collected several pounds of pebbles, it will take many weeks to polish them all.

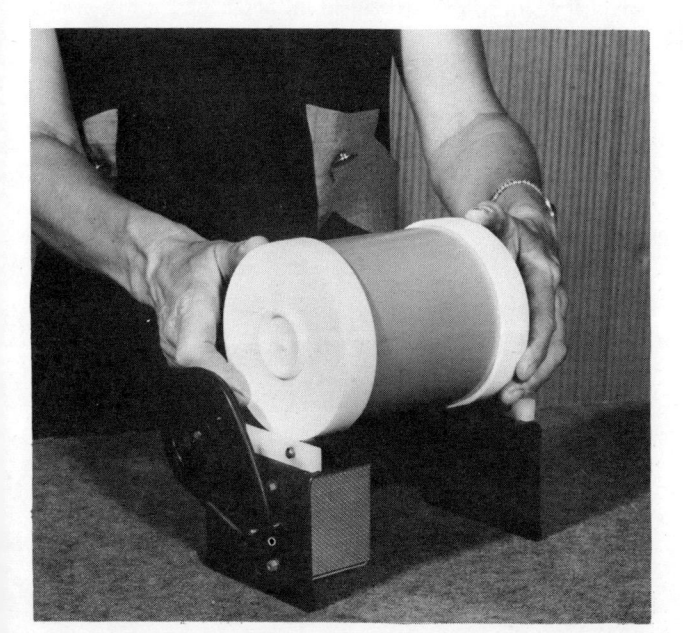

Advantages and disadvantages of different models

Fig. 14 A tumbler with a single 3-lb barrel

2. *A small tumbler with a single three-pound barrel:* Although slightly more expensive, this little machine will do twice the work of No. 1. You will be able to polish 200 or so pebbles at once and you will be able to include half a dozen slightly larger pebbles.

Its disadvantages are:

(*a*) once again you will have to wait three weeks between each batch of hard and soft pebbles;

(*b*) you will have to collect 200 pebbles before you can start the process. This is not difficult in summer when weekend trips to the coast are a regular feature of family life, but it is worth bearing in mind as winter approaches.

3. *A larger tumbler with two one-and-a-half pound barrels:* This twin-barrelled model has the advantage of a total capacity of approximately 200 pebbles, but what is more important is its ability to do two jobs at once. You can load one barrel with hard pebbles, the other with soft, and three weeks later they are all ready for making into jewellery. As will be explained in the chapter on polishing

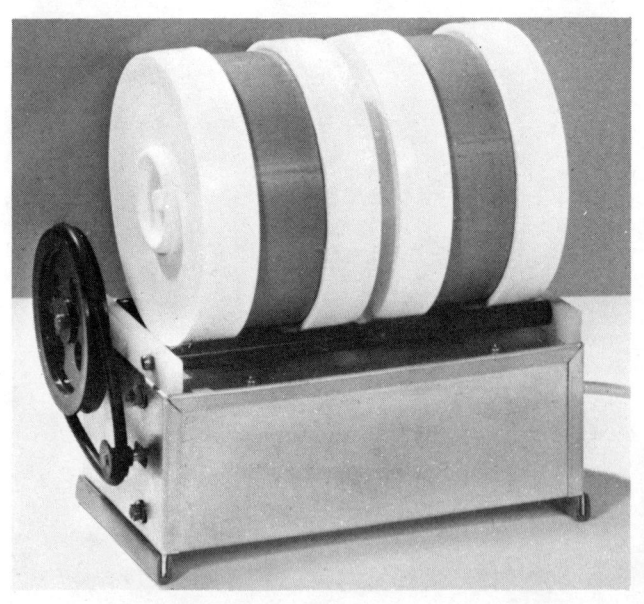

Fig. 15 A tumbler with two 1½-lb barrels

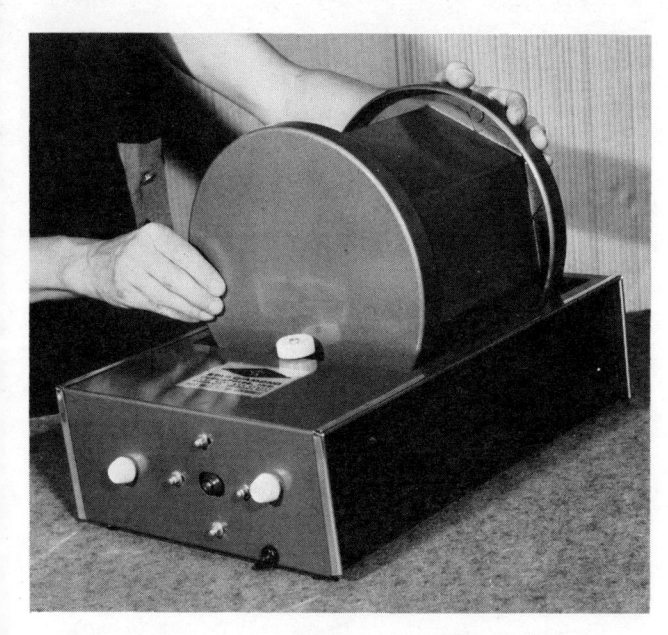

Fig. 16 A small commercial tumbler: ideal if you are starting up in business

pebbles, there are certain advantages in keeping one barrel solely for use in the final polishing stage of the process. With this machine you can do that and still have your second barrel working on grinding other pebbles.

The only disadvantage worth mentioning with this machine is that you are, of course, limited on pebble size to the requirements of a one-and-a-half pound barrel.

4. *A larger tumbler with one three-pound barrel and two one-and-a-half pound barrels:* This is a de-luxe machine with the single disadvantage of being fairly expensive. However, its advantages more than justify its greater cost. Total capacity is around 400 pebbles, but if you happen to be low on supplies you don't have to wait until you can get down to the beach again. Simply use one of the small barrels as you would with No. 1 above. If you have a good stock of pebbles you can add some larger ones when using the three-pound barrel; you can keep one of the small barrels just for polishing; you can put three pounds of pebbles through the first and second grinding stages and then carefully select the best of the batch to fill one of your one and a half pounders. Indeed, a very versatile machine.

5. *A very large tumbler with a twelve-pound barrel:* This giant will polish 800 pebbles in one cycle, enough to keep the average home jewellery maker going for many months. As the barrel must be filled with either hard or soft

Summary

Tumbler capacity	Barrels
1½lb	One, taking approximately 100 pebbles
3lb	One, taking approximately 200 pebbles
3lb	Two, taking approximately 100 pebbles each
6lb	Three, one taking approximately 200 pebbles two taking approximately 100 pebbles each
12lb	One, taking approximately 800 pebbles

Anyone contemplating starting a business in tumble-polishing stones is recommended to give large tumblers careful consideration. Similarly, their ability to polish quite large pebbles must not be overlooked. If you plan to use pebbles for projects other than jewellery-making and you need large quantities of bigger pebbles, a big barrel is likely to be your choice.

But whatever your choice—large, small or in-between—I advise you strongly against metal barrels unless they are adequately lined on the inside with hardwearing rubber. Chemical reactions which produce gas can be set up in an unlined metal barrel if it is filled with pebbles, water and abrasive and made to revolve for any length of time on a

pebbles you will need 1600 pebbles in stock, almost too many unless you are going in for jewellery-making on a commercial scale. It will, of course, polish much larger pebbles than any of the four previously mentioned.

Advantages	Disadvanatages
Inexpensive; easy to fill; very economical on grits and polish	Can only tumble one load of hard or soft pebbles in one four-week cycle; limitation on pebble size
Will take *some* larger pebbles	Can only tumble one load of hard or soft pebbles in one four-week cycle
Can polish hard and soft pebbles at the same time in separate barrels	Limitations on pebble size
Extremely versatile; large total capacity, but can also be used for tumbling small loads. Can grind hard and soft pebbles, and polish a third batch at the same time	More expensive than any above
Will polish larger pebbles. Ideal for commercial use	Difficult to fill owing to large capacity; can only tumble one load of hard or soft pebbles in one four-week period. Expensive

machine. The gas, usually hydrogen, is produced by a reaction of the acids normally present in water and pebbles with the particles of metal which are removed from the inside of the barrel by abrasion. The danger from explosions is negligible, but the possibility of the lids being forced off or seams failing under pressure is quite high in an unlined metal barrel. The mess which results from a lid coming off a barrel unexpectedly is a quite sufficient reason for avoiding such barrels. If you *must* use metal, make absolutely sure that the lining seals off as much of the inner surface of the barrel as is possible from contact with grits, water and pebbles.

Plastic barrels are almost problem-free as far as gas is

concerned. There is no reaction between acids and metal in plastic barrels and the small amount of gas which is generated by grinding pebbles in water is dissipated when the lid is removed for regular inspection of the pebbles during the polishing process. Some recently introduced barrels have safety valves built in to provide a suitable gas vent.

The final point I wish to make about choosing a tumbler applies to all models, whatever their size or method of construction. Remember that all machines are subject to wear. There will come a time when a component needs replacing or the whole machine needs servicing. At such times it is comforting to know that your supplier can help; that he has in stock any replacement part you need. If you buy a tumbler made in Timbuktu you will probably have to take or send it back to Timbuktu if a fault develops. If, on the other hand, the manufacturer can be reached quickly by letter or telephone you will have few problems when the need for servicing arises.

Home-made and more advanced machines

It would be unfair to close this chapter without a brief reference to home-made tumblers and more sophisticated machines now being developed for the hobby market. Many mechanically-minded enthusiasts have made their own tumble polishing machines and produced excellent polished pebbles. But it is not a project to be undertaken lightly. Pulley sizes, belt length, speed or rotation and size of barrel must all be carefully calculated if a home-made machine is going to be a success. Unless you are accustomed to tackling such design problems or you can enlist the help of a knowledgeable friend, I would advise against a home-made job. You can buy a small but very efficient tumbler complete with electric motor and ready to go for less than ten pounds. You might save half of that sum if you made your own successfully. An excellent book for those contemplating making their own tumbling machine is *Gem Tumbling and Baroque Jewellery Making* by The Victors, available from lapidary shops.

The next generation of tumble-polishers are likely to have many new design features to make the job of achieving a perfect polish much easier. I have already mentioned other methods of driving the rollers, and barrels with gas vents. Other new ideas include variable speed drives which can make the rather difficult job of achieving a good polish on softer pebbles much simpler. The barrel can be slowed down during critical periods such as polishing and the final result can be carefully controlled. No doubt, these new machines will cost a little more than conventional tumblers; but for readers seeking easier methods of achieving perfection they are worth considering.

Fig. 17 The 'Vari-speed' tumbler, which can be adjusted to turn faster or slower according to the kind of pebbles you are tumbling

4 Perfect polishing

We have now arrived at the exciting moment when you start to polish. You have collected several pounds of pretty pebbles; perhaps even learned the names of and begun to recognize the more interesting ones; and you have bought yourself a tumbler and a supply of grits and polish. You are ready to start.

The first important question to settle is where you are going to keep your machine. It makes a certain amount of noise so I do not recommend a bedroom unless you are a heavy sleeper. Take a handful of pebbles and pour them from one hand to the other half a dozen times. That should give you some idea of the noise you will get from the machine when you start tumbling.

Next you should consider where you least mind a bit of mess. Remember you will be filling and emptying the barrels with pebbles, water, grits and polish many times during the machine's life.

Finally, has the spot you have selected a nearby electrical point where you can safely plug in your machine? You do not want yards of cable lying around for other members of the family to trip over. You should find a place at about table-top height where you can get at the machine comfortably to change grits, inspect barrels, oil bearings, and generally fuss over the thing without getting in anyone's way.

I suppose most tumblers are set to work in a quiet corner of the kitchen and if you can find such a spot it should prove ideal. Spread out a dozen sheets of newspaper and stand your tumbler on them. A sheet at a time can be removed during cleaning-up operations and they will also help reduce noise by cushioning vibrations when the barrel is turning. You can fit a three-pin plug at this stage. Make quite sure you wire it correctly and make the earth connection. Tumblers are perfectly safe to run from the household electricity supply but remember you are using water in the process. To disregard safety measures which the manufacturer has built into the machine would be very foolish.

For the purpose of writing this chapter I have assumed

that you have bought a tumbler similar to the six-pound model with one three-pound and two one-and-a-half pound barrels described in the previous chapter. If you have bought a different model you will find that the basic polishing process is the same with all machines and I have added notes where necessary to guide owners of smaller or larger machines. The one I have chosen has the advantage of versatility and incorporates both small and fairly large barrels so much of what follows will apply to everyone.

Grits and polish

We will have a closer look at these. Silicon carbide is a man-made abrasive substance which is extremely hard. You will remember the reference to Moh's Scale in the chapter on selecting pebbles (see p. 19). Silicon carbide has a hardness of more than 9·5 on that scale and is many, many times harder than the toughest pebble in your 'hard' bag. It also has the advantage of forming, when made, into wedge-shaped grains, which makes it an excellent grinding material.

When manufactured by heating and then crushing a mixture of silica sand, carbon, salt and sawdust, it is then graded by being passed through a series of fine mesh

Fig. 18 Grinding and polishing compounds. Densities range from (*left*) very coarse to (*right*) finest polish

screens. The familiar No. 80 grit with which almost all tumble-polishing starts gets its name from the fact that it has passed through a screen with 80 meshes to the inch.

You may have bought two or three grades of silicon carbide, depending on the manufacturer's instructions. The point to bear in mind is that the coarse grit has the *lowest* number and the finer the grit, the higher its grade number. A quick examination of the particles in each container will soon resolve matters if you are in any doubt about which is coarse and which is fine. Some manufacturers recommend mixed grades which gradually break down inside the barrel and these are excellent if the manufacturer's instructions are followed.

The two most common polishes are cerium oxide and tin oxide and you should use whichever the manufacturer recommends. *These are not grinding materials.* Their purpose is to add a permanent polish to the perfectly smooth pebbles you have produced in the earlier stages. No amount of polishing will remove any roughness you allow to remain on your pebbles after grinding. If there *is* roughness you have not ground your pebbles long enough and you will merely waste polish if you do not put matters right by going back to an earlier grinding stage.

Last minute checks Your tumbler should have reached you in perfect condition, but you should check carefully before you switch on, especially if it reached you by mail. Check that it has been oiled and that the rollers are parallel and there are no obvious signs that the machine has received a severe blow in transit. There should be no loose wires hanging about and the belt should sit squarely in the grooves on the pulleys. If all seems well, plug in and switch on. The drive roller will turn much faster without a load and you should allow the machine to run for a few minutes like this. All moving parts should turn smoothly. If you hear odd scraping noises or if the rollers turn intermittently, something is not as it should be. Switch off at once and check your plug wiring and the manufacturer's instructions. If the machine does run smoothly, we will have a closer look at the barrels.

Take the lid off one of your barrels and look inside. The inner walls should be perfectly smooth. If your barrels are metal and have rubber linings make sure that the lining is correctly fitted and there are no bulges or loose seams. If the lid is fitted with a gasket or rubber seal this too should be correctly seated.

You will have already sorted your pebbles into hard and soft groups so let us start with your hard ones. Go through them once again to seek out any that have slipped through into the wrong bag. Now is the time to discard badly cracked specimens. The first grind is a tough operation and any cracked specimens are unlikely to survive. For a one-and-a-half pound barrel you will need approximately one hundred pebbles, the largest not more than one inch across; the smallest approximately a quarter of an inch. Try to select a range of shapes—ovals, spheres, discs— because the grinding action is more efficient when different shapes are mixed together.

A three-pound barrel will require approximately two hundred pebbles and you will be able to include half a dozen larger specimens—up to a maximum size of two

Loading your barrels

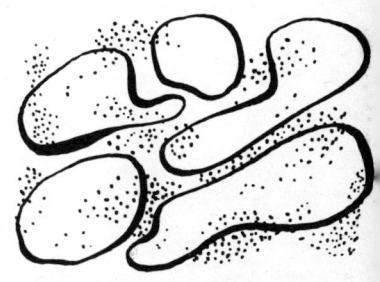

Fig. 19 (a) and (b) A variety of shapes and sizes is the key to success when selecting pebbles or rocks for the tumbler. The small stones grind into the hollows of the large ones

Fig. 20 It is vital that the barrel is loaded correctly, to about three-quarters full

inches. Similarly, larger barrels will take more pebbles with a proportionate number of big ones. All, however, require a grading of sizes from large to small, with plenty of variety in shape.

Note that I headed this section, "Loading your barrels" —*not* filling them. Tumbler barrels must never be filled as cans of beans are filled. If they are they will never polish pebbles. The tumbling action depends on there being sufficient space inside the barrel to allow the pebbles to fall, one over the next, as the barrel revolves.

Too much space and too few pebbles is quite as bad as overfilling. If you do not put sufficient pebbles into the barrel they do not ride up the walls to the point where tumbling commences. They slide back to the bottom and all you get out of the barrel are badly polished flattened discs. So do make a point of getting the amount right. A little under three-quarters full of pebbles of different shapes and sizes should be your aim. This applies to any size of barrel. Place the pebbles inside gently. You spent a long time selecting perfect specimens and it would be a pity to crack or scratch them now. Shake the barrel gently to settle them as you put them in and stop when you near the three-quarters-full point.

Many books and articles emphasize that tumbling is a mechanical process and that the operator has no control over the finished results. I emphatically disagree with this argument. *You* are in control of the operation from start to finish. You select the pebbles; you decide when they are ready for the next stage; you polish them. You may not see the entire operation, but how well you conduct and control the process determines the quality of the polish you achieve. You should keep this in mind as you proceed. Learn by observation, trial and error the best ways of doing each operation. No book can tell you when a particular batch of pebbles is ready for the next stage. You must learn to judge this by experience, learning all you can from your early mistakes and aiming with each new batch of pebbles to improve on your previous results.

There are two excellent ways in which you can start on this road to success now. The first is to keep back a small selection from each batch of pebbles you put into the barrel. Half a dozen will do. Make sure they are representative of the ones you do polish in collecting location, type, colour and size. Put them into a small box or bag and label it so that you know from which beach you collected them. If you have come across any pebbles you were unable to identify on that particular beach and you wish to know how they will polish, you have only to wait and see. This type of comparison—unpolished pebble with finished result—is worth a hundred coloured illustrations in any book and you will soon be able to recognize those pebbles on a particular beach which polish well. Incidentally if you have more than one barrel and they look alike, stick a strip of adhesive tape or plaster on each lid and number your barrels a, b, c, etc. This will avoid confusion later.

The second helpful suggestion is to keep a simple progress chart so that you can record the dates and times you commence and finish different stages in the process, together with comments on results achieved. This information will prove invaluable when next you polish a batch of similar pebbles and you wish to try variations in grinding and polishing times in an effort to better your previous

A grinding and polishing chart

Description of pebbles. Types, where collected	*Barrel number*	*Days on coarse grind*	*Days on medium grind*
EXAMPLE: Flints, quartzite and agates from beaches around Hastings, Sussex	1	5	4

results. Keeping such records and retaining a few pebbles from each batch for comparisons will very soon lead you to perfection in polishing.

You can work out a log similar to the one above for any make or type of tumbler. Read the manufacturer's instructions first—particularly with regard to the number of stages in progress—and prepare your chart accordingly. A school exercise book suitably ruled makes an excellent log. Hang it up somewhere near the machine and get into the habit of keeping entries up to date. It will prove to be a mine of information during the months ahead.

The first grind Now that you have loaded your barrel with pebbles you must add the coarse silicon carbide. The amount of grit depends on the barrel's capacity. A one-and-a-half-pound barrel requires a heaped table-spoonful, while a three-pound barrel requires twice that amount. Check the manufacturer's instructions for other barrel sizes and act accordingly. You should never put too much or too little grit into the barrel as this will upset the grinding process. Use a clean, dry spoon to measure the amount required and shake it evenly over the pebbles in the barrel.

It is of the utmost importance that you do not contaminate the grits and polish, especially by getting any of the coarse grit into the finer material or polish. Keep them well apart. If you can find a few old cocoa tins or similar containers they make excellent holders for your materials. Label the tins and keep them out of harm's way.

The next step is to run tap water into the barrel until it

Days on fine grind	Days on polish	Hours on final wash	Results and comments
4	4 Polycel added	6	Good polish

Might have been improved by longer medium/fine stages |

just covers the top of the pebbles. Don't *fill* the barrel with water. Stop as soon as you see the water cover the pebbles and put the lid on the barrel. You must replace the lid so that it forms a watertight fit on the barrel. Some lids will screw on; other will be a push fit; and some will be fixed by nuts and bolts. All can be prevented from fitting correctly if grains of grit are allowed to remain on the lid or the part of the barrel which comes into contact with the lid. Wipe this area carefully before putting the lid in place and read the manufacturer's instructions for achieving a watertight fit before putting the barrel on the rollers. When you have the lid on, wipe the outside of the barrel to remove water and grit and check that water is not

Fig. 21 Adding the correct amount of silicon carbide

Fig. 22 Remember not to overfill the tumbler with water. Just make sure that the pebbles are covered

leaking around the cap. If all is well switch on the tumbler and place the barrel onto the turning rollers. The rollers will immediately slow down under the weight of the barrel but should settle down at once to a steady speed of revolution. Watch the barrel for a minute or two, checking for a steady rotation and no water leaks.

Although you cannot see inside the barrel as it turns on the rollers, you can tell a great deal about what is happening inside by listening to the sound of the pebbles as they grind. The pebbles should be tumbling or rolling one over the next as they near the top of the barrel in a continuous, rythmical motion. If you have proceeded this far and followed all the advice given above, that is the gentle, rolling sound you should hear. If you hear bangs and knocks, or the sound of pebbles falling and hitting each other, something is wrong. You have not put sufficient pebbles into the barrel, or you have put too many of the wrong size. If you hear little or no movement you have put too many pebbles into the barrel and the tumbling action is not operating.

You are about to discover that tumble-polishing requires a good deal of patience because now you must allow the barrel to turn on the rollers for the next twenty-four hours without interruption. This is always difficult for beginners who find it hard to resist taking the barrel off the rollers every hour or so to see what has happened to their precious pebbles. Very little happens in one hour. But slowly, gradually, your pebbles are being worn to smoothness. When twenty-four hours has passed you can take the barrel off and carefully open the lid. You will probably find it easier to switch off the motor when removing the barrel during the first few days, but you should soon get the knack of lifting the barrel cleanly and neatly from the rollers without stopping the machine—and replacing it just as expertly when you have finished your inspection.

Once the lid is removed you should see a dark grey liquid. Working over the kitchen sink, and with the tap turned on, carefully lift out half a dozen pebbles. Shake off as much of the slurry as possible before moving them clear of the barrel. Put the barrel to one side and run the pebbles you have removed under the tap to wash away all traces of the grey liquid. Now examine the washed pebbles carefully. Already they will feel smoother to your fingers, but they have a long way to go to perfection. Select one of the pebbles and dry it carefully. Now examine it under a good light and you will see the tiny pits and cracks on its surface.

Back into the barrel it must go, along with the others you removed. Wash the lid and the top of the barrel to remove all traces of grit and replace the lid as you did before. Once you are satisfied that you have a watertight seal switch on the tumbler and replace the barrel on the rollers. Again, watch it for a minute or two to check for leaks. If all is well, wait another day and repeat the inspection.

You alone must decide when your pebbles are ready for the next stage. Fairly smooth beach pebbles composed mainly of quartz will take between three and six days to grind to the required smoothness. The aim is to remove all surface blemishes, pits and cracks from every pebble in the barrel, but this perfection is rarely, if ever, achieved. If you continue coarse grinding until the worst pebble in the barrel is perfectly smooth, the remainder will be too much reduced in size. Indeed, the smallest could be ground away completely if you allowed the first stage to go on too long. A compromise is what you should aim for.

When the day comes that four, or possibly five, of the half-dozen pebbles you remove for inspection satisfy you by their smoothness and blemish-free appearance that they are ready, it is time to call a halt. Remove all the pebbles from the barrel and place them in the sink with the tap running. A plastic sink tidy or colander makes an excellent container for the pebbles at this stage. Let the tap run onto them to wash away all traces of grit.

You must not under any circumstances pour the sludge in the barrel down the waste pipe. It will very quickly block your drains and you will be faced with an expensive plumbing job. The best way to dispose of it is to find a suitably-sized plastic bag and carry it, with the barrel, out to the dustbin. Pour the contents of the barrel into the bag and put the bag into the dustbin.

Now, back to the kitchen and wash everything— pebbles, barrel, lid, your hands, and then wash the pebbles again. If you have made a mess around the machine remove one of the sheets of newspaper after cleaning the rollers on the tumbler. Now is probably a good time to lubricate the roller bearings and carry out any other weekly maintenance recommended by the manufacturer.

Fig. 23 The end of the first stage. The pebbles should now be perfectly smooth

Do this before you remove a sheet of newspaper and you will be ship-shape for the next stage in the process.

Step by step through the first stage

1. Check your tumbler.
2. Load barrel just less than three-quarters full with suitably sized pebbles.
3. Add correct amount of coarse grit.
4. Add water—just covering pebbles.
5. Clean cap and barrel.
6. Replace cap and check that it is watertight.
7. Switch on tumbler and place barrel on rollers, again checking for leaks.
8. Inspect daily—remember to carry out steps 5 and 6 each time.
9. When pebbles are ready remove them from the barrel.
10. Dispose of sludge in the dustbin.
11. Wash everything very carefully.
12. Carry out machine maintenance.

Quality control

We have now arrived at a point where many beginners fall by the wayside along the path to perfect polishing. The task is simple: dry your pebbles carefully, spread them out on a sheet of newspaper, examine them and reject every one that retains a blemish, pit, or crack. Ruthlessness is what is required and many beginners lack it. They allow poor quality pebbles to slip through to the next stage instead of eliminating them at this stage. When, at the end of the process, they gaze forlornly at the final result they blame the machine, the manufacturer or their own bad luck when all the time the fault is their own. So do be ruthless. The pebbles you reject now can be put back into the barrel when you start your next coarse grind and you will probably be delighted with the result. Meanwhile, put them aside.

This rejection process will of course reduce the bulk of your pebbles by about five or ten per cent. The coarse silicon carbide will also have rendered each pebble smaller

Fig. 24 Quality control. Eliminate badly cracked and pitted pebbles now

in size and the combined effect of rejection and wear will probably reduce the entire batch by up to fifteen per cent of its original volume.

If rejection has been high, or wear very great, and you only have one barrel on your tumbler this can mean that you are unable to load it correctly for the next stage. This ceases to be a problem when you have been tumbling for some time. You will always have odd polished pebbles lying around which for one reason or another you have not made into jewellery, and these can be used as fillers to make up the bulk of the load. If you have a very small, single-barrelled tumbler there are two courses of action you can take if the bulk of your pebbles falls below the minimum two-thirds loading line and you have not built up a stock of polished pebbles from which to draw to make up the load.

1. Put to one side the pebbles you have already processed through the first stage and start again with a new load of pebbles. When this second load has been coarse ground you will have more than enough pebbles to continue to the next stage.

2. Accept that you will not achieve perfection at your first polishing attempt and continue to the second stage

with all the pebbles you have put through the first stage.

If you are lucky enough to have a tumbler with large *and* small barrels and you loaded one of your large barrels to begin with, you will now begin to see the advantages of your machine. Simply load a smaller barrel from the pebbles you have left after rejecting all the cracked and pitted specimens and continue with the next stage.

The second grind

Some manufacturers suggest that the second grind with medium grit is unnecessary and that you can proceed direct from the coarse to the fine grit. However, to maintain a gradual grinding process and to eliminate scratches caused by the coarse grit it is recommended that a second grind with medium grit is adopted as follows:

Ensure your barrel is completely clean and that no traces of the coarse grit remain, and load it to just less than three quarters full with pebbles. Take your container of medium grit (220 grade), add the correct amount to the barrel and then cover the pebbles with water. Ensure the cap is secured and that the barrel is running freely and place the loaded barrel onto the rollers. This stage of tumbling is important because it eliminates the scratches caused by the coarse grit so that when the pebbles go into the third stage of tumbling they are relatively smooth.

Continue this second grind for approximately seven days and at the end of this time examine the stones to ensure that the scratch marks have disappeared.

Step by step through the second stage

1 Make sure that all traces of the coarse grit have been removed from the pebbles, the barrel, cap rollers and even your hands and nails.
2 Load barrel to just under three-quarters full with selected pebbles from the first run. (Or continue with all the pebbles if you only have one barrel and this is your first attempt at tumbling.)
3 Add correct amount of medium grit.
4 Add water—just covering the pebbles.

5 Replace cap and shake barrel to check that it is watertight.

6 Switch on tumbler, make sure it is running smoothly and place barrel on rollers—again check for leaks.

7 Inspect stones daily—check each time that the barrel top is clean and the lid fits securely and is watertight.

8 After six or seven days inspect pebbles to see if they feel smooth and imperfections have been removed.

9 If satisfactory remove pebbles from barrel and dispose of sludge in dustbin.

10 Carefully wash pebbles and remove all traces of sludge and grit and make sure that the barrel, the barrel top and the stones are completely clean.

The third grind You now have a barrel of unpolished and fairly smooth pebbles and your aim now is to eliminate all grit marks so that the stones are perfectly smooth for the final polish.

Once again check that the barrel is completely clean and free from all traces of medium grit, then load once more to just less than three-quarters full with pebbles. (If this is your first attempt at tumbling, at this stage you will have lost some of your bulk and this must be restored to just under three-quarters full with a filler such as sawdust or wallpaper paste.)

The third stage of tumbling is the most important of all. It is also the stage at which many attempts at perfection fail because most beginners are apt to regard it as a grinding process similar to the first and second grinds with coarse and medium grits. But it is much more.

During the first two or three days the fine silicon carbide *does* in fact continue the grinding process begun by the coarser grit. Scratches and tiny imperfections—some of them made by the medium grit—are gradually worn away. It is at this point that the real work of the third stage begins. The fine grit starts to break down. It loses its power to remove scratches and pit-marks and now prepares the pebble for the final polish. You will see now why there is little to be gained from leaving badly pitted pebbles in the barrel at the end of the first stage. So little grinding takes place during the third stage that any deep imperfections cannot be removed. What you must also see is the importance of continuing the third stage until the pebbles *are* ready for polishing. Be patient. Be prepared, if necessary, to run this stage twice as long as the medium or coarse grind. Your final results really do depend on it.

Fortunately, it is quite easy to decide when the pebbles have been long enough in the barrel on this stage. You will, of course, be checking their progress daily by opening the barrel and carefully washing half a dozen pebbles under the tap before examining their surfaces. What you are looking for is absolute smoothness over the entire surface of each pebble. The smallest pit marks will ruin the final polish so examine your samples very, very carefully. At the end of this stage the pebbles should look exactly as they will when polished—except for their lack of shine. A matt-finish probably best describes what you must aim for. When it will come depends on a number of variable factors, but you might begin to expect it five or six days after commencing your third stage. If, on examination, you think that your samples are ready, take a small piece of felt and soak it under the tap. Next, sprinkle a small amount—half a teaspoonful would be more than enough—of your polishing powder onto the wet felt.

Fig. 25 Test-polishing on a piece of felt impregnated with polishing compound

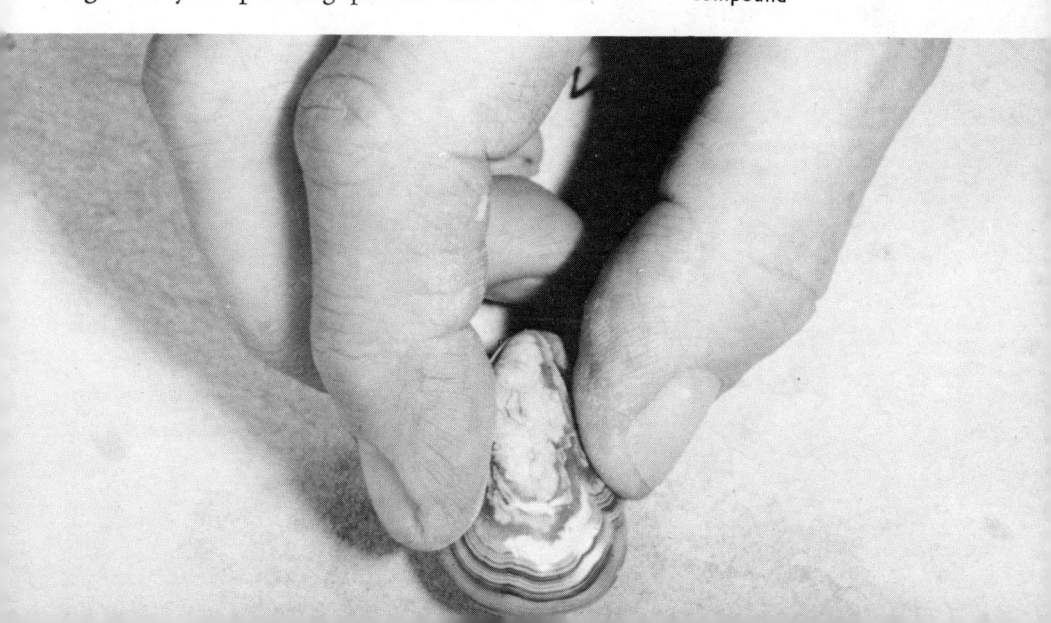

Take one of your sample pebbles firmly between finger and thumb and rub it vigorously backwards and forwards over the impregnated felt forty or fifty times. Now, carefully dry the area of pebble you have polished and examine it very closely in good light. Look for tiny pin-pricks or scratches on the polished surface. If you see even one you must continue the third stage for at least a further twenty-four hours before test-polishing another pebble. If you are quite satisfied that the surface you have polished is perfect the third stage is complete.

Incidentally, if you do see tiny pin-pricks or scratches when you examine your sample, do not under any circumstances add more fine grit to the barrel in the hope that you will speed up the process. You will do quite the reverse. After five or six days of third stage tumbling your pebbles are nearing their final smoothness and even fine silicon carbide will scratch them. If you add more grit now you will have to begin the third stage again. The correct procedure is to put the pebbles back into the barrel and continue until you can achieve a perfect polish on the test specimen.

Step by step through the third stage

1 Make sure you have washed away all traces of medium grit from pebbles, barrel, caps and rollers.
2 Load barrel just less than three-quarters full with selected pebbles from the first run. (Or continue with all pebbles if you have only one barrel and this is your first attempt at polishing.)
3 Add correct amount of fine grit.
4 Add water—just covering pebbles.
5 Clean cap and barrel top.
6 Replace cap and check that it is watertight.
7 Switch on tumbler and place barrel on rollers, again checking for leaks.
8 Inspect daily—remember to carry out 5 and 6 each time.
9 After five or six days, test polish one pebble on a piece of felt impregnated with polishing powder.

10 If satisfactory, remove pebbles carefully from barrel.
11 Dispose of sludge in dustbin.
12 Wash everything very carefully. Take even more care than you did after the first and second grinds.
13 Carry out machine maintenance.

The final polish

You now have a batch of unpolished but perfectly smooth pebbles and your aim should be to impart a mirror-finish to each one. Handle them very carefully at this stage. Don't pour them from one container to another. When washing them to remove every trace of silicon carbide, don't allow them to knock one against the other. The smallest scratch or chip will show up when they are polished, so do handle with care.

Owners of versatile, multi-barrelled tumblers will be able to keep one barrel solely for final polishing without additional expense and, although it means further outlay on equipment, I recommend buying a second barrel for this purpose to owners of single-barrelled machines. If your aim is perfection in polishing, a second barrel is a worthwhile investment because it reduces to nil the chances of odd particles of silicon carbide remaining in the barrel after the third stage has been completed. Very careful washing of the inside of the barrel will do much to prevent this if you must limit expense, but remember that tiny scratches on the barrel's inner surface can trap grit particles which will resist your efforts to remove them with water.

Having made sure that the barrel you are going to use is absolutely clean, place the pebbles carefully inside, one at a time, until you have the required load—that is, just under three-quarters full. There will have been little reduction in volume during the third stage because, as already explained, so little grinding takes place. If you had the correct load at the beginning of the third stage you should have just the right amount now.

Take your container of polishing powder and add the correct amount of polish to the barrel. Cover the pebbles with clean water, replace the cap, make sure that everything is clinically clean and return the barrel to the rollers.

As already pointed out, sound plays an important part in tumble-polishing. During this final stage you should pay particular attention to the sound of your pebbles as they tumble in the barrel. A steady and rhythmical motion inside the barrel will produce the steady and rhythmical sound of pebbles tumbling one over the next. Any harsh banging or unrhythmical striking of pebbles together is a sure sign that the tumbling action is not being carried out. If this is allowed to happen during the polishing stage it will certainly produce cracks and scratches on the pebble's surfaces.

The commonest cause of cracks and scratches at this stage is an insufficient load. With too few pebbles in the barrel the load is thrown about violently, causing one pebble to strike against the next so harshly that cracks and scratches are the inevitable result. This should not happen if you have followed all the advice given so far, but if you do hear any irregular sounds during the first twenty-four hours of the polishing stage you should take remedial action at once.

Remove the barrel from the rollers, take off the lid and add a small amount of wallpaper adhesive to the mixture. The aim is to thicken the liquid in the barrel so that it cushions the fall of each pebble. Do not make the mixture too thick, otherwise the effectiveness of the polishing agent could be reduced. A thin cream consistency is ideal and it is better to err on the side of thinness rather than add too much at the outset. The addition of the paste will, you may notice, reduce the noise your pebbles make as they tumble. It also increases the time you must allow for the polish to do its work because movement inside the barrel is reduced owing to the greater viscosity of the thickened liquid. A polishing stage of four days without paste might take seven days if paste is added.

The noise reduction question is often in the minds of beginners—especially if they live in flats or cannot find an out-of-the-way spot for their machine. The noise is not very considerable and you should never disregard safety or the final results you wish to achieve when considering noise reduction. Do not put your machine into a padded box. The motor will overheat if adequate ventilation is not provided. Pads of rubber or felt under the base of the machine will do almost as much in the way of reducing noise and they will not prevent ventilation. You should regard the noise reduction achieved by the addition of wallpaper paste at the polishing stage as incidental. The paste is put in to prevent cracking and scratching of the pebbles. Do not, by the way, add paste during the earlier grinding stages in an effort to reduce noise—unless you are prepared to accept very long first and second stages.

Daily inspection of your pebbles is just as important at the polishing stage as it is during grinding so do not neglect it. The process should take from four to seven days to complete and only experience will tell you when the polish has done its work. There comes a time in the process when no amount of further polishing will improve the finish. Indeed, if the barrel were allowed to turn for an excessively long period the final polish would deteriorate. Daily inspection, your log book and experience will guide you on this point. If you examine half a dozen pebbles each day and stop the process on the day you see no improvement on the previous day's polish, your results should be satisfactory.

Step by step through the final polish

1 Double check that all traces of silicon carbide have been removed from your pebbles by thoroughly washing them in running water.
2 Place your pebbles very carefully into the polishing barrel. (If you are using the same barrel it *must* be clinically clean.)
3 Add correct amount of polishing powder.
4 Add water—just covering pebbles.
5 Replace cap and check that all is watertight.
6 Switch on the tumbler and place barrel on rollers, again checking for leaks.

7 If tumbling action sounds harsh add a small amount of wallpaper paste to the barrel.
8 Inspect daily. Remember to carry out 5 each time.
9 When polish cannot be improved upon carefully remove pebbles from barrel.
10 Dispose of sludge in dustbin.
11 Wash everything very carefully.
12 Carry out machine maintenance.

The last wash   The polishing powder leaves a film on the pebbles which is removed by placing the pebbles in the cleaned barrel, covering with water, and adding not more than half a teaspoonful of detergent to break down the surface tension of the water. Run the barrel for four to eight hours, then remove the pebbles very carefully and wash off the detergent in running water. Place all the pebbles on a soft cloth and allow them to dry.

If you keep a careful log of all your tumbling for three or four months you should certainly be able to achieve perfection at the end of that time. Experiment with longer or shorter runs, different amounts of grit and polish, and pebbles of different hardnesses. This is the best way to serve your apprenticeship in tumbling and it will soon make you a master or mistress of the art. Nothing should go very wrong if you follow each step, each process, logically. If it does, reference to past experience should soon put matters right. Below, for quick guidance, is a list of common faults and suggested causes.

Fault finding

Fault	Possible cause
Machine runs intermittently, or stops	Badly wired plug; lubrication of bearings not carried out; oil on drive belt or rollers
Pebbles still rough after first and second grind	Overloaded barrel; insufficient grit; barrel slipping on rollers; hard and soft pebbles mixed
Pebbles badly cracked after first grind	Underloaded barrel; poor specimens

Fault	Possible cause
Inferior polish achieved	Second stage grind not long enough; insufficient polish; hard and soft pebbles mixed in barrel
Flats develop on pebbles	Underloaded barrel; speed of revolution too slow
Leaking barrel	Caps not fitted correctly; grit particles not removed from cap and/or barrel

5 Jewellery making

Let me make one point absolutely clear at the very outset: jewellery made with tumble-polished pebbles is not imitation jewellery. Each piece you make—ring, pendant, brooch or bracelet—is exclusively yours. No two pebbles are exactly alike and nobody else will ever make or own jewellery exactly the same. Select your pebbles carefully, choose your fittings wisely, make the piece to the best of your ability and the end product will be an object of beauty and originality which will give pleasure forever.

Baroque jewellery, as all jewellery made from tumble-polished pebbles is known, is extremely simple to create. Essentially it involves nothing more than gluing pebbles to fittings and perhaps bending a few pieces of wire; yet at the same time it allows you to use your artistic flair to decide the colour, size, shape, balance and final appearance of every piece you make. All of the art which goes into the making of costly pieces in diamond, emerald or pearl can be found in the best pieces of baroque jewellery and the fact that you found your 'gems' on a beach should in no way lower your artistic aims.

Basic equipment

You have just spent several weeks producing perfectly polished pebbles so a little time spent getting together the other basic materials of the craft should not be begrudged. There are not many, so let us go through them carefully:

A pair of short, thin-nosed pliers are all you should ever

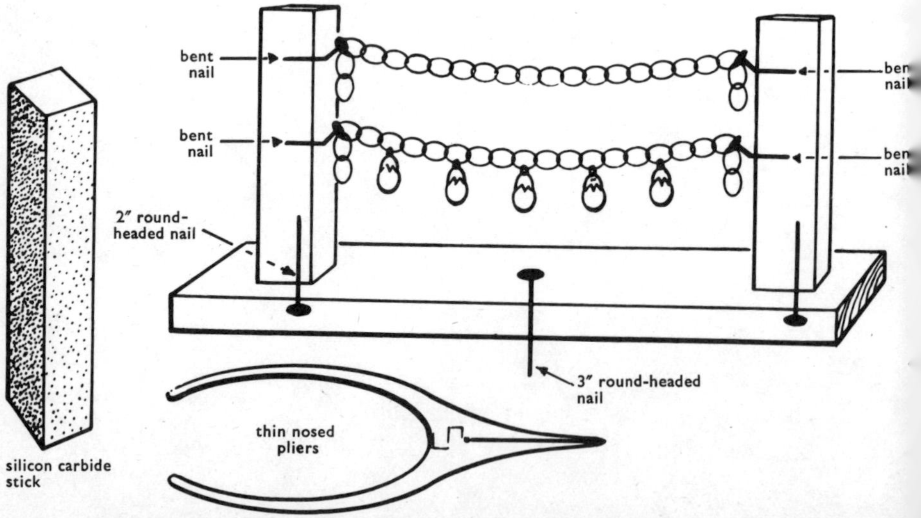

Fig. 26 Essential equipment

need for bending or straightening wire and they are a worthwhile buy for two reasons. They will save time and will do a neater job than fingers alone could ever do. Luckier readers might find an old pair in a tool box or garage, but if you have to buy, they should cost no more than about £1.

A silicon carbide abrasive stick is nothing more than a solid piece of the very abrasive you have used already to grind your pebbles to smoothness. In stick form it is ideal for roughening up fittings and stones prior to gluing. It costs very little.

A wooden jig will provide you with a very useful second pair of hands to hold chains and bracelets when attaching mounted stones. It can be made by anyone capable of using a hammer and nails. Buy three pieces of 2 in. $\times$ 1 in. softwood, all nine inches long. Hammer two one-and-a-half inch, narrow-headed nails about halfway into the narrower side of one of your pieces of wood. The first nail should be fixed two inches from the end of the block; the second near the middle. Next, do exactly the same to your second piece of wood. Now nail your third piece across the top of the two pieces you have hammered nails into, making sure that the protruding nails point inwards towards each other. Now turn the whole thing upside down, bend the protruding nails upwards to an angle by tapping them with your hammer, and your jig is made. If you are lucky enough to have a workbench you can nail the jig to the bench for extra support.

Item four on your list should be very easy to get hold of. This is an *old grill pan* or *shallow roasting tin*. The lid of a biscuit tin would serve almost as well, though it is rather shallow and the grill pan's handle will be found most useful. The container is filled with sand and its purpose is to hold pebbles while fittings are being glued to them. The pebbles are pressed firmly into the sand, thus leaving both hands free for placing the glued fittings in position. As the adhesive used takes some time to set, the sand tray ensures a safe place for the pebbles during the hardening period and leaves you free to continue with other tasks.

Fig. 27 The grill pan makes an ideal container for the sand and pebbles

A small piece of glass or *plastic-laminated board* is useful as a mixing palette when preparing the adhesive. Both can be easily cleaned after use and, their surfaces being non-absorbent, there is no danger of contaminating the adhesive.

The adhesive is an epoxy resin (e.g. Araldite). It is an all-purpose adhesive and you are quite likely to have some already either in the garage or your tool box. If not, a box should cost less than 40p. and for this you will obtain sufficient to make many hundreds of jewellery items. The box contains two tubes—one the resin, the other the hardener. Before use, correct quantities from each tube must be thoroughly mixed together on a clean, dry, non-absorbent surface (hence your piece of glass), and the resultant mixture must be used within a very short time. Unlike ordinary glue, epoxy resin sets and hardens by a chemical process which cannot be stopped once the hardener and resin have been mixed. For this reason only very small quantities, ideally the exact amount you need to make a particular batch of jewellery items, should be mixed at any one time.

For applying the epoxy resin to the fittings before gluing I have found different-sized *darning needles* to be ideal. Push the points into small corks and use the eyed ends to pick up the small quantities of adhesive used to glue each piece.

Fig. 28 More useful equipment

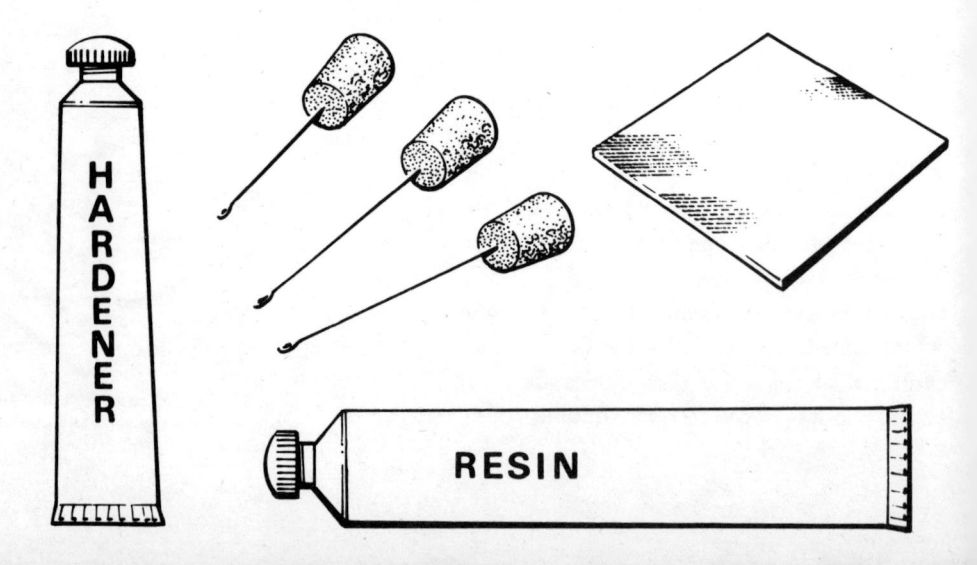

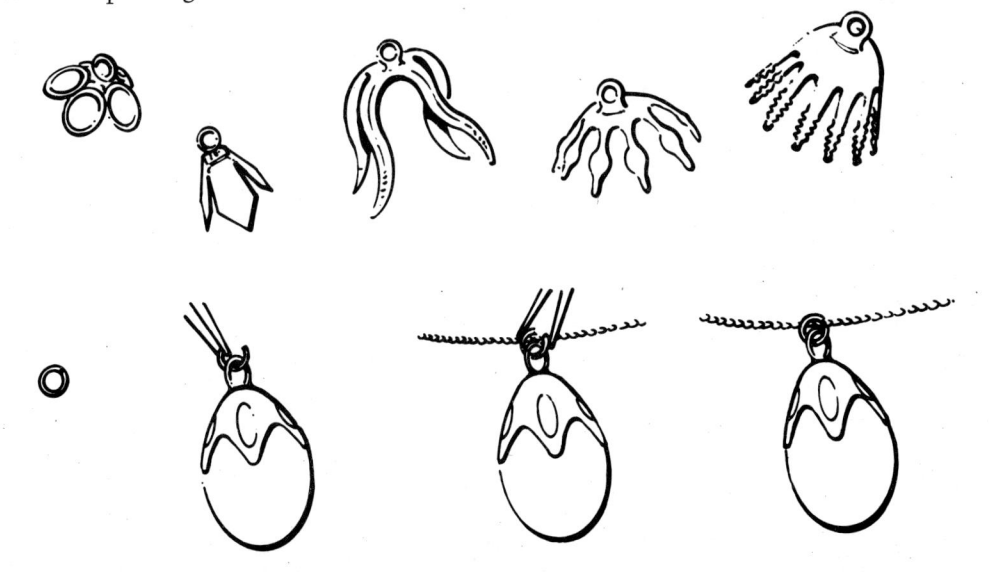

Finally, we come to the jewellery fittings themselves. (*See* p. 78.) There are hundreds for you to chose from—rings, bracelets, chains, earwires, earscrews, brooches, cuff-links, tie bars, tie tacks, keyrings, necklaces—all in a wide variety of styles and finishes. They can be purchased in a selection of metals—sterling silver, gold, silver-plated, gold-plated, stainless steel, or simply gold and silver coloured alloy—and your choice depends on what you wish to pay. But whatever metal or style of fitting you select, there are only two basic ways in which your pebbles are attached to the mountings. They are the *bell cap* method or the *pad* method.

A bell cap is used to make pendants, necklaces, bracelets and earrings. It consists, as its name suggests, of a hollow, bell-shaped body surmounted by a tiny ring and it is secured, cap-like, onto the pebble. The bell-shaped body is made up of flexible, petal-like prongs of metal which are very easy to bend.

They can be moulded with the fingers to fit snugly over the end of any pebble where they are secured with epoxy resin. The bell-capped pebble can then be fixed to a chain, bracelet, or earwire by means of a *jump ring*. This is a small circle of springy metal which can be opened, using a pair of thin-nosed pliers, to allow the ring at the top of the bell cap and a link from a piece of chain or a bracelet to be coupled together.

Fittings

Fig. 29 Bell caps (*top*) and jump rings (*bottom*)

Plate 6 Jewellery fittings

Plate 7 Jewellery to be proud of

Fig. 30 'Pad' type fittings, useful for rings, brooches and cufflinks

Both bell caps and jump rings come in several sizes. The smallest bell caps are no longer than match heads while the largest can be half an inch long. Jump rings to suit each size available and the size required depends on the size of the pebble, the aim always being to use the smallest possible bell cap and jump ring whatever the piece being made.

The *pad* method of fixing is used to make rings, brooches, cufflinks and other items in which the pebble is attached directly to the fitting and not hung onto it by means of a bell cap. Once again sizes differ, particularly in rings and bracelets, and the choice of fitting is determined by the size of pebble you wish to use for the job.

Making the jewellery

Let us now go step-by-step through the work involved in making some pieces of jewellery using both methods of fixing. First find yourself a clear working area in the kitchen and lay out your equipment as follows:

Pebbles. Select the very best of your round and pear-shaped pebbles for bell-capping and set aside any with a flat side for pad mounting.

Sand tray. Prepare this (salt can be used if sand is not readily available) by filling to a depth of two inches and shaking until level. Press your pebbles into the sand to about half their depth, making sure that the more pointed ends are upwards. Space them evenly across the tray.

Bell caps. Take various sizes, spread the prongs and sit one on top of each pebble. Experiment with different sizes and types to achieve the best possible artistic effect. Bear in mind that the position of the eye on the top of the cap determines how the pebble will hang from the jump ring. If you want a particular side of a pebble to face 'forwards' you must position your bell cap accordingly.

Do not touch the tops of your pebbles with your fingers at this stage. Hold them around their middles. The oil in your skin can prevent a good bond when you cement the bell caps in position.

Epoxy resin. Do not start to mix this until you are quite satisfied that all bell caps selected are suitable. Then, having read the instructions carefully, squeeze the correct amount of resin and hardener on to your glass plate and mix very thoroughly.

Needles. Take a corked needle and pick up a small amount of mixed adhesive on the 'eye' end. Lift up your first bell cap and carefully place a blob of adhesive inside the cap. Replace the cap on the pebble and press down firmly. At this stage the adhesive is *not* holding the cap in position. The cap is balanced on top of the pebble and it is important that it remains balanced for the next hour so do not set it at an odd angle on the pebble.

Continue to lift and replace each pebble with its blob of adhesive until you have worked your way through the tray.

Leaving your tray on the workbench, light the grill of your cooker and turn it as high as possible. Let it burn for a few minutes, then carefully carry your tray of bell-capped pebbles from the bench and place it under the burning grill. Watch the prongs of the bell caps very carefully at this stage. After thirty seconds or so you will see the adhesive begin to flow from underneath the bell cap. The moment this happens pull out the tray. This must be done quickly, but gently. If the tray is knocked, all the bell caps will fall off.

Place the tray on a level surface away from heat and do not touch it for the next hour. When one hour has passed every bell cap will be firmly cemented to its pebble and the adhesive will have dried clear, colourless and almost unnoticeable.

If working with children or in a spot where access to a

Plate 8 Rough Foreign stones
Snowflake obsidian   Sodalite   Amethyst   Rutilated quartz
Red tiger's eye   Rose quartz   Blue lace agate
Aventurine   Rhodonite   Amazonite

Plate 9 The polished versions

Snowflake obsidian   Sodalite   Amethyst   Rutilated quartz
Red tiger's eye   Rose quartz   Blue lace agate
Aventurine   Rhodonite   Amazonite

hot grill is impossible, the tray of pebbles can be left to bond without heat quite successfully. Proceed as above until every bell cap has been replaced with its blob of adhesive on its pebble and leave the tray undisturbed for twenty-four hours. An equally good bond should be the result.

To return for a moment to the faster 'grill' method it is most important that the adhesive is not 'overcooked'. Remove the tray from under the grill the moment you see the epoxy begin to run. If this is not done it will discolour on hardening to an unpleasant brown.

The jig. When gluing is completed you can proceed to make necklaces, pendants and bracelets. Hook pieces of chain or bracelet onto the bent nails of your jig; work out the correct spacing of each pebble; and slip jump rings through the links on the chain or bracelet where required with the aid of your pliers. Select bell-capped pebbles according to shape, size and colour, and, using your pliers once again, couple them to your chain or bracelet by means of the jump rings.

Although slightly different methods are used for pad fittings, the aim remains the same: a perfect bond between fitting and pebble. This is best achieved by roughening the two surfaces to be joined with your *silicon carbide stick*. A few scratches on the pad and two or three strokes of the stick across the pebbles are all that is required.

Rings should be scratched in this way and then set in the sand tray in the same way as the pebbles were set for bell-capping. Scratch the area of the pebbles you wish to join to the ring pad *before* you mix your adhesive and proceed as for bell-capping. If using the quicker 'grill' method for bonding it will be found that the epoxy takes a few seconds longer to flow because it is protected from the heat by the pebble. How much longer depends on the size of the pebble because a larger pebble shields the resin from the heat far more than does a small pebble. It is probably better, therefore, to make rings with similar-sized stones in one batch.

Cufflinks and earscrews should be dealt with in the same

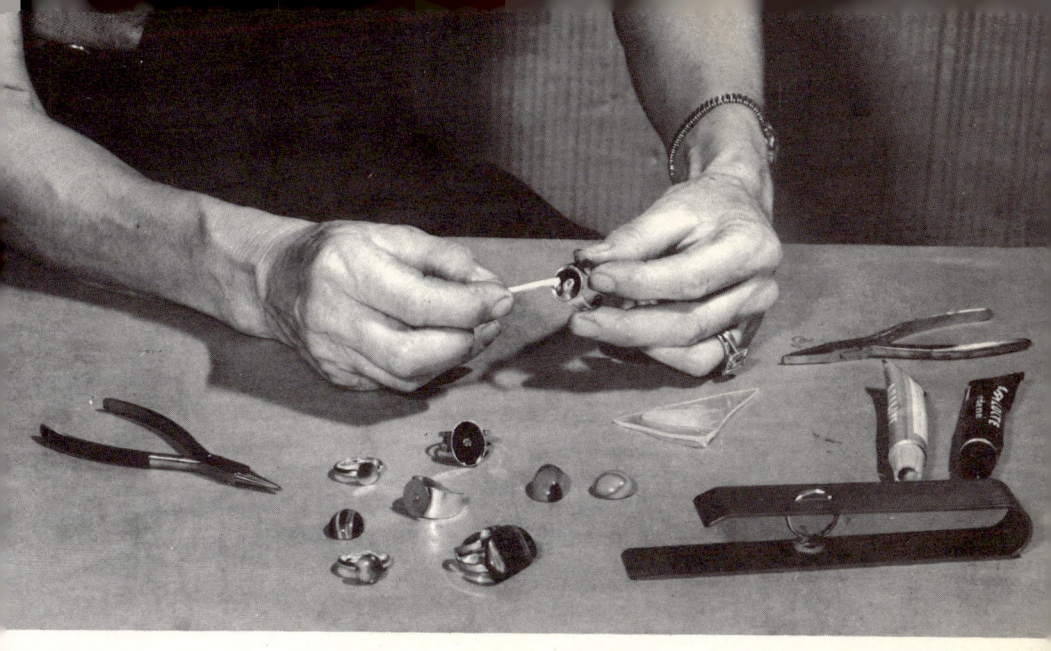

way as rings. Set the fitting in the sand tray after scratching the pad with the abrasive stick and glue the pebble to the fitting.

Bracelets should be laid out on the sand after each pad has been scratched. Pebbles of different sizes, shapes, and colours can then be tried on the pads before they are scratched and cemented. Again, it is probably better to work with pebbles of similar sizes.

Figs. 31 (a) and (b) Another method of ensuring a perfect bond between pebble and fitting without using heat. The spring steel clip on the right of the pictures holds the fitting and pebble securely in position until the adhesive has hardened.

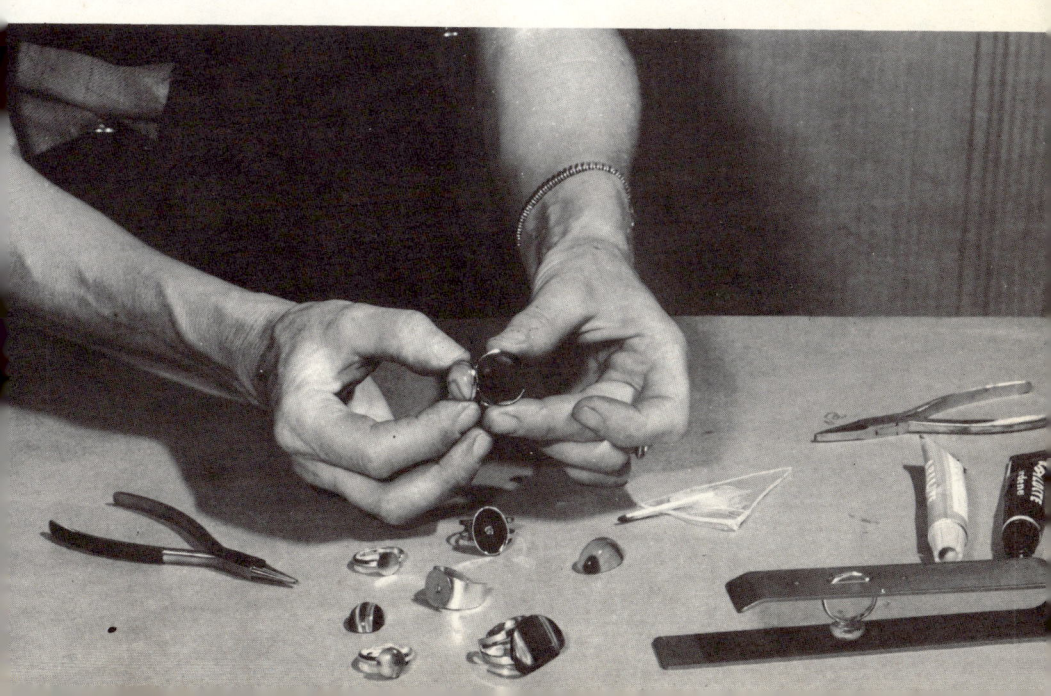

Fig. 32 Attaching a polished pebble to a bell cap fitting to make a pendant. Again the spring steel clip will hold both in position until the adhesive has hardened

There are so many different types of *brooches* available that the choice of whether to place the fitting or the pebble in the sand tray must be left to you. If you can balance the brooch on top of the pebble without fear of it slipping or falling off before the adhesive has dried, I would recommend that method. But if you feel safer with the fitting in the sand, allow a few seconds longer under the grill.

Finally, remember that the standard of jewellery you make rests entirely with you. If you use poor quality fittings, chipped or poorly polished pebbles, and far too much adhesive, the end product will be Junk! If you follow carefully the instructions set out above and use only your very best pebbles for jewellery-making the end product will give you great pleasure for many years.

6 Exotic stones from foreign lands

Once you have achieved success at polishing British pebbles you might like to turn your attention to pebbles and stones from other lands. These are within everyone's reach whether or not you take holidays abroad. Lapidary shops are opening in all parts of the country and if you visit one you will be able to buy rough broken fragments of a suitable size for tumbling from many parts of the world. I have not yet come upon a shop selling foreign pebbles, but this does not present a great problem for the tumble-polishing enthusiast. Rock fragments can be used to load a tumbler barrel if the first stage coarse grind is lengthened to allow the silicon carbide to remove rough edges and transform the rough rock to pebble shape.

If you are able to take a holiday on a foreign coast you will find all the exotic pebbles you can carry home in a rainbow range of colours that will delight your eye, captivate your imagination—and grossly overload your luggage for the journey home! I will repeat my earlier warning about not overloading yourself, though I realize the temptation will be great if your collecting in Britain has been confined to a few miles of coastline. You must, of course, still be ruthless in rejecting cracked or badly pitted specimens. However attractive, they will not polish well. Again, the rules about size and shape apply equally on a foreign beach. You will be making jewellery with the pebbles you select once you get them home and this must be kept in mind when collecting.

Grouping

The pebbles you collect can be sorted into 'hard' and 'soft' groups, using the steel file and penknife blade, and you will be able to polish all pebbles in your 'hard' bag together without difficulty. Best results will be achieved with softer pebbles if they are polished separately because variations in the hardness of 'soft' material can be very wide; whereas most of the 'hard' material is likely to belong to the quartz family. Bear in mind that you will often come across familiar pebbles however far you go. Jaspers and agates and other easily recognizable varieties are to be found all over the world—though in deeper or more striking shades and colours. They can be treated in the same way as those found in Britain.

I must emphasize the importance of keeping careful records when polishing unfamiliar foreign pebbles. Retain unpolished specimens of each type for later comparisons and, if stocks are plentiful, experiment with different grinding and polishing times.

Incidentally, I know of one enterprising young lady who has never spent a holiday south of Dover and yet she has foreign pebbles galore in her unpolished stocks. She hit on the bright idea of acquiring penfriends who live near the coast in half a dozen foreign countries and they keep her well stocked with pebbles in exchange for 'British-home-made' jewellery at Christmas and birthday times. It is an idea well worth copying if it is not possible to travel.

Lapidary shops

Readers who are able to visit lapidary shops or buy rough rock fragments by mail order will be delighted at the varieties obtainable in Britain. The first thing to do is write for lists and catalogues, which are available from most suppliers, and compare stocks and prices. A number of suppliers sell only in large quantities which would be uneconomical if you are using one tumbler with a single

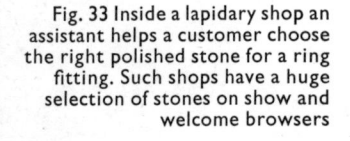

Fig. 33 Inside a lapidary shop an assistant helps a customer choose the right polished stone for a ring fitting. Such shops have a huge selection of stones on show and welcome browsers

barrel; but the price saving, particularly on postage, makes bulk buying an attractive proposition for clubs and groups. However, I do not recommend the purchase of unbroken rock which, although much cheaper, is very difficult to reduce to tumble-polishing size unless you have a crushing machine. It is most unwise to attempt to break large pieces of rock with cold chisels and hammers, but if you are tempted, protect your eyes by wearing goggles.

Ready broken rock for tumble-polishing comes in a number of grades and I recommend the purchase of First Grade material wherever possible. This will be a little more expensive but badly cracked and poor quality material will have been rejected before weighing. If you buy Second Grade material you will have to do the rejecting yourself and this could reduce by as much as one-third the amount of suitable material you get for your money.

Terms such as 'First Grade' and 'Top Quality' are relative and their meaning depends on the overall quality of the material the supplier handles. In time you will acquire the knowledge to judge quality for yourself, but in the meanwhile you should buy from a supplier who sells under a 'Money back if not satisfied' guarantee. All reputable suppliers sell under those terms.

Vast quantities of semi-precious rock are imported into Britain each year for use in the jewellery and lapidary trades. Many of the varieties are far too costly to be considered suitable for polishing in a tumbler. They are used by jewellers who cut and facet them and often set them alongside precious gems in rings, bracelets and pendants which sell for many hundreds of pounds. Nevertheless a wide choice remains open to the amateur tumble-polisher who requires something beautiful at only pence per pound. Some of those stones you should look out for are listed below. When polishing these materials aim for the same perfection you should now have reached with British beach pebbles and do not be afraid to experiment with longer or shorter grinding and polishing stages. Trial and error backed by detailed notes and records will soon lead you to perfection with these unfamiliar foreigners.

Summary of foreign stones

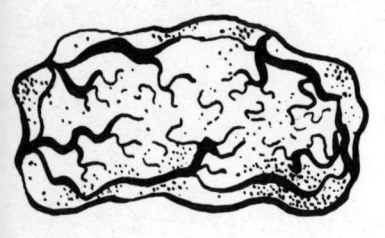

Fig. 34 Section through a moss agate

Fig. 35 A scenic agate

Fig. 36 Malachite

Name	*Description*
Moss agate	Translucent with mossy, fernlike 'growths' which are best seen when the rock is held up to light. Usually green.
Blue lace agate	Opaque and very finely banded. A delicate light blue in colour; the 'lace' effect best seen in rough rock
Scenic agate	Opaque to translucent with internal forms which suggest forest and mountain scenery
Plume agate	Transluscent. Internal formations suggest smoke and feathers
Banded agate	Opaque to transluscent. Distinctive banding in a wide colour range including white, blue, yellow, green, brown, red, and black
Malachite	Opaque. Rich deep green in colour with feint banding best seen when polished
Sodalite	Transluscent. Deep blue, often with white streaks
Snowflake obsidan	Opaque. Black with snowflake patterns
Tiger eye	Opaque. Silky yellow and brown with a 'catseye' effect when turned in light. Red and blue varieties are also available

Tumbling hints
Agate has a hardness of 7 on Moh's Scale and all rough agate is difficult to grind smooth. It does, however, take a wonderful polish if the first grinding stage is not cut short. Tumble three or four times as long as you would first-grind beach agates. If your first attempts at polishing agate are unsuccessful try putting the stones through two long coarse stages and change the grit after the first run. Some agates are often badly cracked when purchased in tumbling sizes and it is best to tumble two loads on the first grind and select the best for second stage grinding and polishing. All rough agates can be tumbled together

As above

As above

As above

As above

A very soft stone (Hardness 4) which should be tumbled separately. Inspect every twelve hours when first-stage grinding and do not overrun. A fairly expensive stone which might tempt you to underload the barrel. Beautiful when polished well

Softer than agate but harder than malachite (Hardness 5). Probably best tumbled separately but should be successful with snowflake obsidian and rhodonite

Hardness 5—although variations in hardness occur in varieties from different parts of the world. Do not overrun on the second stage

This stone (Hardness 7) should always polish well, but much inferior material is on the market. Buy only First Grade and do not underrun the first stage. Will tumble with other quartz material

Name	Description
Amethyst	Transparent and semi-transparent. Pale to deep purple, often with white markings
Lapis lazuli	Opaque. Blue and white speckled with gold-coloured pyrites
Rose quartz	Transluscent. Pale pink
Jasper	Opaque. Red and brown with coloured patterns
Rhodonite	Opaque. Red and pink with black markings
Rhodochrosite	Opaque. Red and pink band streaked with white
Cornelian	Semi-transparant. Orange to deep red
Aventurine	Transluscent. Green with a sparkl throughout
Bloodstone	Opaque. Deep green with tiny re spots
Rutilated quartz	Transparent. Clear quartz wit golden needles running through
Amazonite	Opaque to transluscent. Deep gree to blue with a sparkle

Note: Many suppliers offer mixed bags of rock of similar hardness for tumbling. They make excellent buys if First Quality material only is included.

Tumbling hints

Another quartz (Hardness 7) which should polish well. Again, there is a great deal of poor quality material on the market. The best quality is usually only available in very small fragments and if you are lucky enough to locate a good supply you should tumble it separately and watch for cracks on the first and second grinding stages

A difficult stone to tumble-polish really well (Hardness 5). Tumble separately and do not overrun the first stage or underrun the second stage

A beautiful stone when polished well (Hardness 7). Should tumble with other quartz. Watch out for cracks during the first grind

An inexpensive stone which can look beautiful when polished (Hardness 6-7). Variations in hardness might present difficulties but should polish with other quartz. If unsuccessful tumble separately with a longer first stage

(Hardness 5-6). Difficult to find good quality material. Tumble separately for best results

Very soft (Hardness 3). Tumble separately with a very short first stage

Polishes perfectly when first stage is not underrun (Hardness 7). Tumble with other quartz

A long first stage should give excellent results (Hardness 7). Tumble with other quartz

Beautiful when polished (Hardness 7). Tumble with other quartz

Tumble with other quartz (Hardness 7)

Tumble separately for best results (Hardness 6)

7 More advanced machines

I said at the beginning of this book that lapidary grows on you. It is a fascinating subject and if you have enjoyed tumble-polishing beach pebbles you can look forward to many years of pleasure should you decide to pursue the hobby at a more advanced level. Machines to help you progress and develop your skills at the craft are not terribly expensive and the jewellery you will be able to make once you have learned the more advanced techniques will quickly repay your initial outlay on equipment, either in sheer pleasure or in a good profit should you wish to sell your products. Whether you choose to teach yourself at home or join one of the many evening classes or lapidary clubs which are now run in most towns, your complete enjoyment is guaranteed.

One of the first tasks beginners like to attempt is slicing a beach pebble to produce two perfectly matched half pebbles to make into cuff-links or earrings. As you have already discovered, pebbles can be extremely hard and the only suitable tool for slicing them is a *diamond saw*. This is a circular metal disc, eight to ten inches in diameter, and

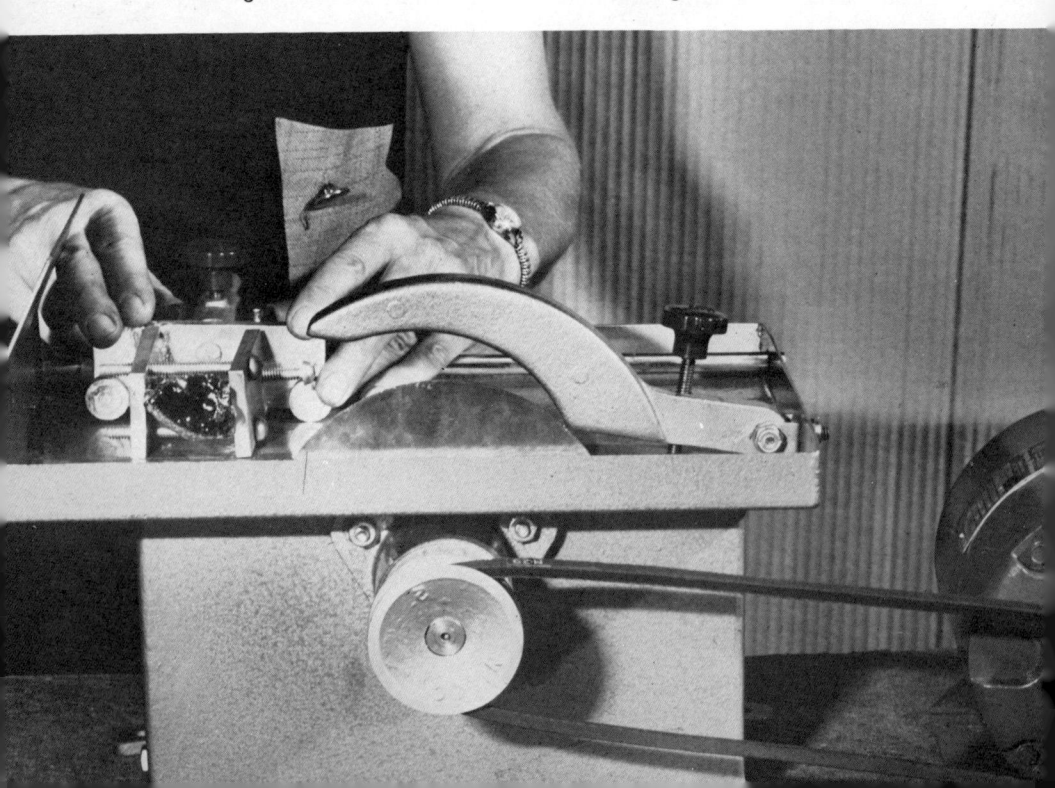

Fig. 37 Slicing a piece of rock on a diamond saw. Pebbles can also be sliced in half to make a pair of earrings or cufflinks

approximately one-tenth of an inch thick. The disc has diamond particles embedded into notches on its rim and when it is made to turn on a shaft connected to an electric motor, it will bite its way through the toughest semi-precious pebble in a few seconds.

The diamond saw used to slice pebbles is known as a trim saw and it is also used to cut pieces of rock to any size required. The stone is usually held in a clamp which the operator guides against the rim of the saw.

Please note that although the word 'saw' conjures up images of dangerous sharp teeth, you need have no such fears with a diamond saw. It has no teeth and will not cut fingers—even when they are pressed against the rim. It actually grinds it way through rock and is completely safe to use even when working with children.

Another method of removing unwanted material from a piece of stone or a pebble is by grinding. For this purpose *grinding wheels* are used. They are made from the same silicon carbide you use when tumble-polishing and they are similarly obtainable in coarse, medium and fine grades. The grinding wheel is also driven on a shaft connected to an electric motor—often the same shaft as the one that turns the diamond saw—and the stone or pebble to be shaped is held against the wheel as it turns. On such wheels

Fig. 38 A selection of sawing, grinding and polishing attachments

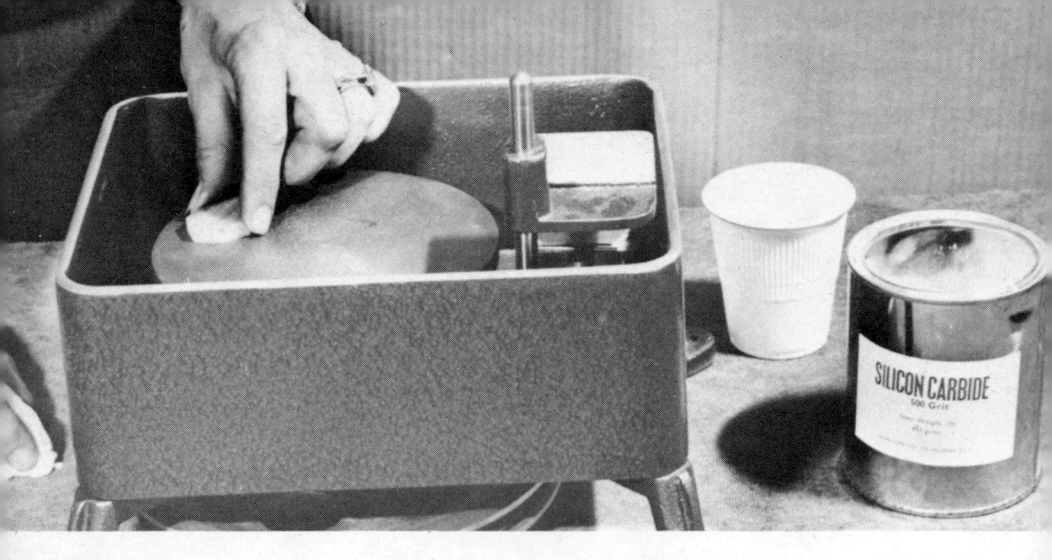

Fig. 39 Grinding a flat surface with a cast iron lap and silicon carbide

stones can be ground flat, or rough edges removed from fragments prior to polishing.

Polishing discs are also turned on a shaft driven by an electric motor. They are made from thick felt which can be impregnated with polishing powder. The stone to be polished is then pressed firmly against the wheel as it spins.

The cutting, grinding, and polishing of pebbles and stones is generally carried out on one machine. It is usual to purchase this 'bare' and add the various attachments as one progresses with the hobby. The great advantage of this idea is that the cost of equipment can be spread over a period of time.

Cast iron laps are used for grinding and polishing flat surfaces, particularly thin slabs of rock previously sliced on a diamond saw. The laps are mounted horizontally on a shaft in the same way as a gramophone record is placed on a turntable. Loose silicon carbide is then sprinkled onto the surface of the disc and the flat slab is pressed against the lap in order to grind it to the required finish. Grits are changed progressively and final polishing is carried out on a horizontal felt wheel.

Cabochon cutting is also carried out on silicon carbide wheels and felt discs. A cabochon is a stone or pebble which has been shaped to a symmetrical oval dome by first mounting the stone on a piece of stick (known as a dop stick) with hot wax and then grinding it to shape by moving it against a revolving wheel.

Faceting involves cutting flat faces on a stone in such a way that the beauty of the stone is revealed when light is refracted through it. Faceting attachments, which ensure the correct angle of cut on each face, can be purchased and attached to many machines; or one can buy a complete machine just for faceting.

Figs. 40 and 41 The techniques of cabochon cutting. It is important to get a smooth, round surface on the dopped pebbles

Fig. 42 (a) Faceting a stone and (b) faceting attachments

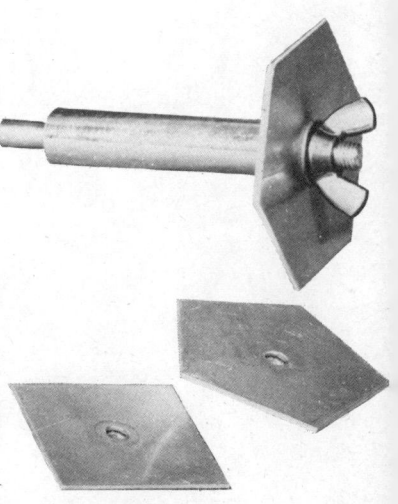

Illustrated here are some of the many versatile lapidary machines on the market today:

Fig. 43 The 'Gem Master', a very popular, versatile model

Fig. 44 The 'Cabochon Master'

Fig. 45 The 'Rock Master' for larger stones

8 Rules and regulations

I must not close this book without a very brief mention of four subjects which might be of importance should you decide to make jewellery on a commercial scale. They are unlikely to affect readers interested only in making jewellery for personal use, but for the commercially minded the four subjects are: V.A.T.; income tax; import duty; and the law relating to the removal of pebbles and rock samples from public beaches and mine and quarry workings.

At the time of writing, sales of jewellery are subject to V.A.T. If you plan to sell large quantities of home-made jewellery you should seek advice on the up-to-date position regarding V.A.T. from your local office where expert guidance is available free of charge. Note that polished pebbles and stones themselves are also subject to V.A.T.

All income is unfortunately subject to income tax and you should always keep careful records of any transactions —both buying and selling—if you aim to earn any income from the hobby. The services of an accountant are recommended if your knowledge of book-keeping is limited and you aim to make substantial sales.

Import duty is not payable at the time of writing on rough rock, pebbles, and minerals purchased from abroad. You should not run into difficulties when passing through Customs points after collecting pebbles or rock fragments while on holiday.

The removal of large quantities of shingle from public beaches is carefully controlled by local authorities. Shingle acts as a natural barrier against erosion and its uncontrolled removal could result in large areas of land and foreshore being eaten away by the sea. A few pounds of pebbles taken home by a tumble-polishing enthusiast will not make the slightest difference, but all collecting should be kept to a minimum.

If you wish to collect rock samples inland, bear in mind that all land, including old mines and quarries, is owned by someone and you will certainly lay yourself open to a charge of trespassing if you climb fences or ignore 'keep out' notice boards. It is rarely difficult to obtain permission to collect a few samples if the correct approach is used. Be polite, explain your hobby, ask first and say 'thank you' afterwards and you should have few problems wherever you go.

Lapidary suppliers This is by no means a comprehensive list of lapidary suppliers, but merely a guide to some of the larger establishments operating throughout the country.
Tumble-polishing machines; rough stones and jewellery fittings:
- Gemrocks Ltd, 7 Brunswick Centre, London WC1.
- Ammonite Ltd, Llandow Industrial Estate, Cowbridge, Glamorgan, CF7 7PB.
- M. L. Beach (Products) Ltd, Church Street, Twickenham, Middlesex; 7 Kings Parade, Ditchling Road, Brighton.
- Kernowcraft Ltd, 21 Pydar Street, Truro, Cornwall.
- Gemstones, 44 Walmsley Street, Hull, Yorks.
- Rough and Tumble Ltd, 20 Front Street, Tynemouth, Tyne and Wear.
- G. & B. Butler, 18b The Pantiles, Tunbridge Wells, Kent.
- Coronet Trading Co., 44 Station Lane, Hornchurch, Essex.
- Gemcraft Lapidary Ltd., 162 Chiswick High Road, London W4 1PR.

Further reading If you have enjoyed reading this book, further pleasure awaits you in the form of more books by Edward Fletcher:

Rock and Gem Polishing
Bottle Collecting
Treasure Hunting For All
A Treasure Hunter's Guide

Maps showing the locations of pebbles

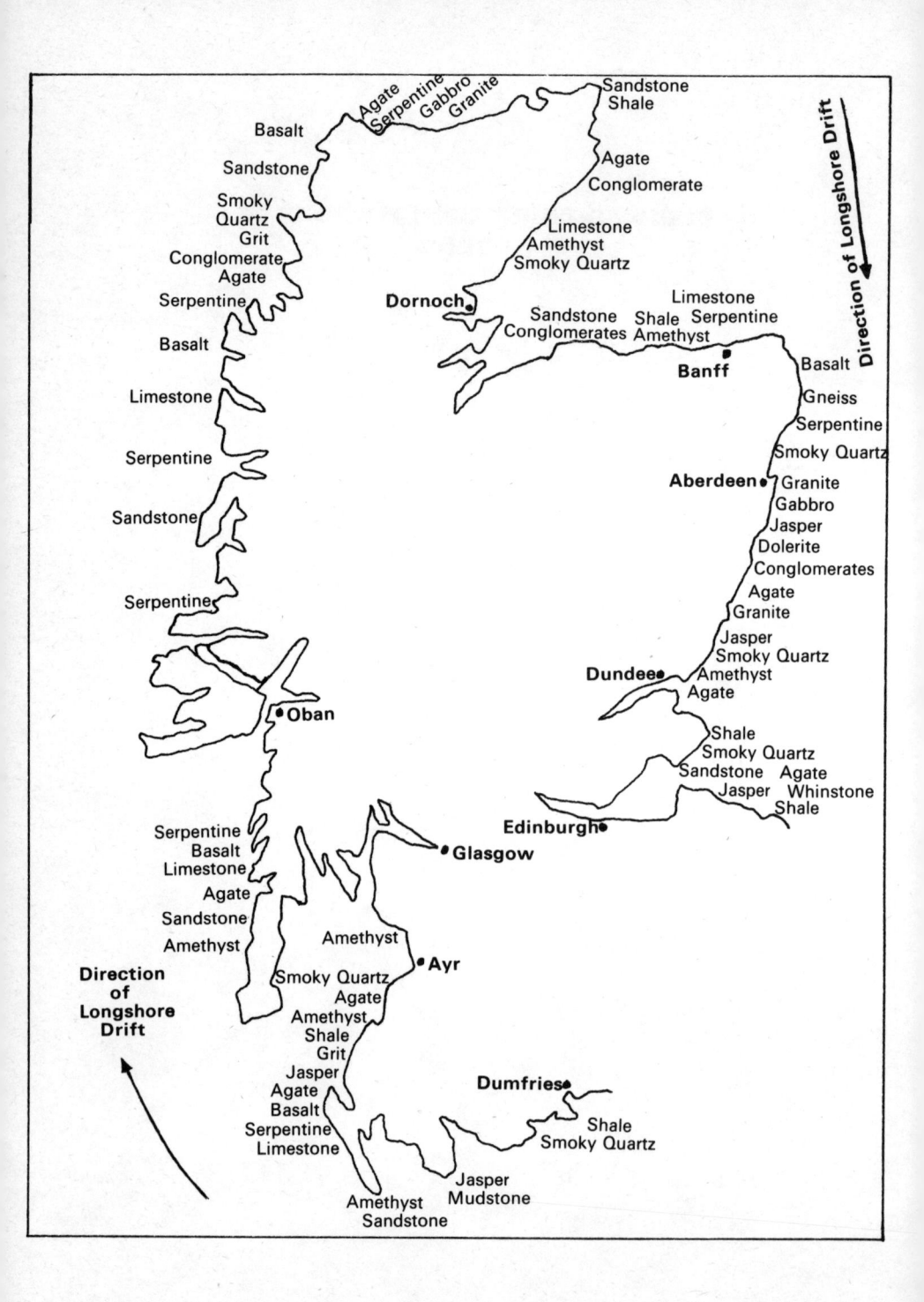

Map of Scotland showing coastal geology and rock/mineral types at locations around the coast.

- **North coast (west to east):** Basalt; Sandstone; Smoky Quartz; Grit; Conglomerate; Agate; Serpentine; Agate; Serpentine; Gabbro; Granite; Sandstone; Shale; Agate; Conglomerate; Limestone; Amethyst; Smoky Quartz
- **Dornoch**
- Sandstone; Conglomerates; Limestone; Shale; Serpentine; Amethyst
- **Banff** — Basalt; Gneiss; Serpentine; Smoky Quartz
- **Aberdeen** — Granite; Gabbro; Jasper; Dolerite; Conglomerates; Agate; Granite; Jasper; Smoky Quartz; Amethyst; Agate
- **Dundee** — Shale; Smoky Quartz; Sandstone; Agate; Jasper; Whinstone; Shale
- **Edinburgh**
- **Glasgow**
- **Ayr** — Amethyst; Smoky Quartz; Agate; Amethyst; Shale; Grit; Jasper; Agate; Basalt; Serpentine; Limestone
- **Dumfries** — Shale; Smoky Quartz; Jasper; Mudstone; Amethyst; Sandstone
- **Oban**
- **West coast (north to south):** Basalt; Sandstone; Smoky Quartz; Grit; Conglomerate; Agate; Serpentine; Basalt; Limestone; Serpentine; Sandstone; Serpentine; Serpentine; Basalt; Limestone; Agate; Sandstone; Amethyst

Direction of Longshore Drift (north-east, top right)
Direction of Longshore Drift (south-west, bottom left)

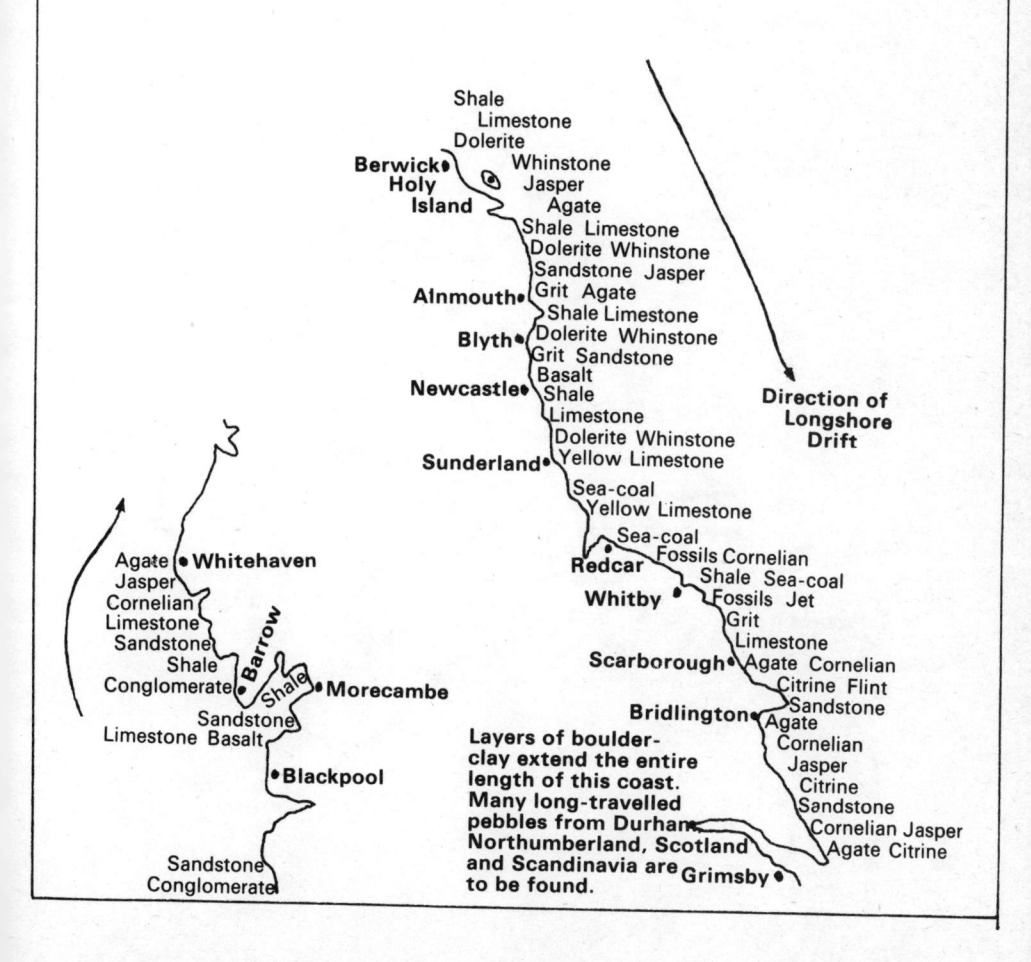

Shale
Limestone
Dolerite
Berwick Whinstone
Holy Jasper
Island Agate
Shale Limestone
Dolerite Whinstone
Sandstone Jasper
Alnmouth Grit Agate
Shale Limestone
Blyth Dolerite Whinstone
Grit Sandstone
Basalt
Newcastle Shale
Limestone
Dolerite Whinstone
Sunderland Yellow Limestone
Sea-coal
Yellow Limestone
Sea-coal
Fossils Cornelian
Redcar Shale Sea-coal
Whitby Fossils Jet
Grit
Limestone
Scarborough Agate Cornelian
Citrine Flint
Sandstone
Bridlington Agate
Cornelian
Jasper
Citrine
Sandstone
Cornelian Jasper
Agate Citrine
Grimsby

Direction of Longshore Drift

Agate **Whitehaven**
Jasper
Cornelian
Limestone
Sandstone
Shale
Conglomerate
Barrow
Shale
Sandstone **Morecambe**
Limestone Basalt
Blackpool

Sandstone
Conglomerate

Layers of boulder-clay extend the entire length of this coast. Many long-travelled pebbles from Durham, Northumberland, Scotland and Scandinavia are to be found.

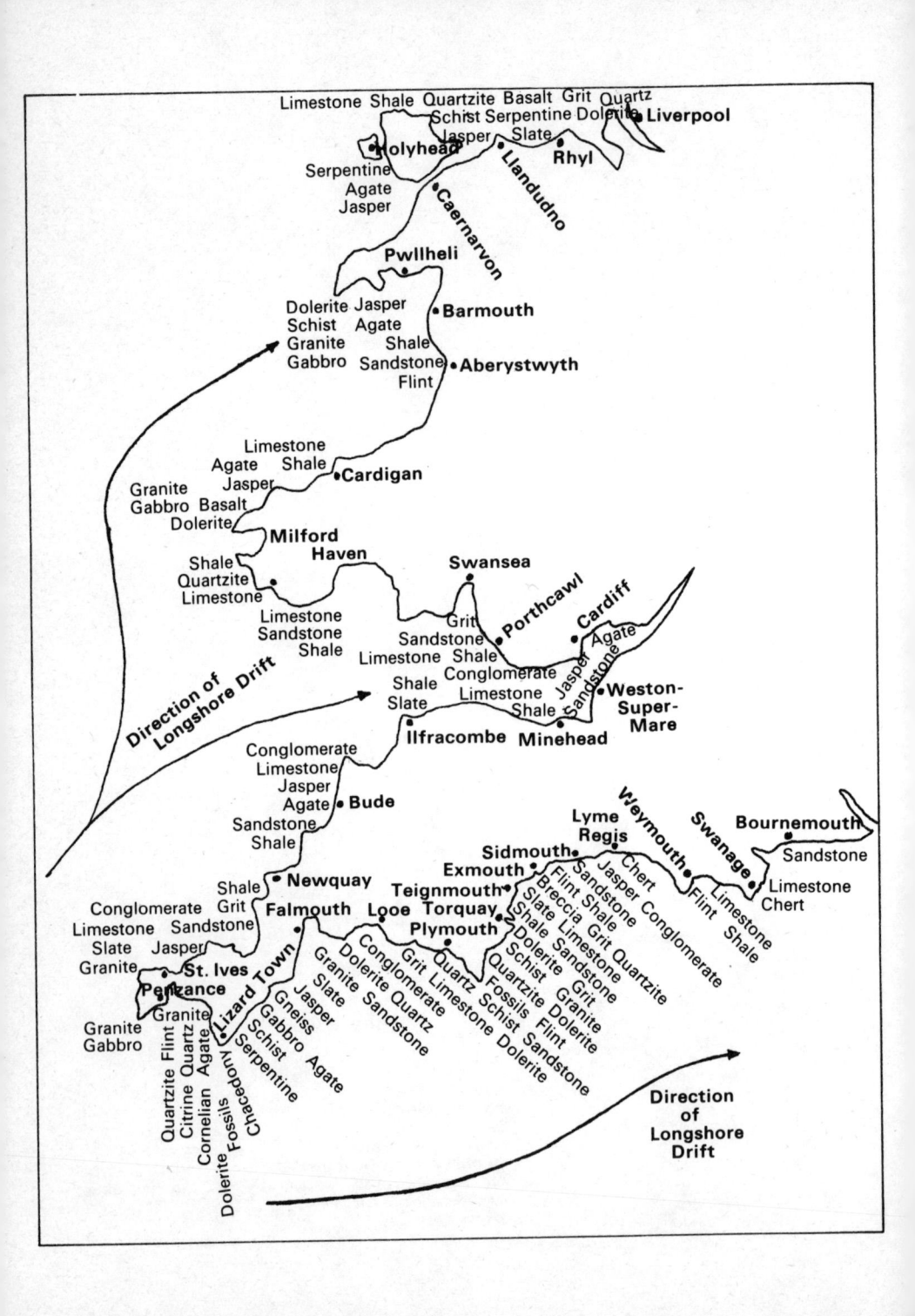

Map of Wales and South-West England: Coastal Rock and Mineral Types

Liverpool — Limestone, Shale, Quartzite, Basalt, Grit, Quartz

Holyhead — Schist, Serpentine, Dolerite, Jasper, Slate

Rhyl

Llandudno

Serpentine, Agate, Jasper

Caernarvon

Pwllheli

Barmouth — Dolerite, Schist, Granite, Gabbro, Jasper, Agate, Shale, Sandstone, Flint

Aberystwyth

Cardigan — Limestone, Shale, Agate, Jasper

Granite, Gabbro, Basalt, Dolerite

Milford Haven — Shale, Quartzite, Limestone

Direction of Longshore Drift →

Limestone, Sandstone, Shale

Swansea

Porthcawl — Grit, Sandstone, Limestone, Shale, Conglomerate

Cardiff — Jasper, Agate, Sandstone

Weston-Super-Mare

Ilfracombe — Shale, Slate, Limestone, Shale

Minehead

Bude — Conglomerate, Limestone, Jasper, Agate, Sandstone, Shale

Newquay — Shale, Grit, Sandstone, Jasper

Falmouth

Looe

Plymouth — Grit, Limestone, Sandstone, Quartz, Conglomerate, Dolerite, Quartz, Granite, Sandstone

Teignmouth — Conglomerate, Quartzite, Schist, Flint, Fossils, Sandstone, Dolerite

Torquay — Slate, Limestone, Shale, Sandstone, Grit, Dolerite

Exmouth — Flint, Shale, Breccia, Grit, Slate, Shale

Sidmouth — Sandstone

Lyme Regis — Jasper, Chert, Conglomerate

Weymouth — Flint, Shale

Swanage — Limestone, Chert

Bournemouth — Sandstone

St. Ives / Penzance — Conglomerate, Limestone, Slate, Granite, Grit, Sandstone, Jasper, Granite

Lizard Town — Quartzite, Flint, Citrine, Quartz, Cornelian, Agate, Dolerite, Fossils, Chalcedony, Serpentine, Schist, Gabbro, Gneiss, Jasper, Slate, Agate

Granite, Gabbro

Direction of Longshore Drift →

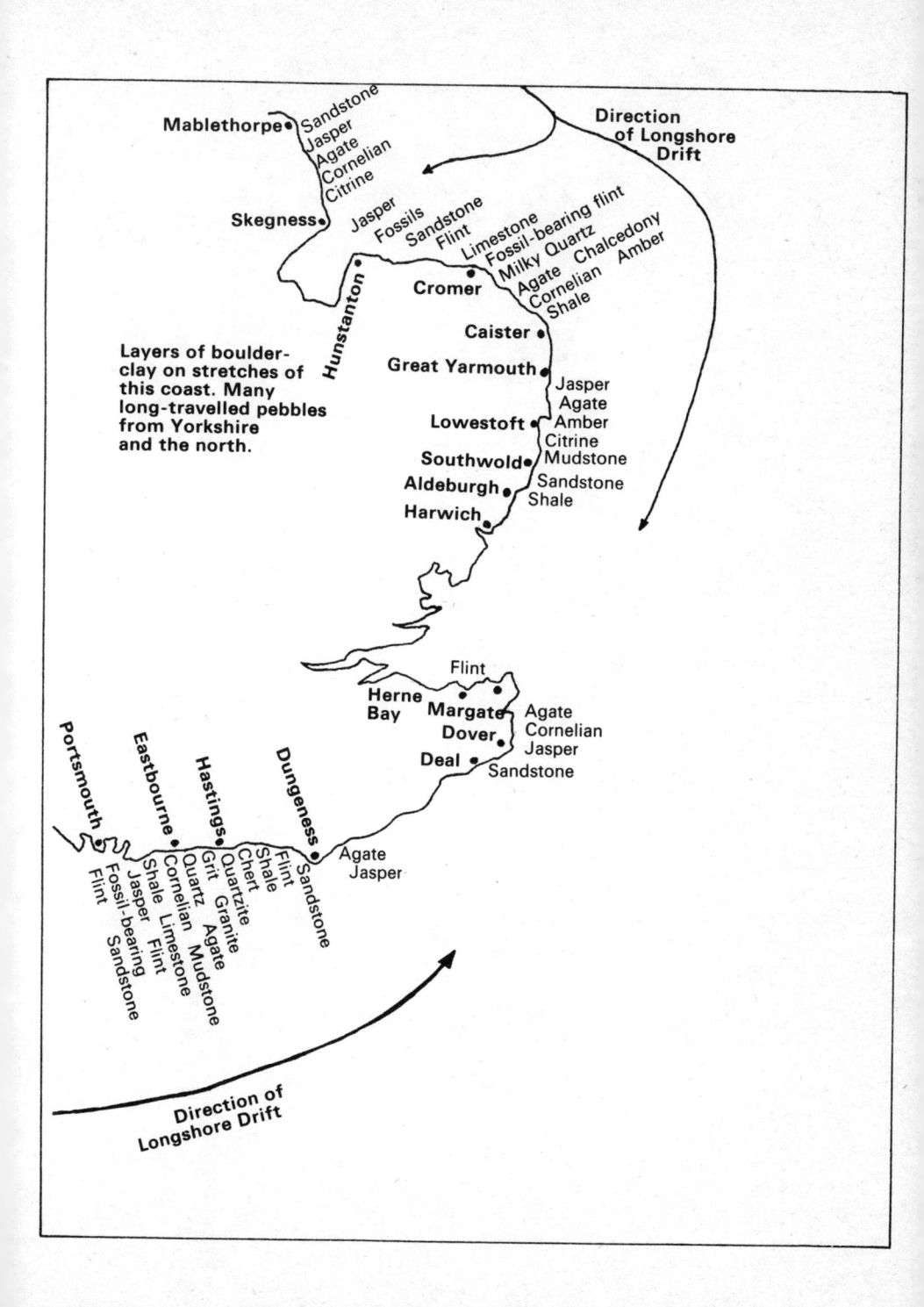

- Mablethorpe
  - Sandstone
  - Jasper
  - Agate
  - Cornelian
  - Citrine
- Skegness
  - Jasper
  - Sandstone
  - Fossils
  - Flint
- Hunstanton
- Cromer
  - Limestone
  - Fossil-bearing flint
  - Milky Quartz
  - Agate Chalcedony
  - Cornelian Amber
  - Shale
- Caister
- Great Yarmouth
- Lowestoft
  - Jasper
  - Agate
  - Amber
  - Citrine
  - Mudstone
- Southwold
  - Sandstone
- Aldeburgh
  - Shale
- Harwich

Direction of Longshore Drift

Layers of boulder-clay on stretches of this coast. Many long-travelled pebbles from Yorkshire and the north.

- Herne Bay
- Margate — Flint
- Dover — Agate, Cornelian, Jasper
- Deal — Sandstone
- Dungeness — Agate, Jasper, Sandstone
- Hastings — Flint, Shale, Chert, Quartz, Grit, Quartzite, Agate, Granite
- Eastbourne — Cornelian, Shale, Limestone, Mudstone, Jasper, Flint, Shale, Fossil-bearing Sandstone, Flint
- Portsmouth

Direction of Longshore Drift

Index

The figures in bold refer to pages on which colour illustrations occur.

adhesives 76
agate 21, 30
  banded 21, **90**
  blue lace **82, 83**, 90
  brown beach 23
  eyed 24
  fortification 24
  moss 90
  plume 90
  scenic 90
amazonite **82, 83**, 92
amber 34, 36
amethyst 24, **26, 27, 82, 83**, 92
aventurine **82, 83**, 92

baroque jewellery 74, **79**
barrel linings 49, 55
  metal 48
  plastic 49
  sizes 44
basalt 37, 38
bell caps 77, **80, 78**
best pebble areas 10
bloodstone 92
bracelets 85
brick 17
brooches **79**, 86

cabochon cutting 96–7
cast iron laps 96
cerium oxide 53–4
chalcedony 25, 30
chert 20, **22**, 28
choosing a tumbler 41
citrine **23**, 24
cleanliness 62
conglomerates 21, 28, 30
cornelian 25, **26, 27**, 30, 92
cracks and scratches 71
cufflinks **79**, 84

diamond saws 94–5
dolerite 36, 38

earscrews 84
earthenware 17
epoxy resin 81
equipment
  collecting 11–12
  for jewellery-making 73–6
erosion 99

faceting 97
  attachments 97
fault finding 73
final wash 72
final polish 69–71
first grind 58
flaky pebbles 16
flint 20, **22**
fossils 34–5, 36

gabbro 37
gas (in barrels) 49
glass 17
gneiss 37, 38
granite **23**, 29, 30
granular pebbles 15
grill pan 75
grinding times 60–1
  wheels 95
grit 36
grouping for hardness 18, 19

hard pebbles 19–31s
home-made tumbler 50

import duty 99
income tax 99

jasper 25, 28, 30, 92
  brown **23**
  green **23**
  red **26, 27**
  yellow **23**
jet **23**, 33, 36
jewellery fittings 77–8, **78**
jump rings 77, **78**

lapidary machines 98
  shops 88
  suppliers 100
lapis lazuli 92
limestone 32, 34
loading your barrels 55–6
longshore drift 11

malachite 90
man-made materials 17
maps 101–105
marble 33, 36
millstone grit 36
mines 99
mixing adhesives 81
mixing palette 76
Moh's scale 19, 53
mudstone 16

needles 87
noise reduction 70

obsidian **26, 27**
  snowflake **82, 83**, 91
onyx 24

pad fittings 80, **78**
pebbles, flaky 16, **22**
  hard 19–31
  pitted 16
  porous 15, **22**
  shape 14, 55
  size 14
  soft 32–6
  veined 16, **22**
pliers 74

polishing discs 95–6
porphyritic pebbles 29, 30
progress chart 57–8
quality control 63–4
quarries 99
quartz 20, 25, 30
  banded crystalline 21, 30
  breccia 21, 28–9
  crystals from Cornwall 24
  green **26, 27**
  milky 21, 30
  rose **82, 83**, 92
  rutilated **82, 83**, 92
  veins in quartzite 22
  veins in slate 16
  white **23**
  yellow **26, 27**
quartzite 20, **22**

record keeping 58
rhodochrosite 92
rhodonite **82, 83**, 92
rings **79**, 84

safety 13
sandstone, coarse-grained 16
  fine-grained 16
sardonyx 24
schist 16
scratch test 19
second grind 65–6
serpentine **26, 27**, 32, 34
silicon carbide 53, 59
  stick 74, 75
slicing on diamond saw 94
sodalite **82, 83**, 90
soft pebbles 32–6

test-polishing 66
third grind 66–9
tiger eye 90
  red **82, 83**
tin oxide 53
topping-up barrels 64
trespass 99
tumble-polishing machines 40–51
  choosing a model 41–3
  commercial 47, 48
  home-made 50
  'Vari-speed' 51
  with 1 × 1½ lb. barrel 44, 45
  " 2 × 1½ lb. barrels 46
  " 1 × 3 lb. barrel 45, 46
  " 1 × 3 lb. and 2 × 1½ lb. barrels 47
  working parts 41

unsuitable pebbles 15, **22**

V.A.T. 99

whinstone 37
wooden jig 74–5

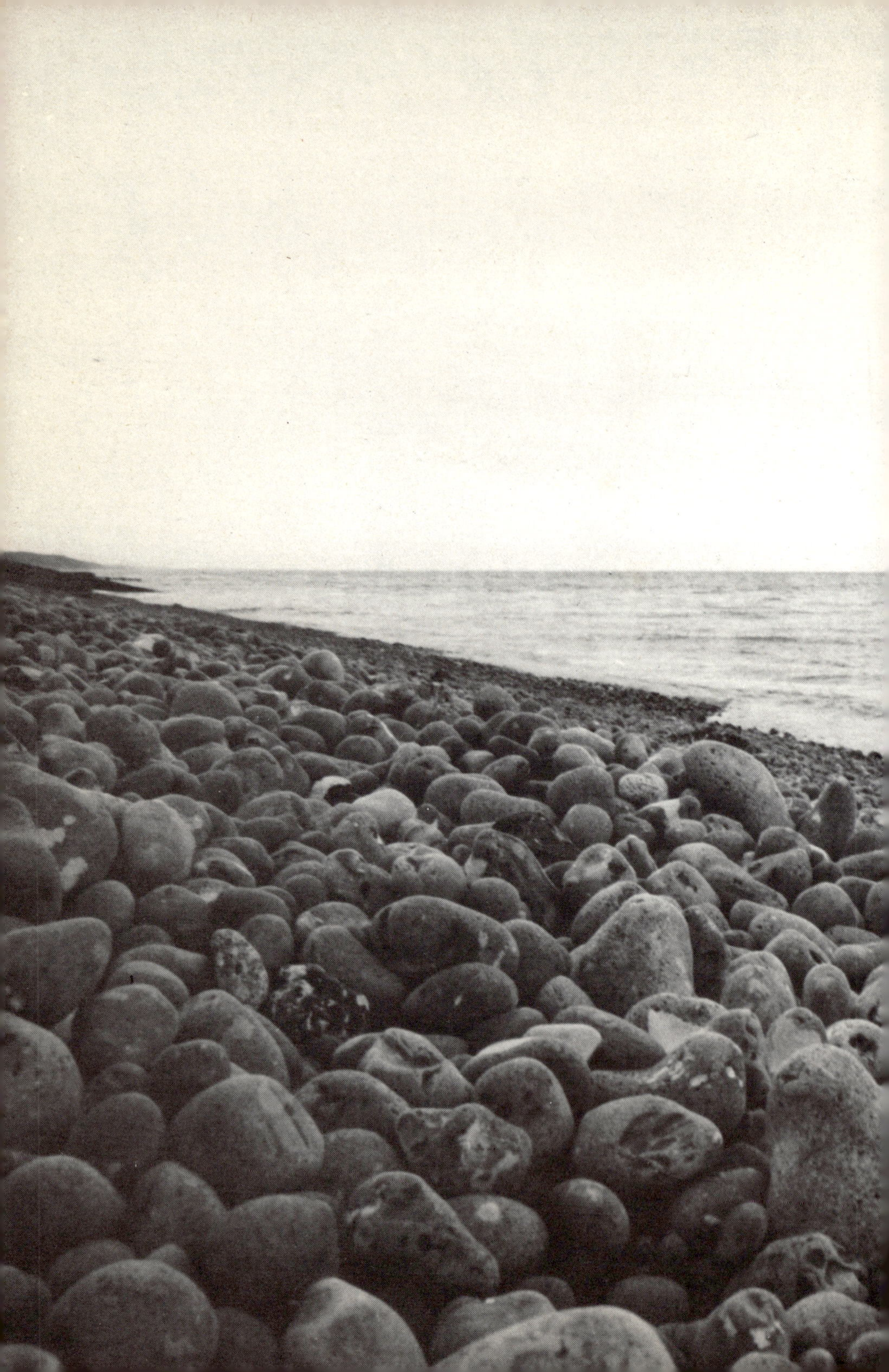

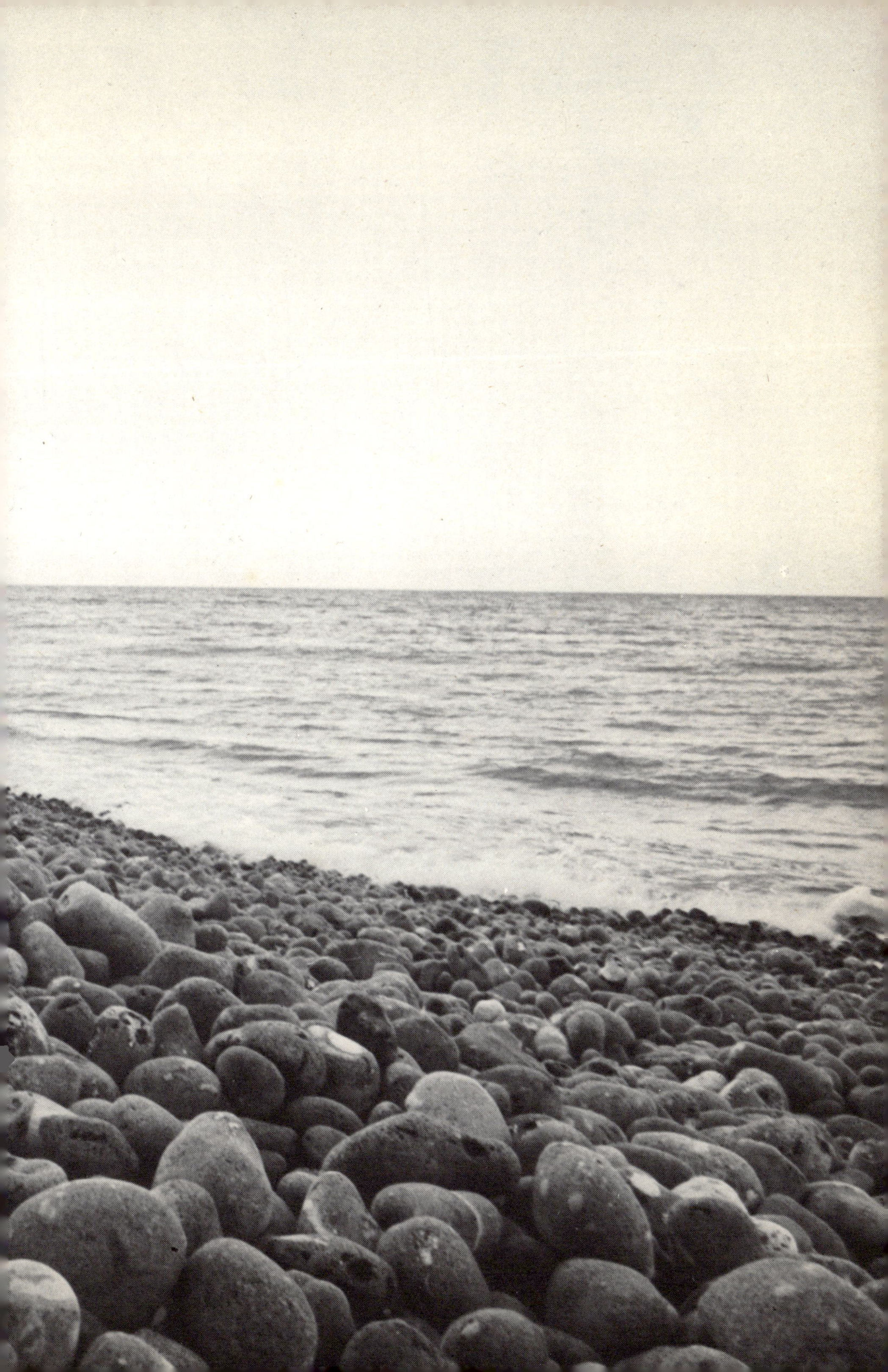

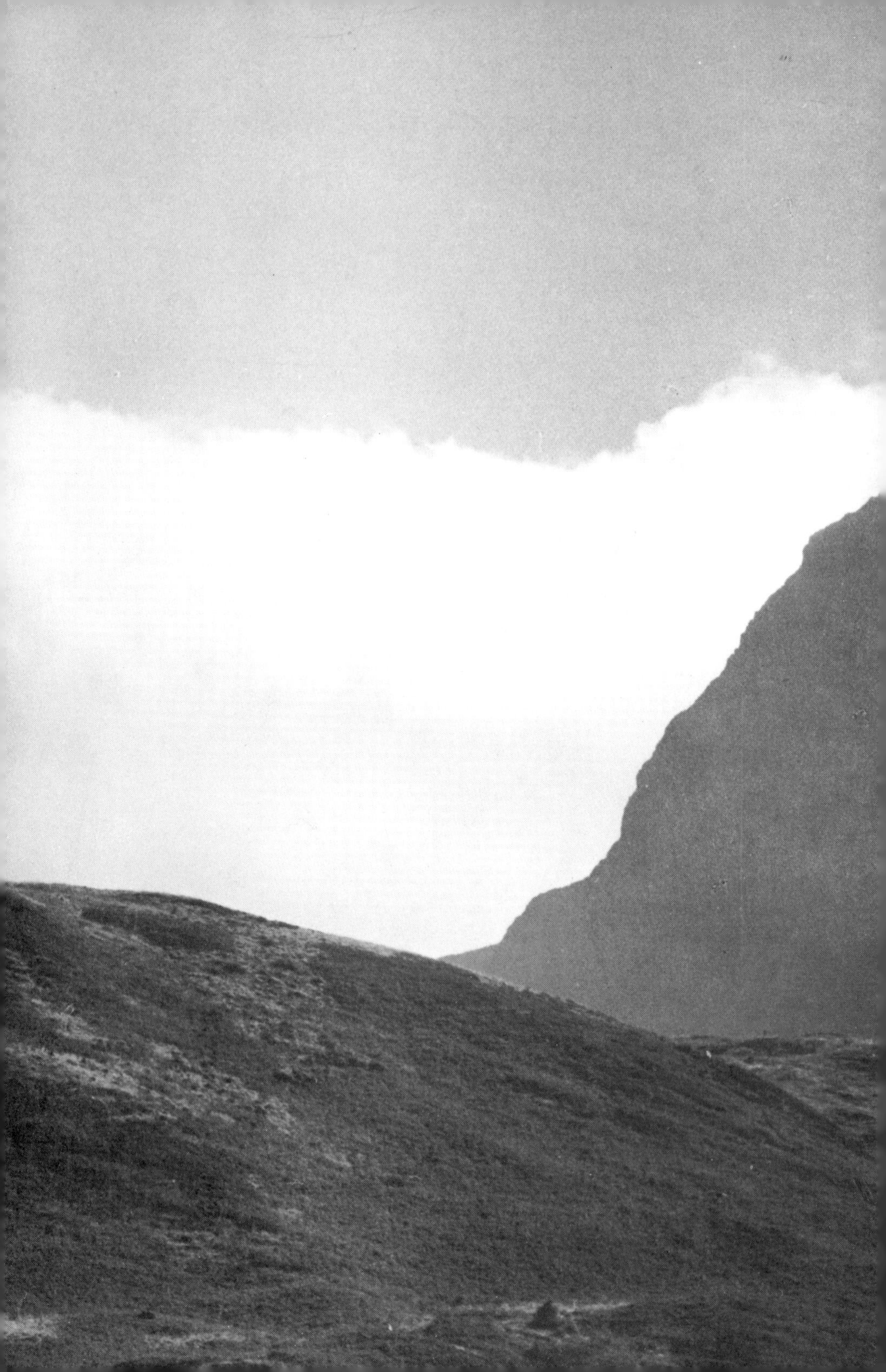

Rock and Gem Polishing

a complete guide to amateur lapidary

Rock and Gem Polishing

a complete guide to amateur lapidary

by
Edward Fletcher

London
Blandford Press

First published in 1973

by Blandford Press Ltd,
167 High Holborn, London WC1V 6PH

Reprinted in 1975

© 1973 Edward Fletcher

ISBN 0 7137 0617 1

All rights reserved. No part of this book may be reproduced or transmitted in any form or by any means, electronic or mechanical, including photocopying, recording or by any information storage and retrieval system, without permission in writing from the Publisher.

Text set in 12 on 13 Bembo and
printed in Great Britain by
Unwin Brothers Limited,
Old Woking, Surrey
A member of the Staples Printing Group

List of Contents

Introduction   7

1 Cutting a pebble in half   10
Diamond blades—Knoop scale—Pulleys, motors and drive belts—Tanks and coolants—Cutting tables and splash guards—Setting up your machine—Last minute checks—Cutting your first pebble—Sharpening the blade

2 Cutting a slab   26
The slab saw—Cutting your first slab—Blade sharpening and sludge cleaning

3 Grinding and polishing a flat surface   34
Cast-iron laps—Other equipment—Using the lap—Polishing—Using your slabs

4 Preforming stones before tumbling   46
Grinding machines—Care of grinding wheels—Grinding your preforms—Using preforms in jewellery-making

5 How to cut a cabochon   57
Machines—Cabochons from pebbles—Dopping the stone—Shaping the dome—Cabochons from slabs—Grinding, sanding and polishing—Jewellery-making with cabochons

6 Drilling a hole in a stone   71
Equipment—Drilling the hole

7 Simple faceting   76
Preforming the stone—faceting or forming the stone

8 Gem collecting   82
The rules for success—Igneous rocks—Summary of rocks to look for—Summary of likely gemstone haunts in igneous rocks—Further study—The gemstones you might find

9 Buying stones and fittings   102
Selection of imported rough rock available from British dealers—Fittings

10 Rock shops and lapidary clubs   107
Suppliers—Magazines—Clubs

11 Maps for Rockhounds   113–120

Index   121

To Edwina Bewkey, for her magic in transforming rough and ready manuscripts into readable books.

Acknowledgements

The author and publishers are grateful to the following who have supplied some of the photographs which illustrate this book:

M. L. Beach (Products) Ltd, Figs. 34, 46
Kernowcraft Ltd, Figs. 11, 35, Plate 6
Ammonite Ltd, Figs. 60, 62
Gemrocks Ltd, Figs. 28, 50
Minerals & Gemstones (Penzance) Ltd, Figs. 10, 16, 24
PMR Lapidary Equipment, Figs. 9, 25
A. & D. Hughes Ltd, Fig. 6
E. P. Joseph Ltd, Figs. 22, 23

The remaining black and white photographs and all the colour plates, except Plate 6, were taken by Michael Allman, F.I.I.P., F.R.P.S.

Thanks are also due to Gemrocks Ltd for their help in supplying stones and equipment for some of the illustrations, and to John Wood who drew the line illustrations and the location maps.

Introduction

Since the publication of my book, *Pebble Polishing*, the hobby of amateur lapidary has grown in popularity by leaps and bounds. Thousands of people who once believed that success at any hobby connected with handicrafts required an artistic flair which only gifted souls possessed have been delighted to discover just how wrong they were. Having bought tumble-polishing machines, and followed half a dozen basic rules, they have produced beautiful hand-made jewellery and proved to themselves that 'artistic flair' is a gift possessed by every one of us and which lies dormant until we provide it with the opportunity to flourish. Now, those same people are asking, 'Where do we go from here?'

I am delighted to report that the further steps in amateur lapidary and home jewellery-making which you are about to take by reading this book are as easy to follow, and equally rewarding, as were those which led to success at tumble-polishing. The equipment—diamond saws, drills, grinding wheels and faceting machines—is as easy and as safe to operate, and will give even more satisfying results. The range of jewellery fittings you will be able to use with the stones you cut and shape is much wider, while the variety of jewellery items you can make is limited only by your own inventiveness.

In *Pebble Polishing* we were concerned with the task of achieving a perfect polish on the outer surfaces of irregularly shaped pebbles and stones which were then attached to simple fittings, such as bell caps, with epoxy resins. In this present book we will examine the various methods of pre-forming rocks and pebbles before putting them into a tumbler, of drilling holes, of slicing pebbles and stones into two equal halves, of polishing large slabs of semi-precious rock to make delightful specimens for a display cabinet, of forming domed cabochons and of cutting steps or facets on transparent and translucent stones.

Readers of *Pebble Polishing* who found the collecting of specimens more exciting than making the jewellery need not despair. The outdoor pleasures of amateur lapidary do not end when one progresses from humble beach pebbles to the more exotic semi-precious gems. It is true that much of the high-quality gem material used in these more advanced techniques comes from foreign lands and is purchased by amateur lapidaries at their local rock shop. Nevertheless, many of the humble beach pebbles described in the earlier book are quite suitable for use with some of the machines we are going to look at. Indeed, there are locations throughout the British Isles where exciting semi-precious gems and minerals can be found by the determined hunter who wishes to cut and polish his own material. Tracking them down is as exciting and as rewarding as searching for amber or cornelians on pebble beaches, and because many are to be found in the wild and remoter parts of Britain, scenic beauty is guaranteed whether or not you succeed in the hunt. Gold, garnets, opal, freshwater pearls, cairngorm, fluorite, amethyst and many other delightful specimens can be found, and detailed knowledge of geology is quite unnecessary in order to track them down. The few basic rules required to locate likely rock formations are given in this book. If you can add to them a certain amount of patience, some careful observation and a little luck, they are as likely to guide you to a valuable gem crystal as is any academic reference book. The collecting maps which I included in *Pebble Polishing* proved so popular with many readers that I have included in this book similar maps to indicate hunting grounds for British gems. They are by no means exhaustive, but will, I hope, lead you to some worthwhile finds.

This book is not a detailed course of instruction in the techniques of advanced lapidary. There are already many books written by experts for experts on the subject, and readers who prefer a more scholarly approach are recommended to look in the reference department of any good bookshop. I have written this book for absolute beginners and for those men, women and children who have tried and succeeded at tumble-polishing and who now wish to take their interest in the hobby a few steps further. It describes in the simplest possible way how to make a start on grinding, drilling, slabbing, faceting and cabochon-cutting. Throughout the book I have concentrated on the least expensive and the simplest machines available at the time of writing, and I have given as many manufacturers as possible an opportunity to provide illustrations and operating instructions for their particular machines. I have also included descriptions and photographs taken during visits to some of the numerous rock shops and lapidary clubs which are now to be found in most towns and cities; and I thoroughly recommend that all readers visit as many shops and clubs as they possibly can. The enthusiasts who run them are mines of information who will be more than pleased to give you the benefit of their experience and knowledge when you decide to buy your equipment or have a question which this book does not answer. Without the help some of those men and women gave me with this present volume, it would probably have remained unwritten.

Finally, a brief word to overseas readers. Lapidary as a hobby is immensely popular in countries such as the United States, Canada and Australia. A number of the machines described in this book are manufactured in those countries and readers living there will have no difficulty in finding a rock shop selling these and many other excellent machines. As for the outdoor aspects of the hobby, I can only say how much I envy you in the wide choice of gem-hunting locations you will be able to visit. The geology in the chapter on gem collecting applies no matter where in the world you live; if you follow the advice given there, your finds should be as exciting as the places you will visit.

1 Cutting a pebble in half

If you have spent a few weekends combing shingle beaches for attractive pebbles you will know how difficult it can be to find matched pairs to make earrings, cufflinks and other items of jewellery which require two stones of similar size, shape and colour. It is a problem which tumble-polishing enthusiasts can only hope to solve by good fortune and patience; and it will come as no surprise, if you have owned a tumbler, to learn that the first task newcomers to more advanced equipment wish to attempt is that of cutting pebbles and small rock fragments into two equal halves. It solves the problem of finding matched pairs at a stroke. Simply select your most attractive finds, cut them in half before loading your tumbler barrel, and you need never again experience the frustration of finding partners for those rare beauties which have a habit of turning up in ones.

The most popular machine for this task is the *trim saw*. It consists of a circular diamond saw blade which is connected to an electric motor by means of two pulleys and a drive belt. The blade is housed in a covered, leak-proof tank which holds sufficient coolant to allow the rim of the blade to be continuously immersed in the liquid as it turns. The top of the tank forms a flat work-table through which the part of the blade which does the cutting protrudes. Behind this protruding part of the blade is a splash guard. This ensures that the spray of coolant which the blade generates as it turns is directed back on to the blade and returns to the tank. A small shield is usually fitted at the front of the machine to protect the operator from splashes.

Fig. 1 Typical diamond saw layout

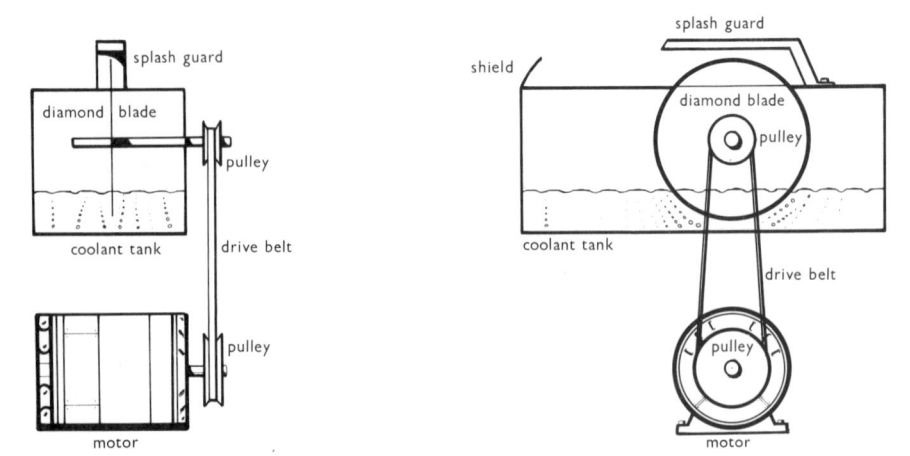

This basic set-up of a motor-driven circular blade partly immersed in a tank of coolant is common to many lapidary saws, and it will be helpful to take a closer look at the various components before we go on to discuss the use of the trim saw.

Diamond blades

Your tumble-polishing experiences will, no doubt, have given you a healthy respect for the hardness of pebbles and semi-precious stones. You will know that it takes many days of continuous rotation inside a barrel to wear away surface cracks and blemishes on tough pebbles, or to grind down the rough edges on crushed rock fragments. How then, you might ask, is it possible to cut a fair-sized beach pebble into two halves in a matter of minutes? The answer is a diamond blade.

Knoop scale

The silicon carbide grits used in the grinding stages of tumble-polishing are extremely hard. On Moh's Scale—the table so often quoted when referring to the relative hardnesses of different gemstones—silicon carbide stands at approximately 9·5. Most of the pebbles and semi-precious stones used in amateur lapidary have a hardness of about 7 on the table and their surfaces can, therefore, be worn down by the abrasive action of silicon carbide which is much harder. Diamond stands at the top of Moh's Scale with a hardness of 10 and it is many, many times harder than silicon carbide, in spite of its proximity on Moh's Scale.

There is another, lesser known table which indicates *comparative* degrees of hardness—unlike Moh's Scale which indicates only *relative* hardnesses—and which shows in a more dramatic way the incredible abrasive power of diamond. On this table, known as the *Knoop Scale*, the average beach pebble stands at 700, silicon carbide stands at about 2,000, while diamond tops the scale at over 6,000, the hardest material known to man.

	Moh's Scale of relative hardness	Knoop Scale of comparative hardness
Calcite	3	135
Fluorite	4	163
Apatite	5	360

Feldspar	6	560
Quartz	7	700
Topaz	8	1,250
Silicon carbide	9.5	2,000
Diamond	10	6,200

Even more remarkable to newcomers to advanced lapidary machines is the fact that diamond blades are absolutely safe to use. Unlike circular saws used in woodwork, lapidary saws hold no dangers for inexperienced fingers. Diamond blades do not have 'teeth' as ordinary sawblades have. Look at one closely and you will see that it is quite smooth on its outer rim, not unlike a gramophone record. The rim is fractionally wider than the remainder of the blade, and it is here that the diamonds which do the cutting are to be found. You cannot see them because they are microscopic in size and consist of tiny fragments of larger diamonds which have been crushed to fine dust, or of man-made diamonds which have been produced by subjecting carbon to tremendous heat and pressure. In the manufacture of some blades, known as *notched rims*, the diamonds are first mixed with metallic powders and inserted into notches cut into the edge of the

Fig. 2 Even when the diamond blade is spinning round, it will not cut your fingers

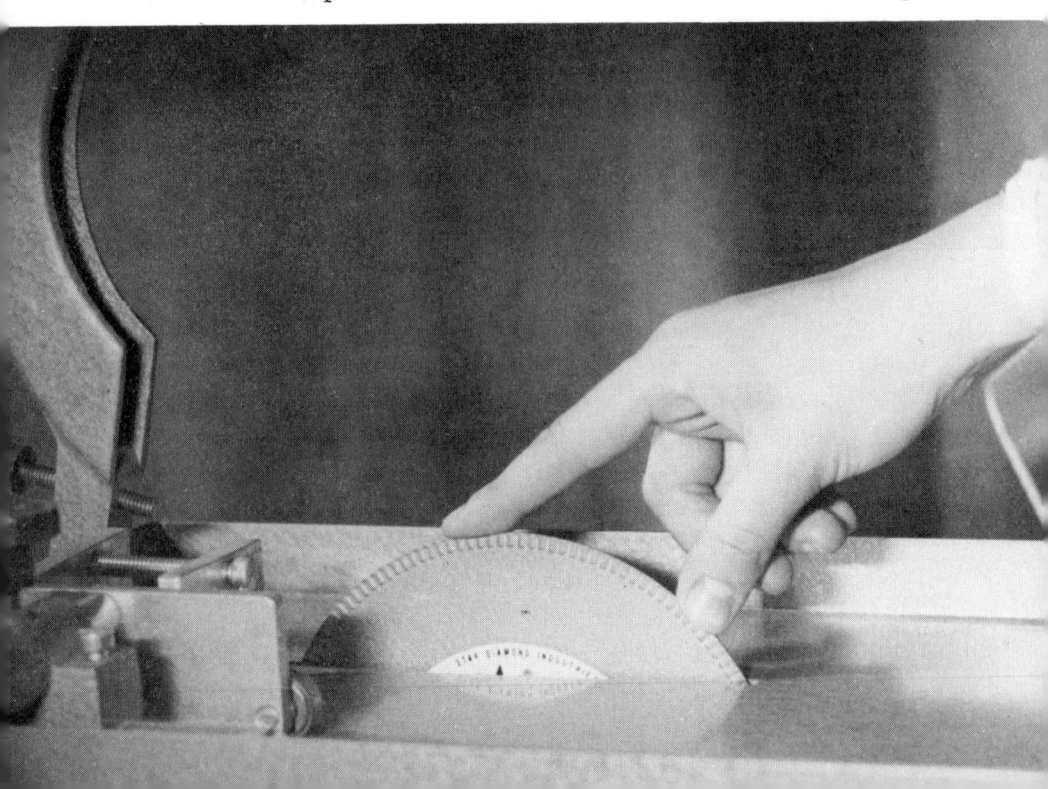

Fig. 3 A diamond sawblade

metal disc. The blade is then heated to a very high temperature so that the diamonds and the metallic powders become fused in the rim. Other blades, known as *sintered rims*, are manufactured by first making thin hoops of fused diamonds and metallic powders which are then soldered on to metal discs to produce the finished blade.

Trim saws are usually fitted with 6 in. or 8 in. diameter blades and, when you buy your machine, the supplier will provide a comprehensive instruction leaflet dealing with the care and use of the blade. These instructions have been written by the blade manufacturer and it is most important that you read them *and* carry them out. An expensive blade can be ruined by failure to do so.

One point which you must be absolutely certain about is whether your blade has been designed to run in one direction only, or is of the type which must be reversed at some time during its working life. Some manufacturers state that their blades must be removed from machines after approximately $\frac{1}{16}$ in. rim wear and reversed so that they cut in the

13

opposite direction to ensure even wear on both sides of the rim. Other manufacturers firmly state that their blades must never be reversed. Hence the need for a very careful reading of instructions supplied with your blade.

Pulleys, motors and drive belts

Some trim saws are supplied without pulleys, motors or drive belts which must be purchased as separate items. It is important that the pulleys fitted to the blade shaft and motor are of the correct size to provide the speed of revolution recommended for the diamond blade. If the trim saw you buy is not fitted with these items, your supplier will tell you the sizes required and will probably stock those which fit your machine.

For the benefit of those few readers who are obliged to work out correct pulley sizes for themselves, let me say that it is a simple calculation. You will find your motor's speed of revolution (r.p.m.) recorded on the small plate attached to the motor casing. It will probably be 1,425 r.p.m. if you are using an ex-refrigerator motor. If the instructions provided with your machine state that the blade speed must be 2,850 r.p.m. and you find a 2-in. pulley connected to the blade shaft, you will require a 4-in. pulley on the motor. This will then drive the blade shaft at twice the motor speed—2,850 r.p.m. In other words, because the pulley on the blade shaft has a diameter half that of the pulley on the motor, it will rotate twice as fast. If you have any difficulty with this calculation, consult a friend with engineering experience or contact a member of your local lapidary club.

Fig. 4 Typical pulley and drive belt arrangement

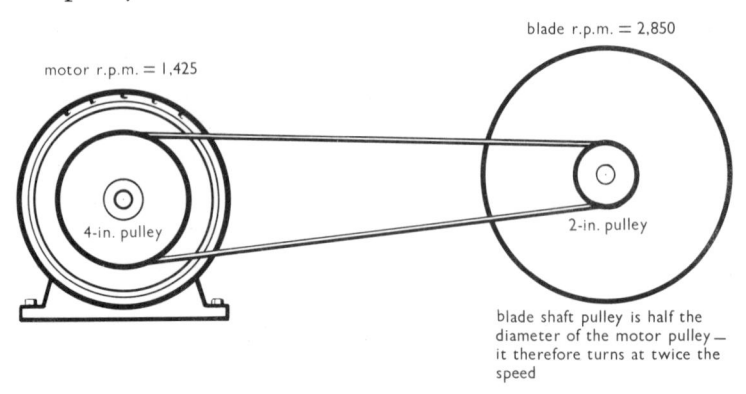

motor r.p.m. = 1,425

4-in. pulley

blade r.p.m. = 2,850

2-in. pulley

blade shaft pulley is half the diameter of the motor pulley — it therefore turns at twice the speed

Many newcomers are perplexed by the fact that the majority of lapidary machines are sold without motors; they are even more perplexed to read in suppliers' catalogues that second-hand refrigerator and washing-machine motors are recommended as ideal for fitting to new saws, grinders and lapping units. The reason why most suppliers prefer to sell machines without motors is simply that if a motor is fitted before despatch to the customer, the weight of the shipping container becomes extremely high. Often it is too high for the container to be sent by mail, and so high that despatch by rail or road proves very expensive. It is fortunately the case that motors fitted to refrigerators, washing machines and spin dryers are ideal for lapidary equipment, and it is also the case that second-hand motors from these appliances can be purchased, for about one-third of the cost of a new motor, at any electrical repair workshop. Furthermore, they can be counted on to give many years of useful life.

Such a motor will usually be what is known as a $\frac{1}{4}$ h.p., continuously rated induction type. This means that it is designed for prolonged running without overheating, that it consumes very little current, that it does not cause radio or television interference and that it will run with the minimum of noise and vibration. Nor does it require much attention during its working life: an occasional light oiling of its bearings, or a spot of grease now and again if it is fitted with grease cups, and long life and hard-working service are assured.

You can, of course, have a motor, pulleys and a drive

Fig. 5 An ex-refrigerator motor is ideal for running a lapidary machine—$\frac{1}{4}$ h.p., induction motor, 240 volts A.C., 50 cycles, 1,425 r.p.m., continuously rated.

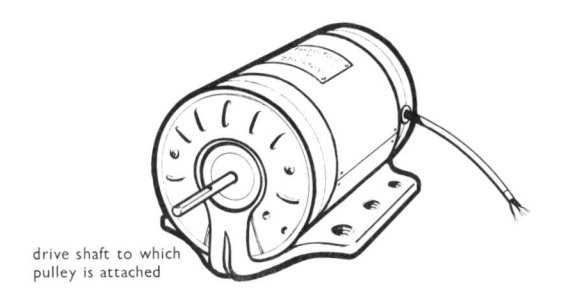

drive shaft to which pulley is attached

pulleys are available in a wide range of sizes

belt fitted to any machine before you buy; but you must expect to pay additional carriage charges. Alternatively, you can buy your machine from a supplier who sells every machine complete and ready to run. Whether you buy a complete machine or fit your own driving attachments, you should always ensure that the drive belt and pulleys are fitted with safety guards, particularly if the machine is to be used by children. The diamond blade is quite safe, but exposed belts and pulleys can be extremely dangerous to small fingers.

Tanks and coolants The tank which holds the liquid coolant is one of the most important parts of any lapidary sawing machine, and it must be absolutely leak-proof. If you cut a pebble or a piece of rock with the tank empty or the coolant level too low the diamond blade will be severely damaged and the stone you are cutting will probably fracture. The liquid coolant must be periodically renewed when it becomes contaminated with rock particles, and the tank must, therefore, be easy to clean. This is usually accomplished by fitting a drain plug, and by ensuring that the cutting table which covers the tank can be quickly removed so that the inside walls may be wiped clean.

The coolant in the tank should always be that recommended by the diamond blade manufacturer. Some makers specify light machine oil, others state that a mixture of oil and paraffin should be used, while some recommend a water-soluble coolant which has to be diluted before use. Whatever the coolant, it performs three vital functions. It keeps the diamond blade cool; it cleans the cut by washing out rock fragments as the blade bites into the stone; and it reduces the heat generated in the stone during cutting. In trim saws the level of the coolant in the tank should be such that approximately $\frac{1}{2}$ in. of the blade's rim is immersed at all times. Too little coolant will reduce cutting efficiency; too much is wasteful. The job of cleaning out the sludge which collects in the bottom of the tank is a task which is often neglected because the sludge cannot be seen unless the cutting table is removed. If you bear in mind the important tasks carried out by the coolant, it will help you remember the importance of this chore.

Cutting tables and splash guards

When choosing a trim saw you should look for a model with an uncluttered cutting table which provides adequate space for you to hold your pebble or stone in *both* hands as you present it to the edge of the blade. The table should also have drain holes drilled through it so that any coolant which finds its way on to the flat surface can run back into the tank. It should also have raised edges to contain coolant which might otherwise drip from its sides.

The splash guard should be as close to the blade as possible so that sprayed coolant is directed back on to the blade. It should also be hinged so that it can be raised when you are sawing pieces slightly larger than pebble size. A shield at the front of the cutting table is also desirable as it will protect you from any sprayed coolant not trapped by the splash guard.

You should find all of the above design features built into the machines sold by any reputable lapidary supplier. If you shop around before buying—either by visiting rock shops or by requesting mail order catalogues—you should soon find a reasonably priced and well-designed trim saw which, if used with care and commonsense, will give years of trouble free service.

Setting up your machine

The ideal situation for your trim saw, once you get it home or have it delivered by the supplier, is in a purpose-built workshop where you can enjoy the pleasures of lapidary insulated from all distractions. Alas, this ideal situation is beyond the reach of most of us; a quiet corner of the kitchen or a few square feet of the garden shed or garage are the best we can hope for. Fortunately, amateur lapidary machines do not take up large amounts of space. Some include a mounting for the motor as a built-in feature so that the unit can be set up in an area no larger than the base of the machine. Others can be mounted

Fig. 6 A 6-inch trim saw complete with motor on portable wooden baseboards which can be stored in cupboards when not required. If using such a board, it is most important that the motor is positioned in such a way that the drive belt connecting the motor pulley and the blade shaft pulley is not too tight. A tight belt will cause unnecessary wear on bearings and can also shorten the life of the blade. Aim instead to have the belt just sufficiently tight to turn the blade shaft pulley without slipping. Incidentally, it is a good idea when making the baseboard to cover the bottom with a sheet of foam rubber which will greatly reduce vibration and noise when the machine is in use. Machines supplied complete with motor will have their pulleys fitted to provide correct belt tension. Do not tamper with them.

Three requirements which the spot you select for your machine should have are a nearby power socket, good light in which to work and access to a tap or sink. *The motor must be wired to a three-pin plug with the earth connection made. Do not use a two-pin plug or connect the machine to a light socket.* On machines supplied complete with a motor, an on/off switch will be provided at some convenient point on the equipment, but if attaching your own motor, a switch will have to be fixed between plug and motor. If you doubt your ability to wire the switch correctly, have the job done by a competent electrician. You can dispense with an on/off switch on the machine if the wall socket is of the type which incorporates its own switch, and if the machine can be situated within easy reach. It is, however, unwise to rely on pulling the plug from the socket as a means of stopping the motor.

If possible set up the machine so that light from a window falls across the cutting table from one side, as this will enable you to work at the machine without obscuring your view of the pebble or stone being cut. Good interior lighting, preferably from an angle lamp which can be directed onto the cutting table, is equally suitable.

A kitchen location for your machine will obviously provide ready access to a tap and sink. Water is used in all lapidary work, particularly with grinding wheels (discussed on p. 47) and it is convenient to have a nearby supply. You can, however, manage quite well with empty washing-up liquid bottles and a few plastic bowls if you are working in a shed or garage. If such a spot has a power supply and good lighting you will not find the lack of a sink and tap an insurmountable problem.

Last minute checks

Before attempting to cut pebbles with your new trim saw, read the supplier's instructions for setting up the machine once again to make quite sure that you have carried them out to the letter. These last minute checks are most important. Do not allow your enthusiasm to 'have a go' blind you to the dangers of operating the machine incorrectly.

It is a good idea to embark upon the more advanced techniques of lapidary armed with a notebook in which you can jot down your comments, questions and other points on machines, methods of cutting and grinding, problems encountered when working with different gemstones or anything else worth noting. When next you visit your local rock shop or lapidary club you can take your notebook and obtain expert opinions and advice on anything you have written down. If the answers to your questions and the comments of more experienced enthusiasts are added to your notes you will have your own 'Book of Lapidary' which will prove invaluable as your interest in the hobby grows. The best time to start such a notebook is now. Make a checklist from the manufacturer's instructions and refer to them each time you use the machine. Such a list might read:

1. Ensure coolant level is correct
2. Check sawblade is secure and correctly positioned on shaft
3. Ensure cutting table is free from rock fragments
4. Check splash guard is secure and does not foul blade
5. Ensure drive belt tension is correct
6. Check that safety guards are correctly fitted over drive belt and pulleys
7. Ensure electrical connections on motor and plug are safe

You will quickly memorize your checklist once you have written it down and you will find that running through the points on it becomes automatic each time you use the machine. Bear in mind that saws and instructions differ. Do not copy out the above list into your notebook. Make your own.

Some diamond blade manufacturers specify that their blades must be broken in before they are used on gemstones by first making two or three cuts in an old and discarded silicon carbide wheel. The purpose of this procedure is to wear away a fraction of an inch of metal on the rim of the wheel in order to expose the diamonds. Few beginners have 'old and discarded silicon carbide wheels' lying around, and a substitute material must usually be found. This should be a piece of *soft* building brick. Find a brick with a sandy texture, break it in half, and try scratching its surface with an old file. If sand grains are removed by the file, the brick is suitable for breaking in your diamond blade. Make sure the coolant level is correct when carrying out this operation, and present the brick to the blade with the same care used when cutting semi-precious stones.

Cutting your first pebble   With a bowl of clean water containing a few drops of washing-up liquid close at hand, you should now select a suitable pebble from your stocks. For your first attempt at sawing choose a pebble with a symmetrical shape—ideally a slightly flattened sphere about the diameter of a 10p piece. It must be free from cracks or flaws suggesting internal weakness which could lead to the pebble fracturing during the sawing operation, and it should be evenly coloured so that once you have cut it in half you will have a matched pair.

Before attempting to saw this first pebble, you must practice the method of holding pebbles when presenting them to the saw. To do this, hold the pebble lightly between your forefingers and roll it back and forth across the kitchen table with the two fingers acting as an axle. When this motion feels comfortable, bring your second fingers into contact with the pebble in front of your forefingers. The remaining two fingers on both hands should now be bent and pressed firmly on to the table top as you push inwards with equal force against the sides of the pebble with fore and second fingers. You will now have the pebble in a vice-like grip which holds it squarely against the table top. Now bring your thumbs into contact with the pebble behind your forefingers and press firmly downwards. Your thumbs should be only slightly apart—just wide enough for the saw blade to pass between them. Some ladies may find that their thumbnails are too long to allow the thumbs to be placed comfortably in this position, in which case the nails will have to be cut. Look on this drastic action as a small sacrifice made in the interests of Art, and comfort yourself with the knowledge that you will not damage an expensive diamond blade if you hold the pebbles in the manner described. (*See* Fig. 7.)

Practice this correct hold half a dozen times and then switch on your trim saw and allow the blade to spin freely for a few moments to ensure an adequate supply of coolant to the rim. You may find it encouraging to touch the blade with your thumbs at this point if you have any doubts about the safety of working so close to a spinning blade. Hesitation caused by nervousness when actually cutting the pebble could damage the saw.

Fig. 7 The correct method of holding a pebble when slicing it on a diamond saw

Hold the pebble firmly and correctly on the cutting table about half an inch from the blade. Sight between your thumbs to ensure that the blade will cut the pebble centrally, and slowly slide your hands forward until contact is made with the spinning blade. Concentrate on holding the pebble squarely on the table and exert pressure *downwards* with your thumbs. Keep your eyes on the blade to ensure that the cut is straight.

It is of the utmost importance that you do not force the pebble on to the blade in an attempt to cut too quickly. It will take from two to four minutes to slice the pebble, and during this time your efforts must be directed towards keeping the cut straight by maintaining firm contact with the cutting table, and towards preventing the pebble riding up the rim of the saw by pressing downwards with your thumbs. Pressure from behind the pebble should be just sufficient to keep the rim of the blade in firm contact with the cut. If sparks begin to fly, or the blade appears to slow down, you are certainly pressing too hard on the rear of the pebble. With the correct amount of pressure applied you should feel firm and regular contact with the blade and just be able to see the slow but sure progress of the cut.

The two commonest mistakes made by beginners when attempting their first cut are first, putting uneven side pressure on the pebble which causes the cut to wander and can lead to a distorted blade, and secondly, parting the thumbs as the blade nears the end of the cut, which causes small flakes of the pebble to chip off as the saw blade breaks through. Make an effort to avoid both mistakes from the outset.

As soon as the cut is completed, both halves of the pebble should be washed in the bowl of soapy water to remove any coolant which has adhered to the stone. Dry the pieces on an old cloth or disposable tissue and then inspect the result. You should have two cleanly cut halves which can now be tumble-polished to produce a matched pair of delightful stones.

After gaining a little experience at cutting symmetrically shaped pebbles you can attempt to cut a small piece of rough rock which you may have bought at your local rock shop or collected on a rock-hounding expedition. The cutting procedure is the same as outlined above, but you must take even greater care when holding the fragment on the saw

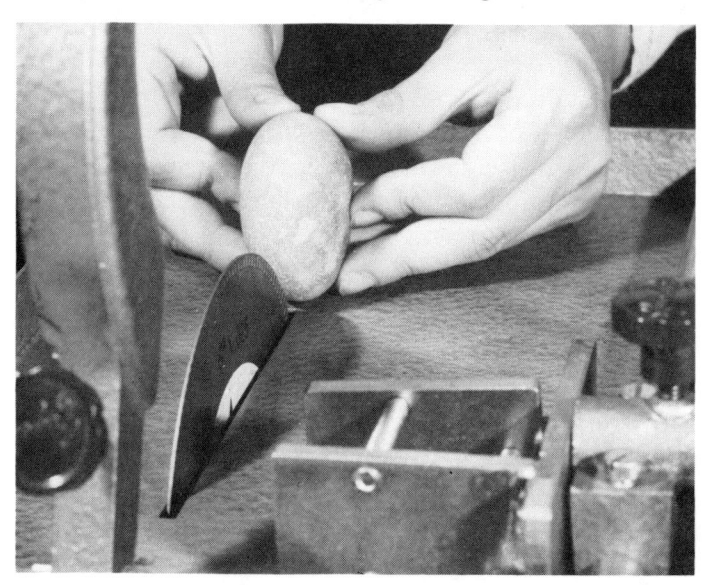

Fig. 8 Slicing the pebble

Fig. 9 Another type of 6-inch trim saw

table and when presenting it to the blade. Always aim to cut a piece of rock in such a way that the largest face is cut first by the blade, and try to have the flattest face against the surface of the table. If you do this, the chances of the blade being deflected as the cut begins will be greatly reduced, and your grip on the stone will be as secure as possible. Two or three hours work with the saw, slicing pebbles and small pieces of rough of different sizes and shapes, should transform you from an absolute beginner to a competent trim-saw operator.

Sharpening the blade

You will be able to slice a very large number of pebbles before your diamond blade needs sharpening, but all blades become blunt when they are repeatedly sawing through hard stone. The first sign of a blunt blade is a much slower cutting action when sawing hard pebbles. This indicates that the diamonds in the rim have become partially covered by metal which has built up around them after being stripped from the rim during cutting. To sharpen the blade, this build-up of metal must be removed in order to expose the diamonds once again. This is done by making two or three cuts in a sandy brick or old silicon carbide wheel. These materials tend to crumble into tiny particles when they are cut, and it is these particles which carry away the build-up of metal on the rim. You *must* have coolant in the tank when making these sharpening cuts which will soon restore the blade's rim to peak condition.

2 Cutting a slab

A slab is a piece of stone taken from a larger mass by making two parallel cuts with the diamond saw blade. It might be a large, thick piece suitable for a book-end or pen stand; or it might be a thin slice which is then cut up into much smaller pieces for jewellery work. Whatever its size, the cutting of a slab involves very similar techniques to those used when slicing a pebble.

The slab saw

The slab saw which does the cutting is also very similar to the trim saws described in Chapter 1. It will probably have a larger blade—anything from 8 in. to 36 in. in diameter—but its basic design will be identical to that of a trim saw. The important difference between the two is that a slab saw is equipped with a vice which holds the stone to be cut by the blade. This is necessary because it would be almost impossible to hold irregularly shaped stones larger than pebble size securely in the hands throughout the cutting action.

You will notice that there is an overlapping of blade sizes in the two types of saw. This has resulted in the production of a hybrid version known as the slab-trim saw which can tackle all of the trim saw's jobs and some of the jobs only carried out on slab saws. A slab-trim saw usually has a blade of 8 in. to 10 in. in diameter, and its vice is removable or hinged at the side of the cutting table so that it can be swung out of the way when trimming work with hand-held stones is carried out. It is, therefore, an extremely useful piece of equipment. If you can afford the slightly

Fig. 10 A versatile slab-trim saw which can be used to cut slabs and trim slices

higher cost of a slab-trim saw fitted with an 8 in. or 10 in. blade I thoroughly recommend it for its advantages over a simple trim saw not equipped with a vice.

Slab saw vices come in a wide range of shapes and sizes, but their basic purpose remains the same no matter how complex their design: that is to hold a piece of rock parallel to the blade so that perfectly straight cuts can be made when slabbing. In its simplest form, the vice consists of two metal jaws which can be screwed together to hold the rock, and which can be made to move along the raised flange or edge of the cutting table parallel to the blade. The jaws are opened and the piece of rock positioned so that it protrudes sufficiently to be cut by the blade. The jaws are then closed again and, with the motor switched on, the vice is pushed along the edge of the table as the rock is fed to the blade. When the cut is completed, the jaws are returned to the front of the table and opened to allow the rock to be moved forward slightly before they are closed and tightened again. A second cut is then made and a parallel-sided slab is thus cut from the rough rock.

The obvious problem with this simple vice is the difficulty experienced in moving the rock forward for the second cut while at the same time keeping the newly cut face parallel to the blade. Less obvious is the problem of side movement which occurs during the cut because the vice is not securely

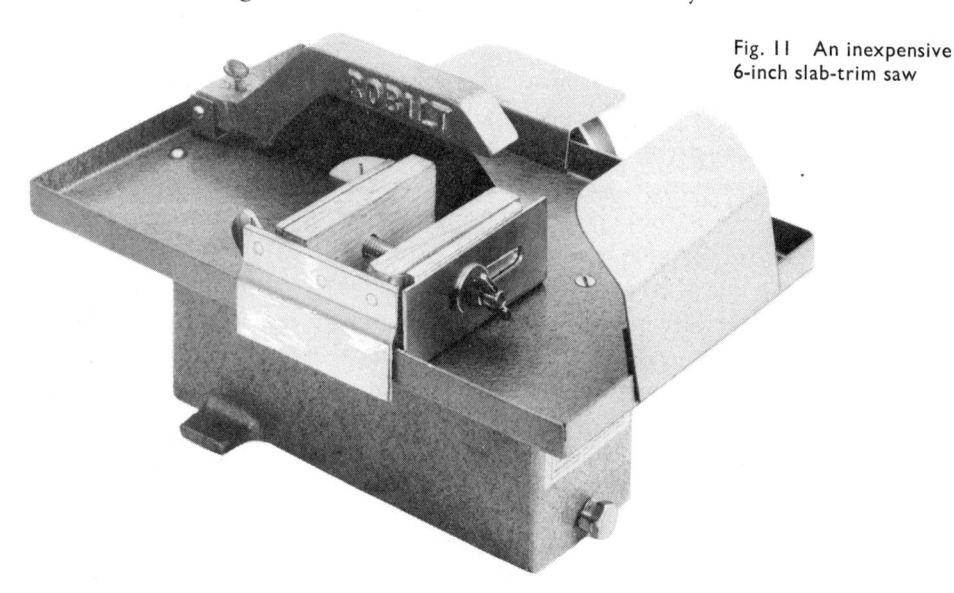

Fig. 11 An inexpensive 6-inch slab-trim saw

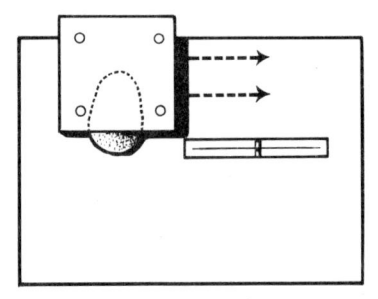

simple vice – jaws fit loosely over raised edge of table. After first cut jaws must be opened and stone moved across table

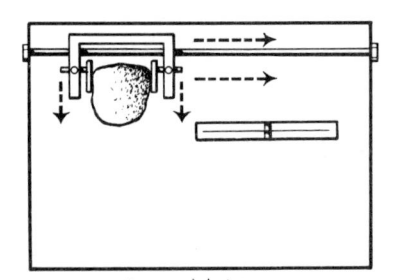

improved design vice – runs on parallel bars bolted to ends of table. Jaws can be moved across the table after first cut without disturbing the stone

Fig. 12 Slab saw vices

attached to the cutting table. To overcome the difficulty experienced in moving the rock forward for the second cut, more advanced machines are fitted with vices which can be moved *across* the cutting table as well as along it. This means that the second cut can be made without moving the rock in the jaws. Instead the jaws themselves are moved across the table while the rock face remains parallel to the blade.

To prevent the vice moving sideways because it is insecurely fixed to the table, more advanced machines have vices which run along the table on firmly bolted parallel bars. This arrangement ensures that the jaws move smoothly and eliminates the possibility of side movement during the cut.

More sophisticated slab saws have vices which are moved along the cutting table by a weight-feed mechanism which drives the vice at the correct speed for perfect cutting. Others have vices which are moved along their guide bars at the correct cutting speed by a drive connected to the same spindle on which the blade turns, while those with blades of 10 in. or more in diameter are also usually equipped with large plastic covers in addition to the splash guard behind the blade. The cover ensures that the substantial amounts of spray thrown up by large blades are contained within the area of the cutting table. Obviously such machines cost rather more than those equipped with smaller blades and vices which are moved by hand, but they are worth considering if large amounts of slabbing work are planned.

Cutting your first slab

The importance of reading the instructions supplied with your slab saw *before* you attempt to use it cannot be over emphasized. Pour the correct amount of coolant into the tank, check that the diamond blade is secure, ensure that drive belt tension is correct and electrical connections are sound and carry out all other pre-running instructions given. The size of rock you can slab on your saw is limited by the diameter of the blade and by the maximum width between the jaws of the vice. The instructions will tell you the largest recommended size of rock which should be worked on your particular model. *Never, under any circumstances, exceed the recommended limit.* You will almost certainly damage the blade if you do.

Familiarize yourself with the way in which the vice works before you switch on the motor. Try clamping rocks of different sizes and shapes in the jaws, bearing in mind that the jaws must hold the rock even more firmly and securely during the cutting action than you held your pebbles when using the trim saw. The slightest movement of the rock in the jaws during cutting will ruin an expensive blade. The jaws of some vices are faced with softwood or leather to improve their grip on the rock. If your vice has unfaced metal jaws you should cut two pieces of softwood or leather which you can insert between the rock and the metal faces as you tighten them. Remember that the thickness of the material will reduce the size of rock which can be held in the vice.

Once satisfied that you fully understand the workings of the vice, select a piece of rock from which to cut your first slab. It must be free from cracks or flaws which might cause it to fracture during cutting, and it should have as few sharp edges as possible. A squarish or oblong piece would be ideal, but is not always possible to find. Examine the shape of the piece carefully to decide the best possible cutting angle, and bear in mind that flat surfaces are held most securely in the jaws. If your saw has a vice which can

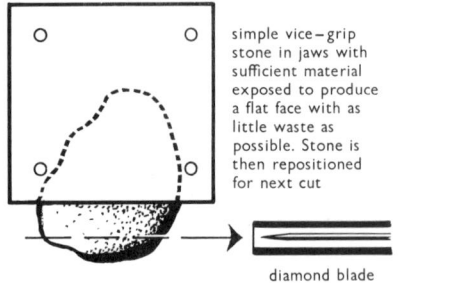

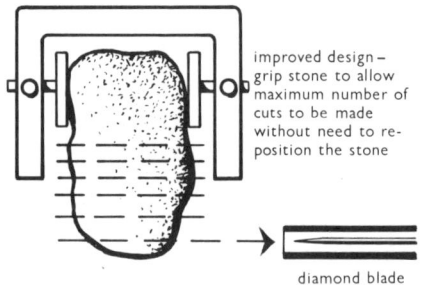

Fig. 13 Holding the stone in the vice

— simple vice-grip stone in jaws with sufficient material exposed to produce a flat face with as little waste as possible. Stone is then repositioned for next cut

— improved design – grip stone to allow maximum number of cuts to be made without need to re-position the stone

diamond blade

diamond blade

be moved across the saw table you should grip the stone between the jaws in such a way that two or more slabs can be cut without the need to re-position the stone. This will ensure parallel sides on each slab cut. If your vice cannot be moved across the table grip the stone so that the first cut will produce a flat face on the stone with as little waste as possible.

When you are satisfied that the jaws have a really firm hold on the stone and there is no danger of the stone slipping during the cut, start the motor and move the vice along the raised edge or guide bar to within an eighth of an inch of the blade. Check that the splash guard will not foul the stone as the cut proceeds and, if necessary, move it rearwards to provide a free run for the vice. With a firm and steady grip on the rear of the vice, ease the stone on to the rim of the blade. The cut must be completed in a single and continuous movement; pressure from the rear must not be so great that the blade begins to slow or sparks fly from the cut. The rate of feed varies with different materials and is largely dependent on the thickness of the rock being cut, but it is better to err on the side of slowness than to try to force the blade to do too much. As you near the end of the cut, place your fingers lightly on the waste piece which is about to fall, and prevent it from slipping into the blade slot on the table. With this first cut completed, slide the vice rearwards and switch off the motor.

When you look at the newly cut face you are sure to be delighted at the beauty the blade has revealed, and you will

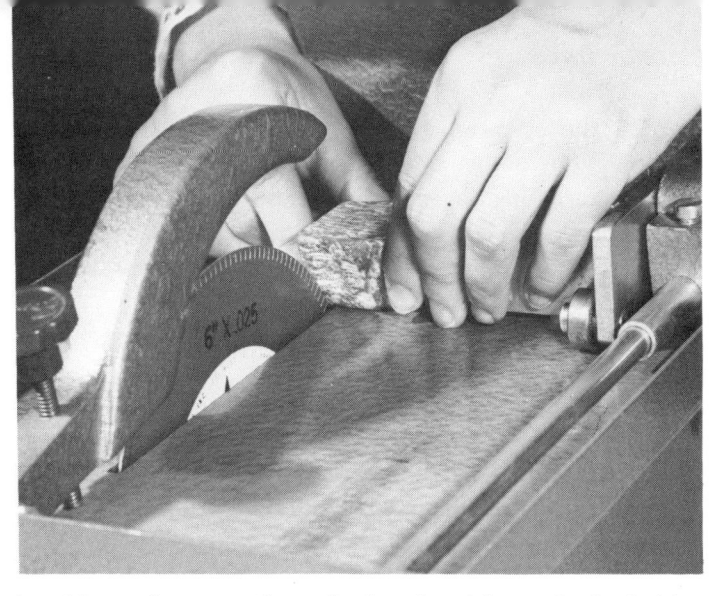

Fig. 14 Cutting a slab

be able to form an idea of what the slab might look like when polished. Run your fingers across the face. It should be fairly smooth and free from deep blade marks which would indicate that the blade, vice or stone had moved sideways during the cut. If all is well you must now decide the thickness of your first slab.

This will depend on how you plan to use the finished piece. Slabs for book-ends, pen stands and other large items will probably be half an inch or more in thickness; slabs which are to be cut into smaller shapes for jewellery-making must be as thin as possible in order to reduce the amount of grinding necessary to form the finished article. Beginners are advised to cut slabs which are intended for jewellery-making a little thicker than more experienced amateur lapidaries might cut them. A slab which is cut slightly thicker than actually required will need more work during the grinding stages, but the surplus material provides an opportunity to correct mistakes made during grinding without spoiling the piece. If, on the other hand, the slab is cut very close to the final dimensions of the finished item, a mistake made during the grinding stages can spell complete ruin for the piece of jewellery. Cut thicker slabs until you have gained experience at grinding.

If your slab saw has a simple vice, you must now solve the problem of moving the stone for the second cut while keeping the face parallel to the diamond blade. One method of doing this is to use an accurately sawn piece of wood which can be held against the opposite side of the cutting table to act as a fence when the stone is loosened in the vice and its sawn face pressed against the wood before the jaws are tightened once again. The wood must be cut to provide the width of slab required, a number of pieces being needed for different slab thickness. If the vice has movable jaws the task is simple: the screws holding the jaws are simply loosened and jaws and stone are pushed across the table to give the required slab thickness. Remember to allow for the thickness of the blade when setting the jaws. Looked at from the vice side of the table it is the *outside* edge of the blade which will determine the thickness of the slab when it is cut.

When the stone has been moved forward and checked for security between the jaws, switch on the motor and proceed with the second cut in exactly the same way as before. Use your fingers as gentle supports as the blade reaches the end of the cut, to prevent the slab from falling, and wash the slab in your bowl of soapy water to remove the smear of coolant left by the blade. If two or more slabs are required, and you have a movable vice, simply adjust the jaws each time you make a cut until you have the number of slabs required or the jaws are fully extended. If you wish to cut slabs of equal thickness, use a wooden guide fence as suggested for use with simple machines each time you move the jaws. This will ensure that the jaws are moved the same distance across the table after each cut.

Fig. 15   Using a wooden guide fence

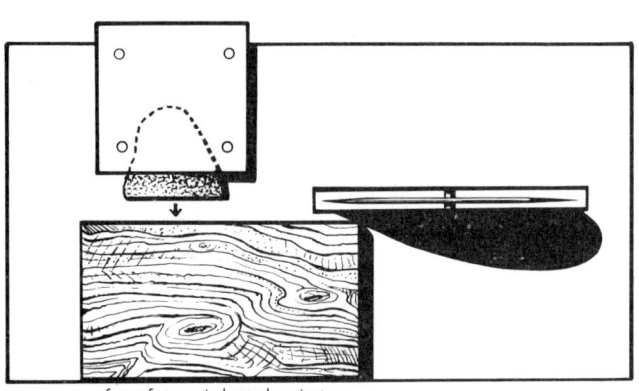

face of stone is butted against accurately sawn piece of wood before jaws are tightened for second cut

Blade sharpening and sludge cleaning

Prolonged use of the diamond blade to slab hard materials, such as agate, will dull the cutting edge. Sharpen in the same way as a trim-saw blade, keeping the coolant level correct during the operation. If yours is a blade which must be reversed at certain times during its working life, do not forget this important task.

You will be able to cut many slabs before it becomes necessary to change the coolant in the tank, but it is wise to develop the habit of checking the amount of sludge build-up regularly. When the coolant becomes so contaminated with rock dust and fragments that it must be changed, proceed as follows. Remove the cutting table and agitate the coolant so that as much of the sludge as possible is washed from the bottom of the tank and held in suspension. Next, take a wide-mouthed glass jar and hold it beneath the drain hole as you unscrew the plug. Allow the contaminated coolant to drain into the jar as you wipe the internal walls of the tank to remove all traces of rock particles. You can now replace the drain plug, tighten it securely, and refill the tank with clean coolant to the required level before replacing the cutting table. Do not throw away the contaminated coolant. Leave the jar undisturbed for a day and the sludge will settle on the bottom. The clean coolant can then be carefully poured off and used again in the tank when next you clean it out. Dispose of the sludge by pouring it into a plastic bag which can then be placed in your dustbin. It should never be poured down drains or sinks.

3 Grinding and polishing a flat surface

Large, flat surfaces, particularly those produced by a slab saw, are usually brought to a final polish on a lapping unit. This piece of equipment is similar in design to a record player and has a flat turntable, or lap as it is known, which is made to revolve by means of an electric motor, pulleys and a drive belt. The lap is made from cast iron and turns at 300 to 500 r.p.m., which is slower than the speed at which your diamond saw works, but much faster than a record player's top speed of 78 r.p.m. The motor is usually similar to that fitted to a diamond saw, the slower speed of revolution being achieved by the use of a larger pulley on the turntable shaft. For example, an 8 in. pulley on the lap shaft and a 2 in. pulley on the motor would produce a working speed of 356 r.p.m.

Cast-iron laps

The cast-iron lap is mounted horizontally inside a bowl or open tank, and loose silicon carbide grits which have been mixed with a little water to produce a light paste are applied to the flat turntable. The motor is switched on and the slab of rock placed face downwards on the spinning lap wheel where it is held in firm contact with the surface

Fig. 16   A well designed lapping unit

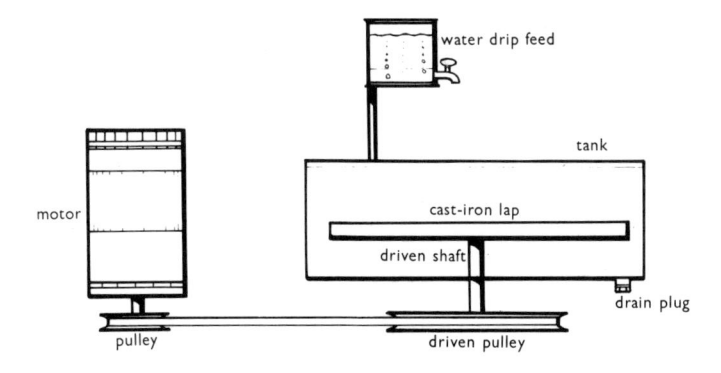

[Diagram labels: motor, pulley, water drip feed, tank, cast-iron lap, driven shaft, driven pulley, drain plug]

Fig. 17 The layout of a cast-iron lap

throughout the grinding operation. As with tumble-polishing, progressively finer grades of silicon carbide are used on the lap until a perfectly smooth surface is achieved. To polish the slab, the cast-iron lap is replaced by another faced with felt or leather which is sprinkled with cerium oxide and a little water. A few minutes work with this will soon produce a mirror finish on the smooth slab.

Cast-iron laps range from 6 in. to 18 in. in diameter and you should consider the size of slab you wish to grind and polish when choosing a machine. If your budget limits your choice to smaller machines, select one which is fitted with a lap without a centre hole or protruding nut as this will mean that the entire area of the lap can be used without damaging the stone. Such laps have threaded bolts on their undersides which screw into the driven shaft.

Another design feature to look for when buying a machine is ease of cleaning. No matter how carefully you apply the silicon carbide to the lap, a certain amount will be thrown off as the wheel spins. This means that the surfaces of the bowl or tank must be cleaned regularly. Some laps are fitted with a drain plug and a waste pipe which can be fed into a bucket placed on the floor near the machine; while others are so designed that water and grits which fly from the lap collect at the front of the container where they can be easily wiped from the surface. Fairly high sides on the rim of the lap bowl are also necessary to catch the drops of silicon carbide paste thrown from the revolving turntable.

As with other lapidary machines, these units are sold with and without motors, pulleys and drive belts, and it is important when buying a machine without these components to ensure that pulleys of the correct size are fitted, in order to achieve the speed of revolution recommended by the manufacturer. A lap which spins too quickly will throw off all the silicon carbide paste; a lap running slowly will take much too long to grind the surface of the slab to a smooth finish.

Some units are fitted with a water reservoir which is mounted above the lap and which incorporates a tap and plastic pipe so that water can be directed on to the lap either as a drip feed during the grinding process, or as a continuous flow to clean the lap between different grinding stages. On other machines, an empty squeezy bottle must be used in place of the water reservoir.

Also available are a number of sophisticated and more expensive units known as vibrating laps which have special bearings and drive shafts enabling them to vibrate in such a way that any slab placed upon their surfaces is moved automatically throughout the process without the need to hold the stone in the hand. Like the conventional lapping units dealt with here, they also use silicon carbide grits for grinding and cerium oxide as a polishing agent; but it is essential when using a vibrating lap that the manufacturer's instructions on grades of silicon carbide to be used and on methods of operation are strictly followed. Ordinary lapping machines offer more scope for experiments with grits, polishes and grinding times.

It is worth mentioning that many rock shops sell a wide range of pre-slabbed stone. If you cannot afford a slab saw *and* a lapping unit, but wish to polish flat slabs, you can get along quite well without the saw if you buy ready-sawn slabs which you can then polish on your own lapping machine. The excitement of cutting a rough rock on a saw in order to reveal its hidden beauty will be missed, but you will be able to select the best slabbed material offered by your supplier to produce your finished specimens and make your jewellery.

Other equipment

Once you have set up the machine in accordance with the manufacturer's instructions, there are a number of other items you must have in order to produce perfectly polished flat surfaces. The first on the list is a supply of ready-cut slabs. Often, when a slab is sawn, the piece breaks from the parent rock a moment before the diamond blade reaches the end of the cut. This leaves a slight projection, or nib, on the edge of the slab which must be removed before it can be placed flat upon the cast-iron lap. Ideally this nib should be ground flat on a coarse grinding wheel, and if you have a grinder it is also wise to grind a very slight bevel around the entire edge of each slab before lapping commences. This will ensure that an absolutely flat surface is presented to the lap each time a slab is worked. If you do not have a grinder, the nib can be successfully tackled with a stout pair of pliers. Grip it between the jaws and give a sharp twist, or hit the head of the pliers smartly with a hammer, and the nib should break off cleanly. You will not be able to grind a bevel on each of your slabs, but if they are presented to the lap carefully this should not present too great a problem.

When buying slabbed stone you should always examine the pieces carefully for cracks, deep imperfections or saw blade marks and reject any piece which is obviously going to break or require a large amount of lapping before it is smooth. You should also reject any piece which has not been cut with absolutely parallel sides. No amount of work on the lapping machine will put matters right if the slab has been incorrectly cut on the saw.

The next item required is a supply of loose silicon carbide in a number of grades from coarse to very fine, together with a polishing powder. As explained in my earlier book, *Pebble Polishing*, silicon carbide is graded by being passed through a series of fine mesh screens. The coarse No. 80 grit gets its name from the fact that it has passed through a screen with 80 meshes to the inch; the higher the grade number, the finer the individual grains. The range of grits available runs from 80 to over 1,000 but you will not need many grades in order to grind your slabs smooth. The best general purpose grades for work on cast-iron laps are Nos. 80, 220 and 400. Cerium oxide is the most widely used polishing agent in all branches of amateur lapidary and it is recommended for slab-polishing on horizontal laps.

The importance of avoiding contamination when working with loose silicon carbide and cerium oxide cannot be over-emphasised. A single grain of No. 80 grit which finds its way into a container holding 400 grit or cerium oxide renders both quite useless for grinding and polishing work. Cleanliness and careful storage will avoid this disaster. Keep your materials in marked containers with secure lids, and check carefully that any spoon or other instrument used when measuring quantities is scrupulously clean.

Finally, you will need a supply of water, a number of plastic containers and a method of applying pastes of grit and water to the lap turntable. If your unit has a water reservoir this should be filled before work commences. Otherwise fill one or two empty washing-up liquid bottles with water and stand them close to the machine. The grits and water can be mixed to light pastes in small plastic bowls and placed nearby ready for application to the lap with a small spoon. Some enthusiasts suggest a paint brush for this last task but, unless a separate brush is used for each grade of silicon carbide, there is a danger that odd particles of coarse grit will be held in the bristles of the brush no matter how thoroughly they are washed. I have seen those small spray bottles on sale at most chemists' shops used very successfully for applying the pastes to the lap but, again, a separate bottle should be used for each grade.

Using the lap Small amounts of each grade of silicon carbide to be used should be mixed with water to form light pastes. Bear in mind the importance of avoiding contamination, and do not mix too much at once. The correct amount depends on the size of your slab and on how cleanly the surface has been cut with the diamond blade. It is better to mix too little than to overdo things and waste expensive grit. More can always be mixed very quickly if needed. Start with a small tea-spoonful of each and experiment with quantities as your experience grows. Do not add too much water when making up the pastes. Additional water can be dripped onto the lap during grinding if you have underestimated; whereas a paste which is too watery to begin with will fly from the lap before grinding commences.

With the motor switched on, a small amount of coarse paste should be applied to the centre of the lap from where it will quickly spread across the surface. Hold the slab firmly by its edges and present the face to the spinning lap in such a way that the front edge, or toe, of the piece, which will be furthest from your wrist, makes contact with the turntable first. The heel is then pressed down gradually until the slab is absolutely flat on the lap. You must *always* place the slab on the turntable *in the direction of rotation* otherwise the slab will be jerked violently from your hand by the spinning lap. It is rather like stepping on to a moving staircase: a flowing action must be developed if a smooth start is to be made.

No hard and fast rules about grinding times can possibly be given; each slab must be treated as an individual grinding and polishing task with each step in the process lasting as long as is necessary. The aim of the first grind, in which No. 80 grit will be used unless otherwise stated by the lap manufacturer, is to remove from the surface of the slab *all* marks left by the cutting action of the diamond blade. This might take as few as three or four minutes if the cut was accurate and the stone relatively soft and free from cracks

Fig. 18 Placing a slab on the lap.

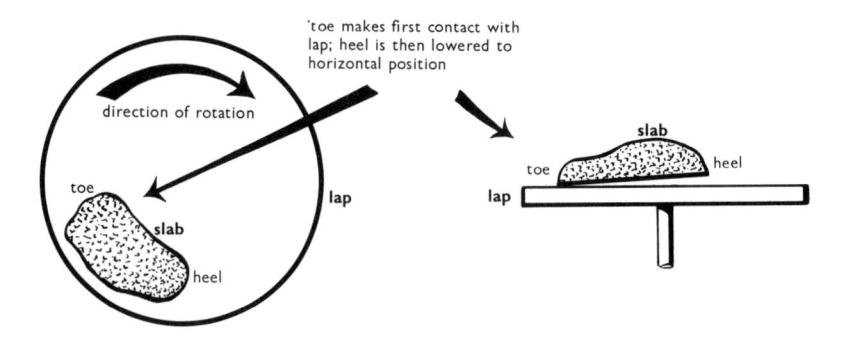

Fig. 19 Holding a slab on a flat lap

and other imperfections, or it might take anything up to half an hour. The key to success lies in having the patience to continue lapping until *all* marks from the previous operation are removed.

The slab must not be allowed to remain motionless on the lap, but should be moved across the surface in a circular or figure-of-eight motion. It must also be turned in the hand as grinding is carried out. This continuous movement is necessary because the outer edges of the circular lap move at a greater speed than the area around the centre. To avoid uneven grinding of the slab's surface it must, therefore, be worked across all parts of the lap.

The amount of pressure which your hand must apply to the slab depends on the slab's weight and its surface area. There is no definite rule, and you will have to experiment with different pressures as you carry out the operation. Certainly your grip on the stone must be sufficiently positive to prevent the slab flying from your hand; but pressure must not be so great that the lap slows down. In practice you will find that you soon develop a 'feel' for the correct pressure. The grits sound as though they are grinding the face when the right amount of downward pressure is applied. If pressure is insufficient, the slab seems to glide across the surface of the lap; too much and it tends to drag.

As surface imperfections are removed, the pastes tend to

thicken because dust and fine particles of stone mix with them during the grinding operation. Small amounts of water must, therefore, be dripped on to the lap as it spins so that the pastes remain fluid in consistency. The slab should be removed from the lap every few minutes and inspected so that grinding progress can be gauged. Rinse the face under running water or wash it in one of your bowls and examine it under a good light. Turn the slab through a few degrees as the light falls on the face, and run your finger across the surface to decide whether or not further coarse grinding is required. Remember that the aim of this first stage is to remove all blade marks. If more coarse grinding is required return the slab to the lap, placing the toe down first, and continue to move it across the surface until you are satisfied that all blade marks have been removed.

When this coarse grinding stage is completed, it must be followed by a thorough washing operation to remove every trace of coarse grit from the lap, the slab and your hands. The lap can be washed by turning the water reservoir tap full on and allowing water to fall on the cast-iron turntable as it spins. Alternatively, a jet of water from one of your plastic bottles can be directed across the surface. On machines fitted with a drain plug, this water will flow down the waste pipe and carry the used grit and rock particles to the sludge

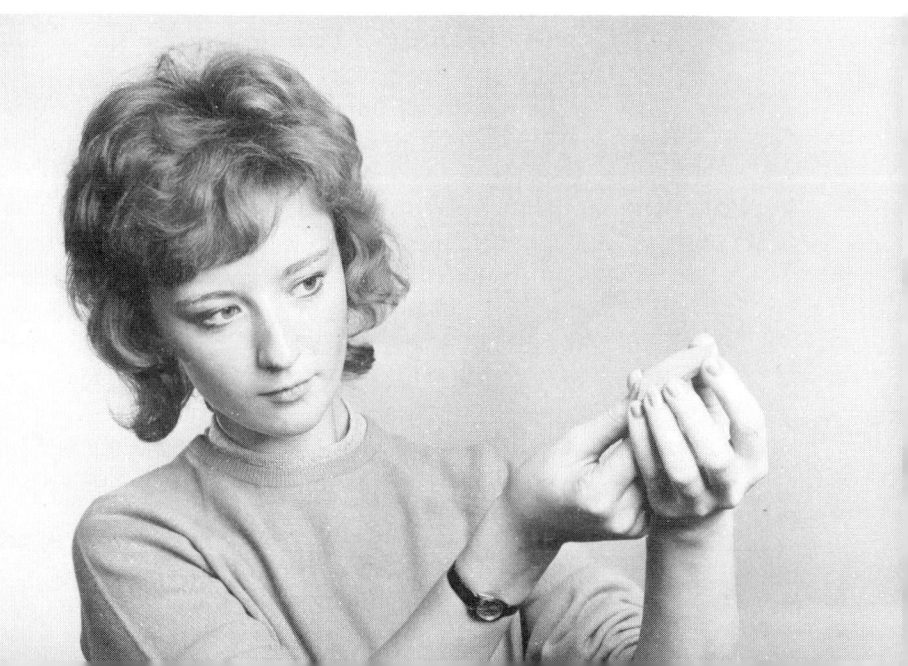

Fig. 20 Examining the surface of a slab to check grinding progress

bucket. Other readers may have to empty the bowl by hand.

After carefully washing the slab and your hands, you are ready to carry out the intermediate grinding stage using No. 220 grit. The procedure is exactly as for the coarse grind, but the aim of the operation is different. You are now attempting to remove all marks left on the face by the coarse silicon carbide. Use the same figure-of-eight motion when holding the stone on the lap and examine the surface repeatedly during the operation for any high spots which might develop if pressure on the stone is uneven. Continue this stage until you are satisfied that all marks left by the No. 80 grit have been worn down, and follow this with a careful washing of the lap, the slab and your hands once again. You are now ready for the final grinding stage.

Silicon carbide grits as fine as the No. 400 grade you will use during the next stage have very limited abrasive powers. Their purpose is to impart an absolutely smooth finish to the flat surface of the slab. They will not remove deep scratches from the surface of the stone and you should only proceed to the third stage when you are satisfied that all scratches have been removed by the coarser No. 220 grit. If you start the third stage too soon you will fail to achieve a mirror finish on your slab when you go on to the polishing process. This third stage is carried out in the same way as the previous stages. Even greater care should be taken to ensure that every trace of grit is washed away before the polishing stage commences. At the end of the process your slab should be absolutely flat and absolutely smooth.

Polishing

On some units a second lap is provided for polishing. This might be a metal or wooden disc which has a leather or felt buff fixed to its surface. The cast-iron lap is unscrewed from the shaft and replaced by the polishing lap. On other units the cast-iron lap remains in position and is covered by a felt disc which is held in place by a clip tightened around the outer rim.

With the leather or felt in position water is dripped onto the surface until the disc is uniformly moistened. Cerium

Fig. 21 Fitting a polishing disc to an 8-inch flat lap

oxide powder is then sprinkled on the pad, the motor is switched on, and polishing then commences. With uniform pressure applied to the slab, it is worked across the surface of the polishing buff using the same motion as in the grinding processes. On no account must the pad be allowed to dry out during this stage. Ensure a steady drip feed of water to the buff in order to maintain a creamy cerium oxide and water paste on the surface. More powder may be added to the lap as required.

Greater downward pressure on the slab is usually needed at this stage in order to impart a polish to the face and great care must be taken to ensure that your grip on the slab does not slip. This can happen quite easily if too much of the slippery polishing paste is allowed to build up on the sides of the stone. Rinse the slab in clean water to reduce this build-up and examine the face regularly to check on the finish achieved. As soon as the entire area of the face has been given a mirror finish you should end the polishing stage. Over-polishing tends to dull rather than improve the finish. A final rinse in clean water should reveal a perfectly polished slab.

When grinding and polishing very thin slabs it is difficult to hold the stone firmly as it is pressed on to the lap. This can result in the slab flying from the hand and being damaged on the side of the bowl. To overcome this problem a block of wood can be temporarily attached to the back of the slab using an adhesive which can be removed later with acetone or methylated spirit when the slab is polished.

Using your slabs   Thick slabs which have been polished on both surfaces and symmetrically shaped on a saw make delightful book-ends. If used as flat bases for penholders or table-lamps only the upper face will require polishing. The base can be covered with baize or felt to prevent scratches on desks or tabletops. Thin slabs which have been polished on both surfaces can

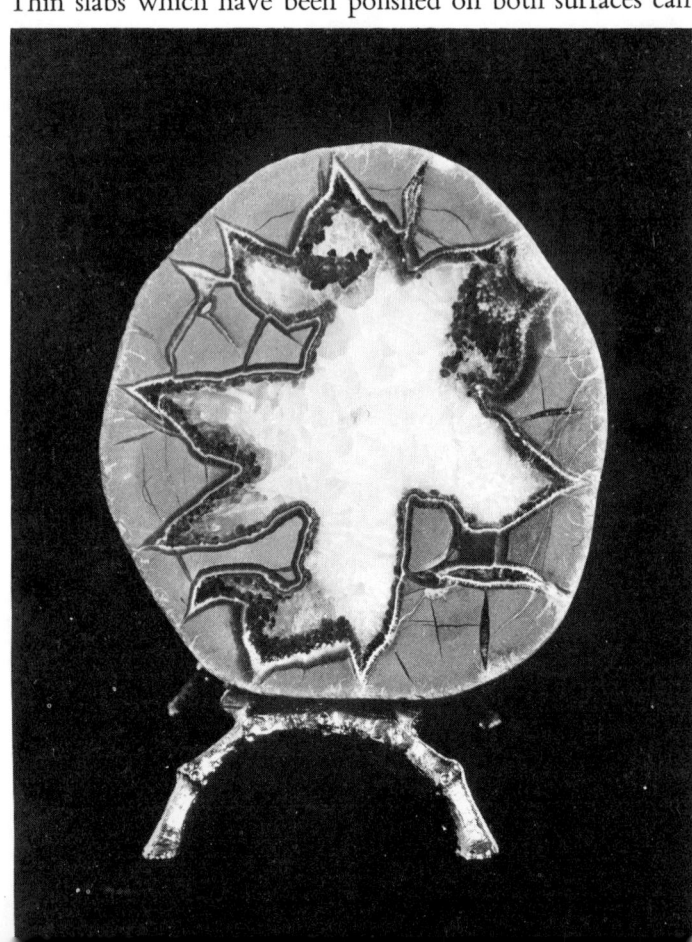

Figs. 22 and (*opposite*) 23 Two delightful polished specimens

Fig. 23

be cut into small squares on your trim saw and used for a wide variety of jewellery items; while smaller slabs with their edges left in a rough and natural state make very attractive pendants. Beautiful display specimens can also be made by simply cutting large stones into two halves and polishing the faces. In contrast, the remainder of the stone is left in its natural state. Such pieces make ideal doorstops, paperweights and unusual ornaments.

4 Preforming stones before tumbling

Your tumble-polishing machine should not be looked upon as redundant when you progress to more advanced lapidary equipment. Indeed, there is an excellent case for investing in a larger tumbler if you propose to take up the hobby enthusiastically because tumblers are far more versatile when used in conjunction with other lapidary machines. This is clearly seen in the production of preforms which will be discussed in this chapter.

Grinding machines

Preforms are stones which have been cut and roughly shaped *before* they are placed in a tumbler barrel. A sliced pebble is one example, but many more shapes including squares, cubes, ovals, hearts, crosses and triangles can also be made. Those having straight edges can be made using diamond saws only and by carrying out all grinding and polishing in the tumbler barrel; but to produce the widest possible range of preforms you will also need a grinding machine. Since this is also the machine on which cabochons are formed it makes a worthwhile addition to your workshop.

Fig. 24 A large tumbler makes a useful addition to a lapidary workshop

Fig. 25 A robust grinding machine with coarse and fine wheels

In its simplest form a grinder consists of a shaft driven by an electric motor, pulleys, and a drive belt in much the same way as a diamond saw is powered. On the ends of the shaft are fitted coarse and fine silicon carbide grinding wheels usually measuring 6 to 8 in. in diameter and 1 in. in thickness, the most popular grades being Nos. 100 and 220. Because water is an essential requirement when grinding, the wheels are surrounded by splash guards and a shallow tray is placed beneath them in order to catch any water used in the process. A drip feed similar to that used with the lapping unit is usually incorporated in the design, though some machines rely on empty washing-up liquid bottles. A drain plug and waste pipe complete the water circulation system. On most units a rubber strip is attached to the front edge of the splash guard to further reduce the spray of

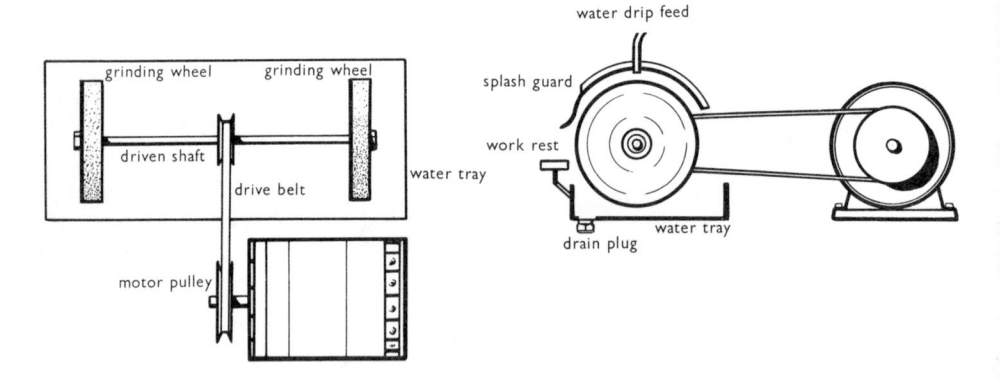

Fig. 26 Basic grinding machine layout

water from the wheels, and some models have a metal work-rest to support the hand during grinding operations.

This basic set-up is quite suitable for shaping preforms prior to tumbling, but other attachments are required in order to produce cabochons which are ground, sanded and polished on the same machine. For the benefit of those readers confused by the terms grinding and sanding let me explain that grinding involves the removal of large amounts of stone in order to bring a particular piece to a regular shape, and sanding refers to the more delicate work of preparing the surface of the stone for its final polish by removing all scratches produced during grinding. A unit designed for grinding, sanding and polishing work usually has its coarse and fine grinding wheels in the centre of the shaft. On one end of the shaft is mounted a sanding disc which consists of a circular piece of wood or metal covered with a hard rubber pad. On to this pad sheets of fine silicon carbide sanding paper are temporarily glued with 'Copydex' or a similar adhesive. The grits on these sheets are graded from Nos. 320 to 600 and because the sheets are attached to a rubber pad they mould themselves to the shape of rounded stones during the sanding operation.

On the other end of the shaft is mounted a hard felt pad which is used during the polishing process in the same way as the horizontal polishing pad is used on a lapping machine. Because the speed at which polishing is carried out is much

Fig. 27 A grinding, sanding and polishing unit

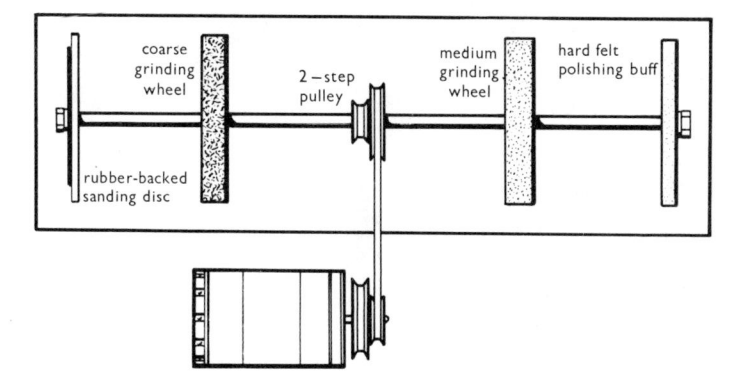

slower than the grinding speed, the shaft and the motor spindles are fitted with two or more pulleys of different sizes so that the speed of revolution can be varied by moving the drive belt. Thus the entire process of grinding, sanding and polishing a stone can be carried out on a single machine. We will return to this three-in-one unit in the next chapter. Meanwhile, let us consider the methods used to produce preforms for tumbling.

If you own a slab saw you can start with large pieces of rock and turn out slabs to your own requirements. They should be cut quite thin because the next step is to cut them into smaller pieces on your trim saw. If you do not own a slab saw concentrate on looking for thin, parallel-sided slabs when hunting through stocks at your local rock shop.

To work out the various shapes you wish to produce on the surface of the slab an aluminium pencil is used. This will leave a clear mark on the surface of the slab which can be used as a guideline when sawing. The pencils can be purchased for a few pence at most rock shops. When marking out squares and oblongs the only other tool required is a ruler, but for shapes such as hearts and circles you will need a template. These are also sold at rock shops, and when buying you should select one made in transparent plastic material in preference to one made in metal. The plastic type enables you to see the surface of the slab as you mark out the various shapes and you will be able to move the

Fig. 28 A combined grinder, sander, polisher

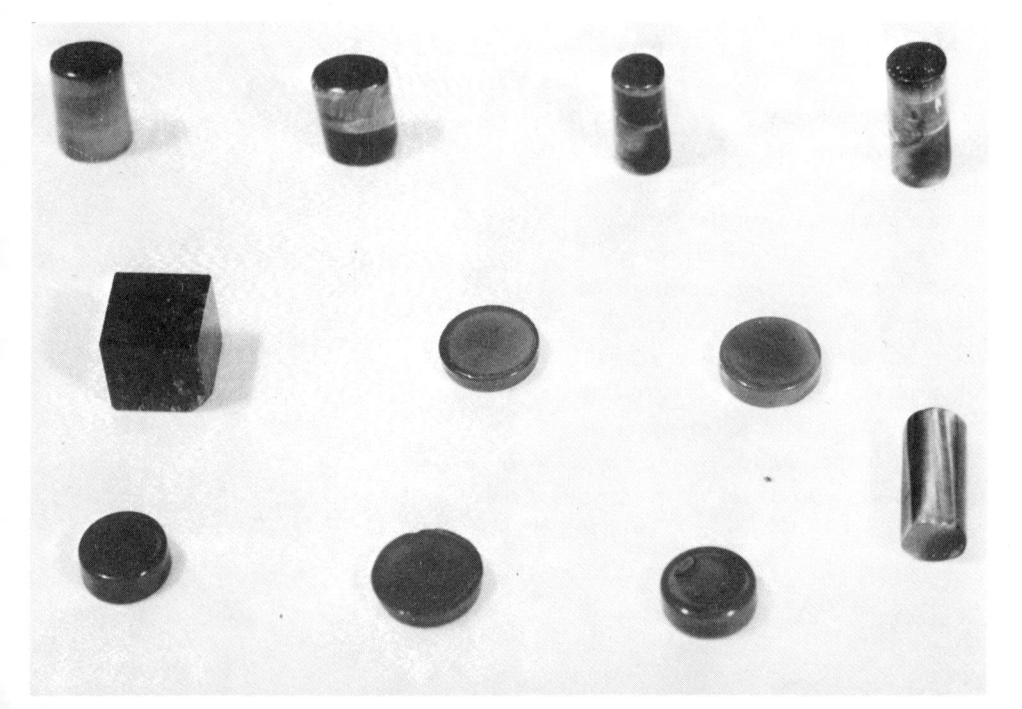

Fig. 29 Preform shapes cut with a trim saw from a larger slab and roughly shaped on a grinding wheel before tumbling

template across the slab to select the most attractive patterns in the stone. After marking out the preforms, the slab is cut into smaller pieces on your trim saw. Remember that the diamond blade must only be used to make straight cuts. *You must never attempt to cut curved shapes with a diamond blade.* Continue trimming with straight cuts around the outline until as much waste material as possible has been removed.

The next step is **to** grind away the remaining waste using your coarse silicon carbide grinding wheel. Ensure that the manufacturer's instructions regarding setting up the machine have been carried out, and if your grinder is fitted with two or more pairs of pulleys, move the drive belt to the pair which turn the shaft at the fastest speed. Fill the water reservoir or your plastic bottles and run the waste pipe from the drain plug in the tray to a nearby bucket. *Do not allow water to run onto the grinding wheels when the motor is switched off and the wheels are stationary.* If you do so the wheels could be thrown out of balance because they will absorb too much water on that part of their rims directly beneath the taps. Here is the sequence of operation when grinding:

1. Switch on motor so that wheels are turning
2. Turn on water feed
3. Carry out grinding operations
4. Turn off water feed and allow water to drain from tray
5. Switch off motor to bring wheels to rest

Fig. 30 Marking and cutting preform shapes with a template

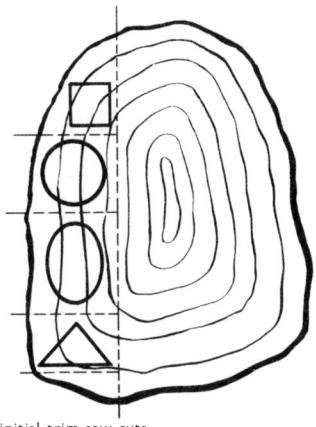

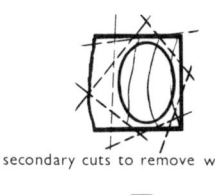

template

initial trim saw cuts

secondary cuts to remove waste

rough shape ready for grinding

Because the grinding wheels are porous, too much water must never be used. On the other hand, the importance of the small amount of water fed to the grinding surface cannot be over-emphasized. Water is as important in grinding as is coolant when using a diamond blade. It cools the surface of the stone which is being shaped and prevents fractures caused by overheating, it washes away particles of grit and stone which would otherwise clog the surface of the wheel and reduce grinding efficiency, and it prevents dust particles rising into the air by carrying all wastes to the water tray beneath the wheels.

Care of grinding wheels

From time to time throughout its life your coarse grinding wheel will require a little maintenance in order to keep its face absolutely flat. Repeated heavy grinding of agate and similar hard materials inevitably results in a number of minor indentations on the face of the wheel. If the stone you are working tends to bounce and bump as you pass it across the wheel it is an indication that the face is not absolutely flat. Putting matters right is known as dressing the wheel, and special diamond-tipped wheel dressers are available which can be passed across the face to re-align it by wearing down the bumps. An equally effective job can be done using a piece of agate slab which has been cut absolutely square. This dressing takes longer but it saves the cost of the diamond tool.

To dress the wheel take the agate slab and present its edge to the spinning wheel at the centre of the rim. Hold the slab firmly and move it gradually towards the wheel until it meets the first of the high spots. Keep the slab square to the wheel and the bump will be worn level with the face. Continue dressing until all imperfections have been removed and remember to use the correct sequence of operation when turning the drip feed on and off. Fine grinding wheels rarely require dressing if used correctly because the really hard grinding work should always be carried out on the coarse wheel. However, should your No. 220 wheel require attention the procedure is exactly the same.

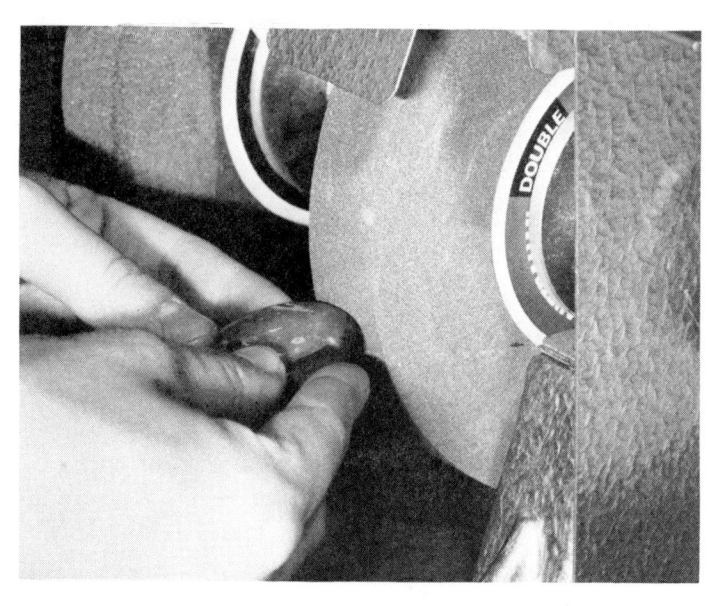

Fig. 31 Presenting the preform to the grinding wheel

Grinding your preforms

With the motor running and the drip feed supplying the correct amount of water to the wheel, stand at the front of the machine with the first of your roughly sawn preforms. Grinding is carried out on the rim of the wheel—that is on the 1 in. thickness of its face—the sides being only occasionally used in cabochon forming. The secret of success is to keep the stone constantly moving from side to side across the rim so that the wheel wears evenly. Grooves and pits will quickly develop if you allow the stone to remain in contact with one point for too long.

Hold the preform firmly between fingers and thumb and present it to the wheel with a light, stroking motion back and forth across the face. Preforms should be shaped on the wheel so that their edges are flat. If sloping edges are formed they tend to fracture during the tumble-polishing stage and spoil an otherwise perfect piece. To produce flat edges on your stones make sure that you carry out all coase grinding at the centre of the rim. If the stone is held above or below this centre line the edge will follow the curved shape of the wheel as it is formed.

Square, oblong and triangular shaped preforms should be held firmly in the hand and passed across the wheel with

correct position for flat edge   too high   too low

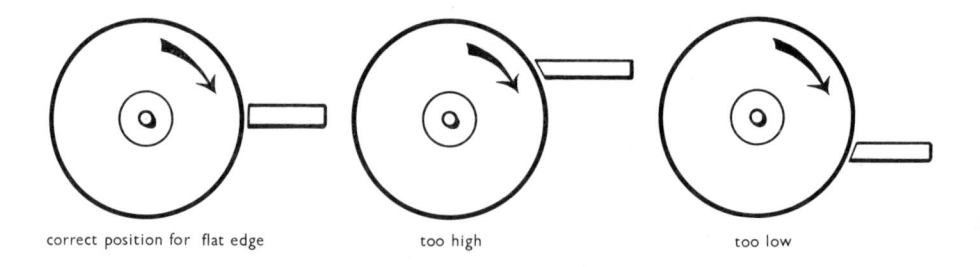

Fig. 32 Grinding preform edges

no movement of the wrist as grinding is carried out. This will ensure that grinding follows the straight lines marked on the stone with the aluminium pencil. Round, oval, and other curved shapes must be held with equal firmness, but your wrist must be swung left and right in a gentle arc which follows the curved pencil line. Endeavour to develop a very light touch when using grinding wheels as this will greatly prolong their working lives.

When the edges of your preforms have been roughly shaped, the faces of the stones should also be passed once or twice across the coarse wheel in order to remove some of the blade marks made during slabbing. Do not overdo this face grinding otherwise the tumbled appearance of the finished preforms might be lost. The aim is to reduce the time it takes to polish the preforms in the tumbler by removing the deeper imperfections on the grinding wheel; but too much work at the wheel can spoil the final appearance of the piece.

Fig. 33 Grinding straight-sided and rounded preforms

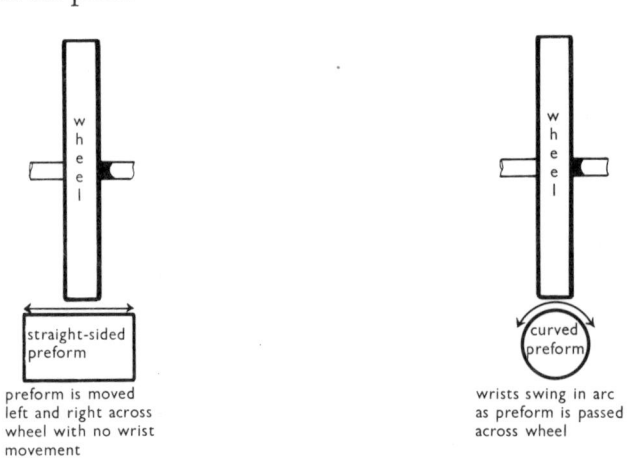

straight-sided preform

preform is moved left and right across wheel with no wrist movement

curved preform

wrists swing in arc as preform is passed across wheel

When you have sufficient roughly ground preforms to half fill the tumbler, place them in the barrel and add a number of small pebbles to bring the load up to just under three-quarters full. These added pebbles will help to carry the silicon carbide to the flat faces of the preforms and greatly improve tumbling efficiency. Add the correct amount of coarse grit and proceed with the first stage of the tumbling operation as outlined in *Pebble Polishing*.

The grinding time will be approximately half that for a load of beach pebbles, and when your daily inspection confirms that most of the preforms have had all traces of diamond blade marks removed you can clean out the barrel and proceed to second stage grinding using fine silicon carbide grit. Again, this pre-polishing stage should take half the time required with a barrel containing beach pebbles. When daily inspection reveals that most of the preforms have a perfectly smooth matt finish you can wash out the barrel and remove the pebbles which you added to make up the load. Thoroughly wash the preforms and inspect each one carefully. Some will have cracked or chipped badly during the grinding stages and they must be rejected now. Others may have minor imperfections which will have to be removed before the polishing stage commences. This can usually be done with a few quick passes across the face of the fine wheel on your grinder.

When this hand-finishing has been carried out, wash all the preforms once again before placing them in the barrel for the final polish. This time the load should be made up to three-quarters by adding some leather off-cuts or small pieces of felt to the barrel. They will help to carry the polish to the flat surfaces of the preforms and also reduce the possibility of further breakages during the final run. Add the correct amount of water and cerium oxide and proceed with the polishing stage.

Angular preforms can be used quite effectively with bell caps to make unusual bracelets and pendants, but most preforms are used with flat pad jewellery fittings to make such things as cufflinks and tie-bars (*see* Plate 7). Flat squares and oblongs are also used for inlay work on trinket

Using preforms in jewellery-making

Fig. 34　Cutting a stone on a horizontal unit

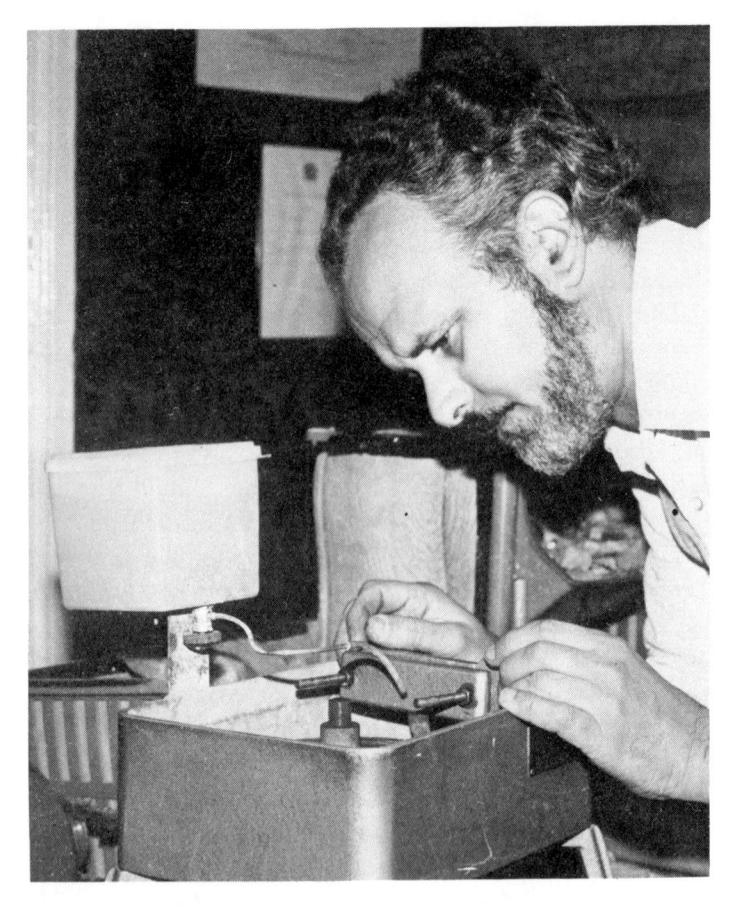

boxes and other small ornaments. Striking 'sculptures' can also be made by bonding preforms on to polished slabs with epoxy resin.

5 How to cut a cabochon

Of all the pleasing shapes and delightful specimens which amateur lapidaries produce in their home gem-cutting workshops cabochons are by far the most popular. The making of these 'beetle-backed' gemstones, so often seen in rings, pendants, bracelets and other items of jewellery, is a relatively simple task and one which is guaranteed to provide hours of pleasure and beautiful results. The skills you have already acquired in slabbing, trimming and making preforms are all used in cabochon cutting, and your familiarity with diamond saws and grinding wheels makes the task of producing your first 'cab' that much easier.

Before we go on to discuss the various steps in shaping the stone I want to introduce you to another machine which can be used in cabochon-making This is the horizontal

Machines

Fig. 35 You can cut, grind and polish stones on this horizontal unit

57

sawing, grinding, sanding and polishing unit: a machine which is relatively inexpensive and easy to use. Like the lapping machine it consists of an open tank in which a spindle or shaft is driven by means of pulleys and drive belt, fitted underneath the tank, which are in turn connected to an electric motor at the rear of the machine. A diamond sawblade is first mounted horizontally on the shaft and the drive belt positioned to give the fastest running speed. The stone to be cut or slabbed is held in a vice which can be raised or lowered on a vertical metal rod at the side of the machine. To cut the stone the vice is swung towards the rim of the blade and, with the water soluble coolant supply directed by means of a plastic tube onto the cutting rim, the stone is pressed against the blade and the cut completed. The vice is then lowered slightly and a second cut made to produce a slab.

Having cut the slab, the diamond blade is removed from the shaft and replaced by a coarse silicon carbide grinding wheel on which the stone is roughly shaped. A finer grinding wheel then replaces the coarse wheel on the shaft and the stone is brought to final shape. Next, a sanding disc is placed on the shaft and the drive belt moved to a pulley which provides a medium speed of revolution. All scratch marks on the stone are then gradually removed.

Finally, the sanding disc is replaced by a felt polishing pad which is charged with cerium oxide paste and the stone is brought to a high polish with the spindle turning at its slowest speed. Thus, by placing different attachments on a single shaft and by adjusting running speeds with various pulley sizes the tasks of sawing, grinding, sanding and polishing are carried out on a single machine.

Cabochons from pebbles

Returning to cabochons, your first attempts at producing these attractive gemstones should be made by slicing several symmetrically shaped pebbles on your trim saw or with the horizontal saw described above. If you use pebbles which have already been tumble-polished, your cabochons can be completed with a few minutes work on coarse and fine grinding wheels to smooth their rough edges and remove

Fig. 36 A horizontal combination unit

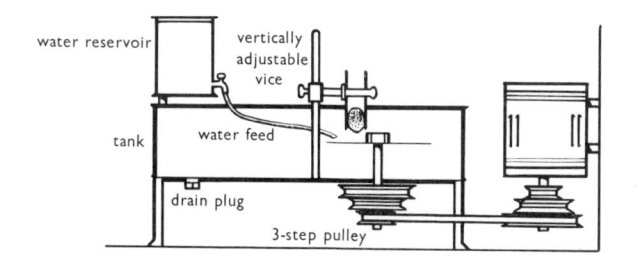

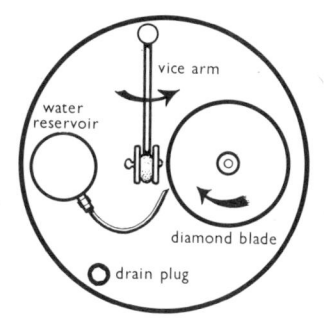

blade marks from their bases. The only problem you will face when making jewellery with cabochons produced in this way is that of finding fittings into which the stones can be set. This is an easy problem to solve if you use the flat pad fittings normally used with baroque stones, but fittings designed for use with cabochons are made in a number of exact sizes. Unless you are extremely fortunate in the range of tumbled stones in your stocks the cabochons will be too large or too small for the fittings.

It is safer to start with an unpolished pebble which can be sliced and then ground to the correct size on a coarse silicon carbide wheel. First you must buy a plastic template stamped out with round and oval shapes in sizes which correspond to those of fittings made for cabochons. These sizes are expressed in millimetres, and each hole of your template will have its length and width clearly marked so that you can select the size to match your fitting.

Fig. 37 Typical cabochon fittings showing exact size requirement of shaped stone

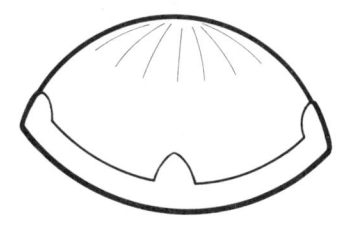

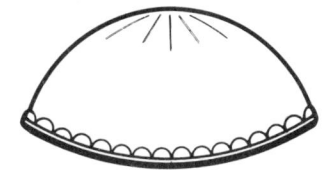

Choose a pebble slightly larger than the hole in the template which corresponds to the size of jewellery fitting you wish to use. Slice the pebble on your trim saw and select the half which has the most pleasing surface appearance and the fewest flaws and imperfections. The base of this half must now be ground absolutely flat. This is best done on a cast-iron lapping unit using Nos. 80 and 220 silicon carbide grits, but if you do not own a lapping unit you can work the stone lightly across the sides of your coarse and fine grinding wheels. This should only be done to remove minor imperfections left by the diamond blade. *The sides of your grinding wheels should never be used for heavy grinding work.*

When the base is absolutely flat, place your plastic template on it and mark the circumference of the cabochon with an aluminium pencil. Ensure that the point of the pencil marks a line as close as possible to the edge of the template hole by holding the pencil at an angle when scribing. If you hold the pencil vertically the shape drawn will be much smaller than the hole in the template.

The next task is to grind the edges of the pebble until they correspond with the line you have marked. This is done on the coarse grinding wheel. Hold the stone with the flat side uppermost and with your fingers supporting the rounded portion underneath. Place your thumbs on the flat base and present the stone to the edge of the grinding wheel. Work in the centre of the wheel and move your wrists to left and right throughout the grinding operation. At the same time the stone must be slowly turned in your hands so that the edge is worn down evenly around the base until the pencil line is reached. You will probably find that a sludge of stone dust and water tends to build up on the edge of the stone, especially when a large amount of waste material must be removed. To prevent this, have a bowl of water nearby and dip the pebble into it frequently during the operation. The water drip feed must, of course, be maintained on the wheels at all times; and do remember the correct procedure for starting and stopping the motor and turning the water supply on and off.

Plate 1 Stones which can be found in Britain

Smoky quartz (Cairngorm)   Agate   Red jasper
Citrine   Amethyst   Jet   Agate

Plate 2 Larger rocks which can be cut and used for jewellery-making

Rhodonite   Amethyst
Rhodocrosite   Polished tiger eye   Rough tiger eye

Plate 3 Imported rocks, available from lapidary suppliers in Britain

Rough sodalite
Polished sodalite
Polished Queensland agate (slab)
Rough Queensland agate
Rough Queensland agate
Labradorite
Lapis lazuli
Bloodstone
Aventurine
Chrysoprase
Moonstone
Rose quartz (polished and unpolished)
Amazonite

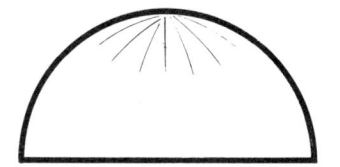

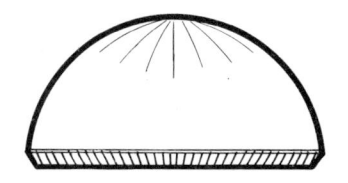

Fig. 38 Shaped stone before and after grinding of chamfer around base

To complete the base of the stone, the sharp edge formed where the flat face meets the sloping sides must be smoothed by grinding a narrow bevel or chamfer around the base. The purpose of this sloping edge is to avoid any splintering of the base during the shaping of the dome, and also to ensure that the finished cabochon will fit neatly into the jewellery mount. The chamfer is easily formed by passing the edge of the base across the grinding wheel at the same angle as you would work when sharpening a knife blade.

Dopping the stone

With the work on the base completed you must now grind, sand and polish the dome. Coarse grinding can be carried out while holding the stone in your hands if it is a fairly large cabochon. This is the usual procedure when using a horizontal grinding wheel, but smaller stones and those which are to be shaped on vertical wheels are easier to hold if they are now attached to dop sticks. Dopping simply means attaching a handle to the base of the stone to make it easier to manipulate, and a dop stick is an ordinary piece of dowel about 5 in. long with a flat end slightly narrower than the base of the stone. Call at your local timber shop and buy half a dozen lengths of dowel in sizes ranging from $\frac{1}{4}$–$\frac{3}{4}$ in.; take them home and cut them into 5-in. lengths with perfectly straight saw cuts and you will have sufficient dop sticks to last a lifetime.

The time-honoured method of attaching the stone to the stick is to use dop wax, and like many such methods it is the best—if you carry out the job correctly. You will be able to buy a dopping unit at your rock shop, or you can make yourself a simple stove with the following items:

Fig. 39 A dopping unit sold by many rock shops

2 empty bean cans (largest size)
1 empty bean can (smallest size)
1 empty can about half the size of your small bean can
flat metal tray
a 2-in. stub of candle
dop sticks
stick of dop wax (available for a few pence at your rock shop)

The dop wax is broken into pieces and placed in the smallest can, the small bean can is punctured on its bottom

62

and sides with as many holes as you can make with a 6-inch nail and hammer, the two large bean cans are filled almost to overflowing with sand, and the metal tray is wiped clean, dried, and placed conveniently nearby. Light the candle and place the punctured bean can over it. Put the smallest can containing the dop wax onto this miniature stove and keep a careful watch until the wax begins to melt. *It must not be allowed to boil and bubble.* If it should do so extinguish the candle immediately by blowing through the holes in the can. Have two or three dop sticks of various thicknesses in your hands and rest their ends on the top of the stove so that the wood is warmed. When you see that the wax has melted, dip each stick into it to a depth of half an inch. Turn the stick in your fingers for a few moments then withdraw it smoothly from the wax and stand it on end on the flat tray. The wax will run down the stick towards the tray and form a conical, flat-topped bed on which your stone will rest evenly.

    Prepare several dop sticks in this way while the wax is molten. As their ends harden on the metal tray they can be removed and stored, wax upwards, in the sand tins until required. Take care that the wax in the melting pot does not become too hot during your dopping operations. It will lose its ability to adhere to your stones if it is allowed to boil. Control the temperature by extinguishing and re-lighting the candle.

    With a supply of waxed sticks in your sand tins you can now dop one of your half-made cabochons. The stone must first be warmed by placing its flat side *upwards* on the candle stove. It will have reached the correct temperature when you can just bear to place your finger on the flat base. Select a dop stick slightly narrower than the base and pass it slowly over the candle stove so that the wax begins to soften. Now, with a swift but smooth movement, press the flat face of the wax against the flat face of the stone and lift it from the top of the stove. Turn the dop stick so that the stone is resting squarely on the top, moisten your fingers by licking them, and gently centralize the stone as you mould the soft wax around its base to form a solid

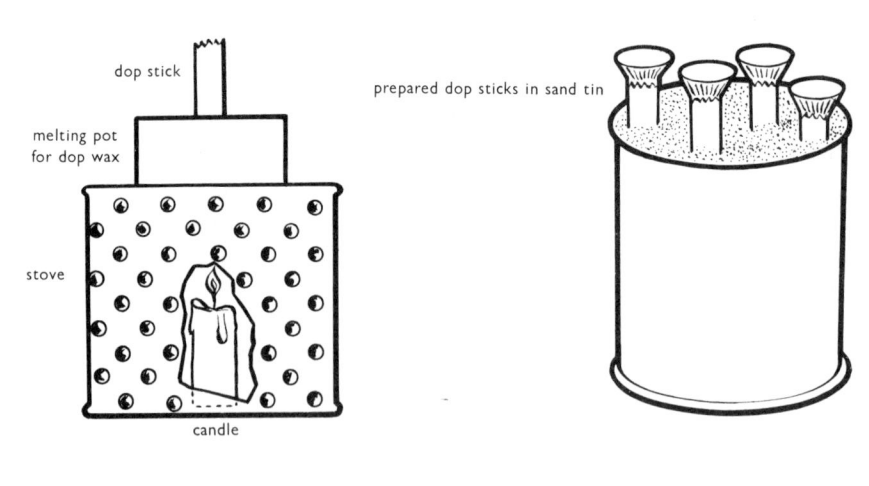

Fig. 40 dop stick / melting pot for dop wax / stove / candle / prepared dop sticks in sand tin

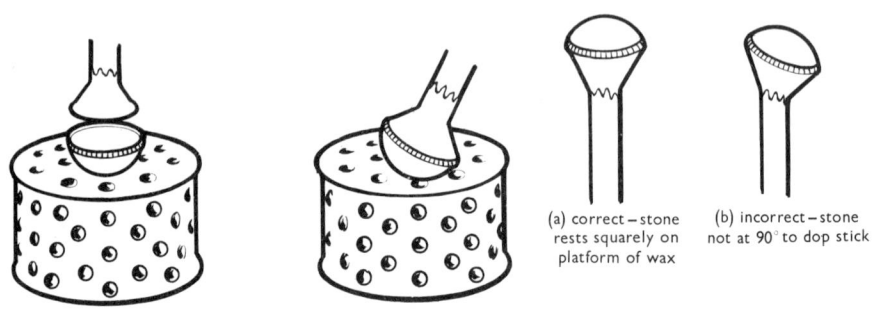

Fig. 41 (a) correct – stone rests squarely on platform of wax (b) incorrect – stone not at 90° to dop stick

Fig. 42 (a) start with dop stick in vertical position (b) gradually work towards top of dome by moving dop stick to horizontal position grind areas of stone which are not symmetrical until a perfect dome is formed

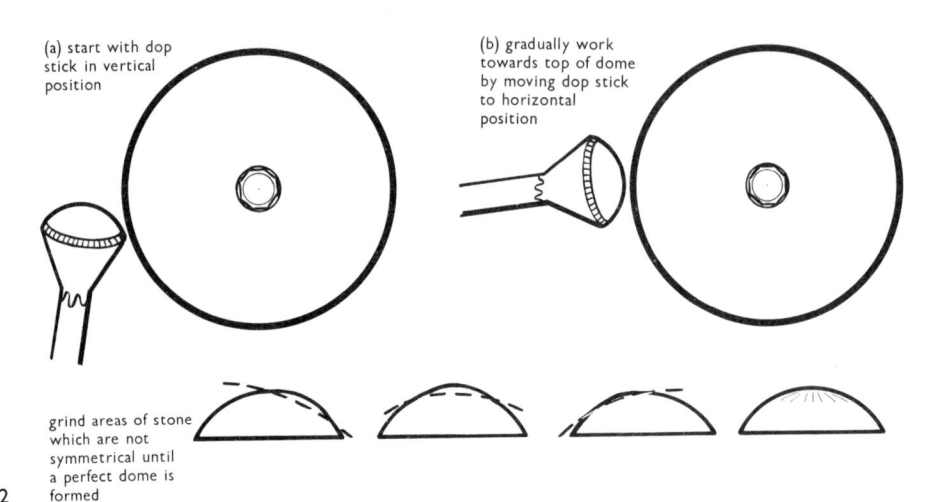

64

platform. Return the mounted stone to the sand tin until the wax has hardened when your cabochon will be ready for grinding, sanding and polishing.

Shaping the dome

Commence on the coarse grinding wheel after examining the stone carefully to decide at which points the shape is not symmetrical. Bring the dome into contact with the wheel slightly below the centre of the rim; sweep it back and forth across the face, at the same time rotating the dop stick between fingers and thumb. Start with the stick in a near vertical position and gradually work towards the horizontal. When turning the stone on the stick you should increase pressure when those areas which are not symmetrical are in contact with the wheel. The aim is to form a perfect dome without flats or ridges.

When you are satisfied with the shape of the dome, wash the stone thoroughly in clean water and proceed to the fine grinding wheel. Go over the entire surface once again in the same manner. At this stage a very light touch is required in order to avoid the grinding of tiny flats. Keep the stone moving across the wheel and rotate the dop stick rapidly in your fingers. When all coarse grinding scratches have been removed wash the stone again in preparation for the next stage.

Sanding is carried out on the vertical sanding disc at the end of your machine. Attach a No. 320 silicon carbide paper-backed sanding sheet to the rubber-faced disc and move the drive belt on the pulleys to give a medium running speed. Use a plastic bottle to apply water to the sheet as it spins, and bear in mind that the aim in sanding is to remove scratches left on the surface of the stone by the fine grinding wheel. Keep the stone moving and roll it across the spinning disc on the dop stick. Change to a No. 400 sheet to produce

Fig. 40 (*top*) Candle stove for dopping stones

Fig. 41 (*centre*) Lifting warmed stone on prepared dop stick

Fig. 42 (*bottom*) Shaping the dome

an absolutely smooth matt finish on the cabochon dome and ensure an adequate supply of water from the bottle throughout the entire sanding stage.

Final polishing is carried out at the other end of the machine using the felt pad, but before polishing commences wash the dopped stone and your hands very carefully to remove all traces of silicon carbide. Move the drive belt on the pulleys to provide the slowest running speed and then apply a thin paste of cerium oxide and water to the pad as it spins and spread it evenly across the surface. Do not saturate the polishing disc with water. It must remain moist throughout the polishing stage, but too much water will cause the cerium oxide to fly from the pad. Rotate the dome of the cabochon across the moist face of the pad for a few minutes and you should produce a mirror finish on the stone.

When satisfied with the polish achieved you can remove the finished cabochon from the dop stick by holding it firmly between your fingers and giving a quick sideways pull. If this should fail place the dopped stone in the freezer compartment of your refrigerator for five minutes and then try again. The wax will contract when cold and the stone should then drop off.

It should be noted that the sanding and polishing stages of forming the cabochon can, of course, be carried out on the horizontal machine already described, or on a lapping unit using loose Nos. 320 and 400 grits and cerium oxide. The procedure for working the stone is identical to that used with vertical sanding and polishing discs.

Cabochons from slabs

Because they are already dome-shaped, sliced beach pebbles are ideal material for beginners with little experience of grinding wheels. Once you have gained some experience at forming symmetrical domes you can proceed to cutting cabochons from slabbed stone and produce even more beautiful specimens. Remember when cutting or buying your slabs that they must be parallel-sided and slightly thicker than the height of the finished cabochon to allow for waste when grinding. They must also be free from cracks and other imperfections which cannot be removed later.

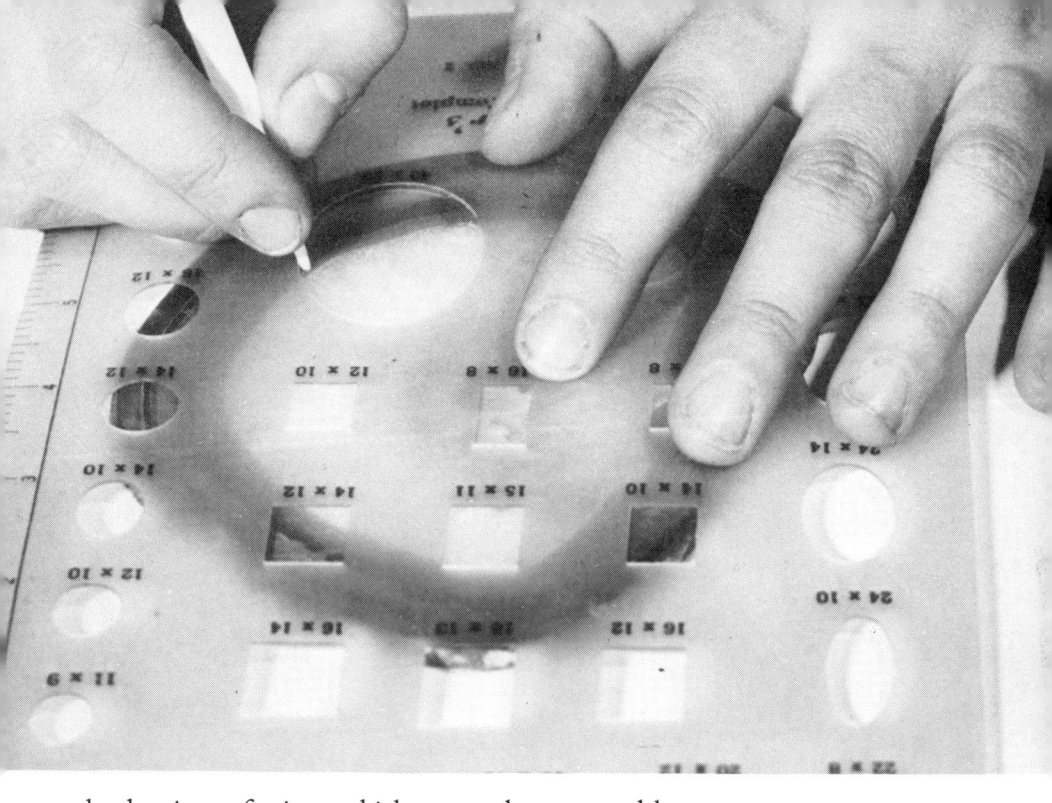

Remove all saw blade marks on a flat lap with loose silicon carbide grit and mark out the cabochon shape with a template and aluminium pencil. The trim saw is used to cut the slab into smaller shapes and to remove as much waste as possible from the trimmed slab. All cuts with the blade must be absolutely straight, and an allowance for the thickness of the blade must be made when trimming. Coarse grinding of the cabochon outline can be carried out with the trimmed slab held in the hands. The method is the same as described for grinding oval preforms, but with cabochons the slab can be held slightly above the centre of the wheel so that the walls are ground with a slightly inward curve. Keep the stone moving across the face of the wheel and when the outline is completed grind a narrow chamfer on the sharp edge. The stone is now ready for dopping. Follow the instructions given for dopping sliced pebbles, and bear in mind that it is the face with the chamfered edge which is attached to the dop stick.

Fig. 43 Marking cabochon shapes on a flat slab with the aid of a template

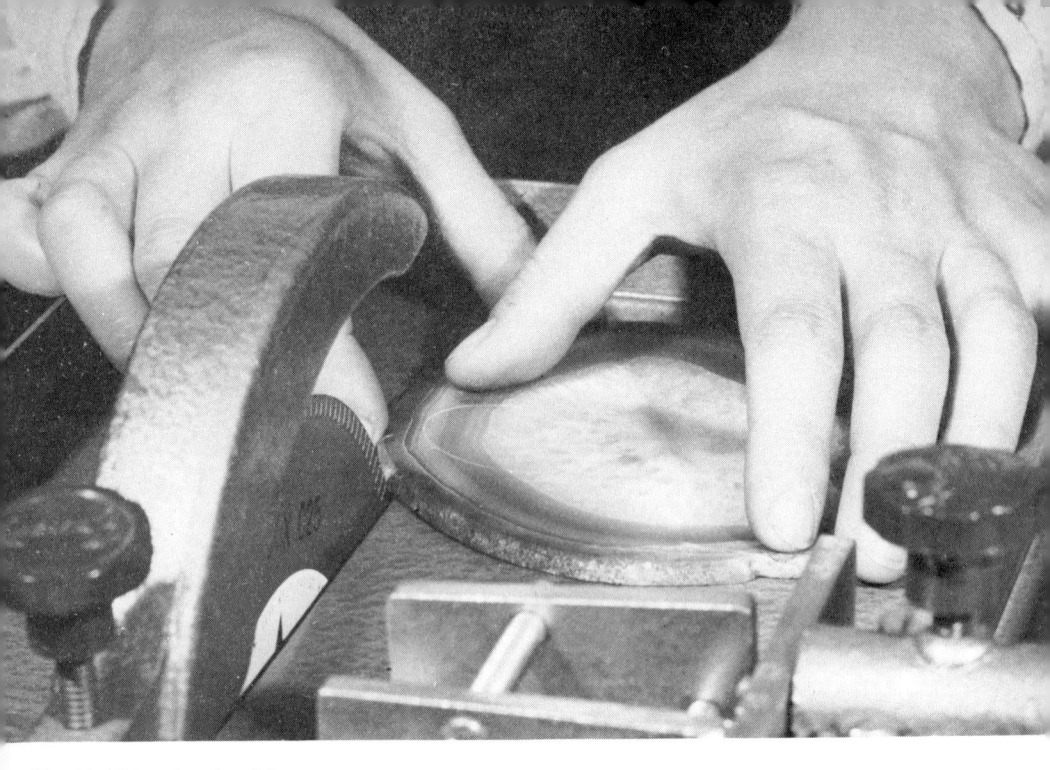

Fig. 44 Trimming the slab to a rough cabochon shape

Fig. 45 Grinding the cabochon

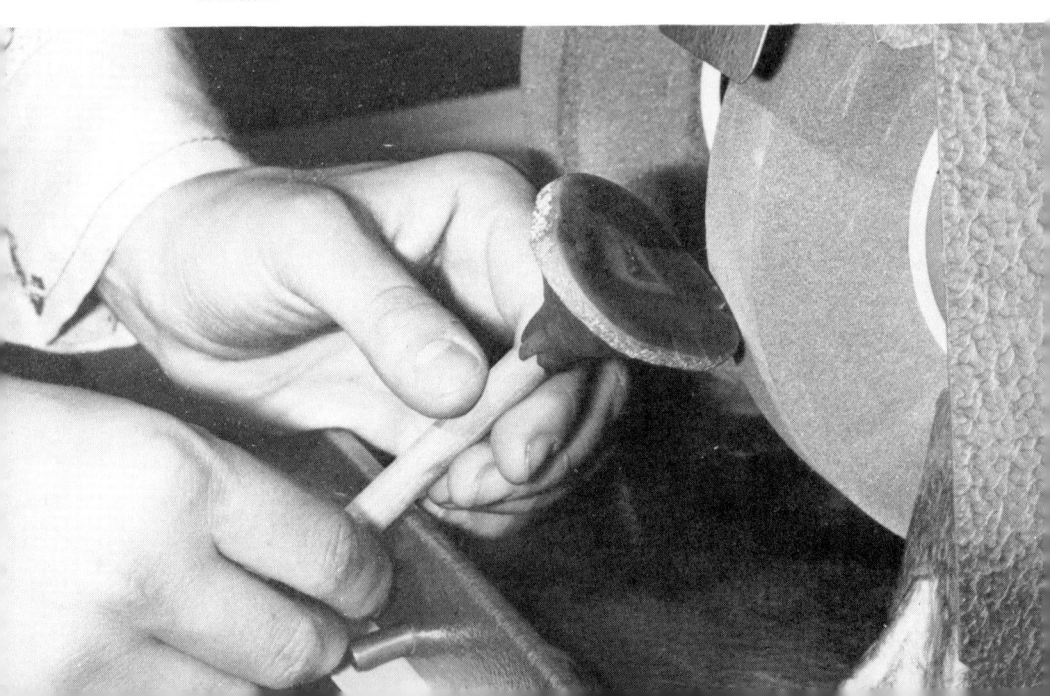

Fig. 46 A small, well designed unit for cabochon making. It has a vertical saw at one end of the shaft, while the grinding, sanding and polishing wheels can be mounted at the other end

Again, the procedure is as for pebble slices, greater care being taken to avoid the grinding of flats during preliminary shaping. Do not make sudden changes to the angle at which the stone is held against the grinding wheel. The aim should be to gradually round the outer walls towards the centre of the stone to produce a perfect dome. Proceed to sanding and polishing only after you have achieved a perfectly smooth cabochon outline with the grinding wheels.

Grinding, sanding and polishing

Fig. 47 The hand-held slab is presented to the grinding wheel slightly above centre line to produce inward-curving sides. The slab is then reversed before dopping

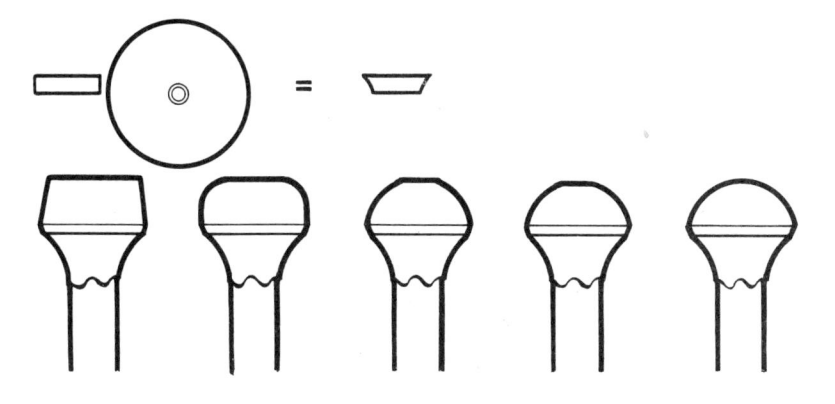

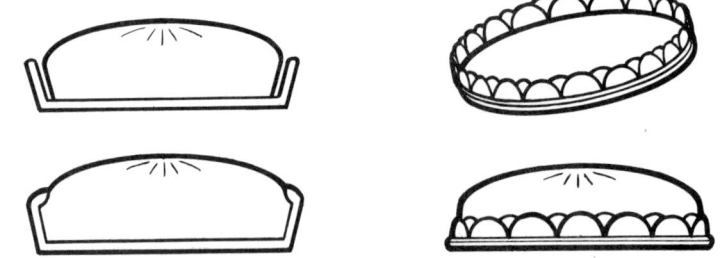

Fig. 48 Plain and fancy cabochon fittings

Jewellery-making with cabochons

Jewellery fittings for use with cabochons differ from the flat pad fittings used with baroque stones by having a raised edge which is rubbed over the stone after it has been cemented in position to give a neat and attractive finish to the piece. The raised edge might be plain or fancy in style and the variety of cabochon fittings is extremely wide. Rings, brooches, cufflinks, pendants and earrings can all be made using cabochons of many different shapes. When buying your fittings ensure that they are of the size to match the cabochons you plan to cut. Mail order catalogues for home jewellery-making equipment always state in millimetres the size of cabochon required for a particular fitting.

In spite of the enormous range of manufactured fittings which home jewellery makers can buy, and the simple efficiency of epoxy resin as an adhesive for bonding gemstones to jewellery mounts, almost every newcomer to the hobby wants to drill a hole in a stone. I believe this is because most absolute beginners imagine that necklaces, pendants and other pieces of jewellery produced by amateur lapidaries are made with drilled stones. They soon realize that this is not so and that drilled stones are only very occasionally used by home jewellery makers. Nevertheless the desire to drill holes in semi-precious stones persists.

Until quite recently the cost of equipment suitable for drilling holes in obdurate stone was so high that most amateur lapidaries were content to leave this branch of the subject to professional workers in commercial lapidary establishments. If they required a drilled stone for a particular item of jewellery, this was either purchased ready-drilled or the stone was taken to a professional who provided a hole-drilling service. Today, thanks to the introduction of inexpensive, battery-operated drilling machines and to the availability of diamond-tipped drillbits the job can be successfully tackled by amateur lapidaries at a fairly reasonable cost per hole. However, you should ask yourself before buying the tools whether the cost of the equipment required is justified by the number of holes you wish to drill. If you own a trim saw you can cut a neat slot in the edge of a stone into which a jump ring can be cemented. This will serve

6 Drilling a hole in a stone

Equipment

Fig. 49 Two methods of mounting a polished slab

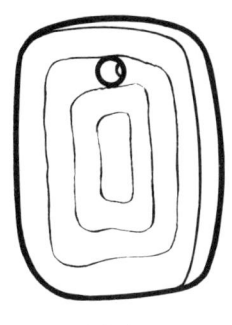

drilled stone

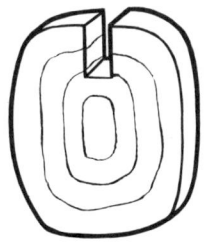

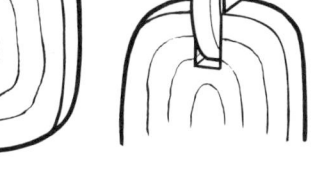

(b) slit stone — cut is made with a trim saw and bolt ring is cemented in position

equally well on almost every occasion you might need a drilled stone for a pendant or necklace. A little imagination used in the creation of other items of jewellery can usually overcome the lack of hole-drilling facilities in your workshop, and the range of manufactured fittings for use with epoxy resin continues to grow. In spite of this you may still feel that a drilling machine is essential, so we will now look briefly at how holes are drilled.

I must stress that special equipment is needed. *You cannot drill gemstones with home power tools used for carpentry or metalwork.* Such machines run at a speed of approximately 2,000 r.p.m. and this is much too slow for gemstone drilling. Furthermore, the drillbits used to drill wood and metal are cutting tools which remove waste material as shavings as the hole is drilled; whereas diamond-tipped lapidary drillbits are really cylindrical grinding wheels with a large number of abrasive points which remove waste material as tiny granular particles.

A small drilling machine with a speed of up to 9,000 r.p.m. and capable of being run on a 12 volt battery can be purchased for less than the price of a home power tool. You will also need a drill stand in which to mount the machine to ensure absolutely accurate drilling. The stand will cost slightly more than the drilling machine, but it must be regarded as essential equipment if you are to avoid breaking the expensive diamond bits.

There are two types of drillbit on the market. The first, which is the least expensive, has a single layer of diamond particles deposited on its shank, and its obvious disadvantage is that once this layer has been removed the drill's working life is at an end. The second type has many layers of diamond particles bonded on its shank and it can, therefore, be used to drill many more holes before a new drill must be purchased. As the top layer of diamonds become worn or blunted fresh diamond points are exposed to prolong drilling efficiency. Initially this type of drillbit costs more than the plated variety, but with careful use it should prove a more economical proposition.

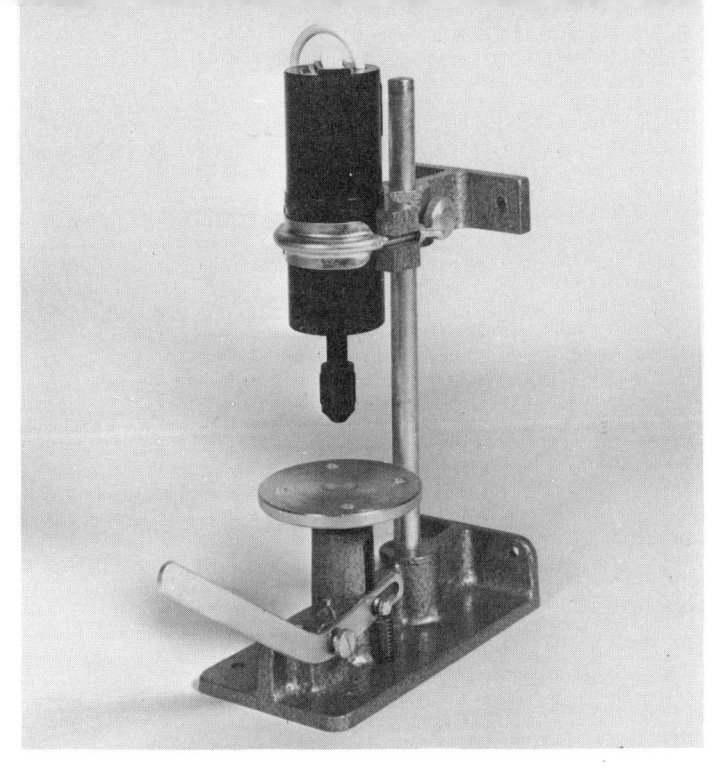

Fig. 50 The Expo drill and stand suitable for lapidary drilling work

Drilling the hole

It is unwise to attempt the drilling of any stone other than a flat slab because of the difficulty experienced in starting the drill on a curved surface. Drill your holes in preforms *before* you grind and polish them and your drill-bits will last much longer. Only thin slabs should be drilled; any slab more than $\frac{1}{2}$ in. in thickness should not be used. Mark out the template shape and cut the piece to rough shape on your trim saw before deciding where you will drill the hole. Mark this spot with your aluminium pencil

Fig. 51 (*left*) Drillbit detail
Fig. 52 (*right*) Drilling without a drill stand can ruin an expensive drillbit

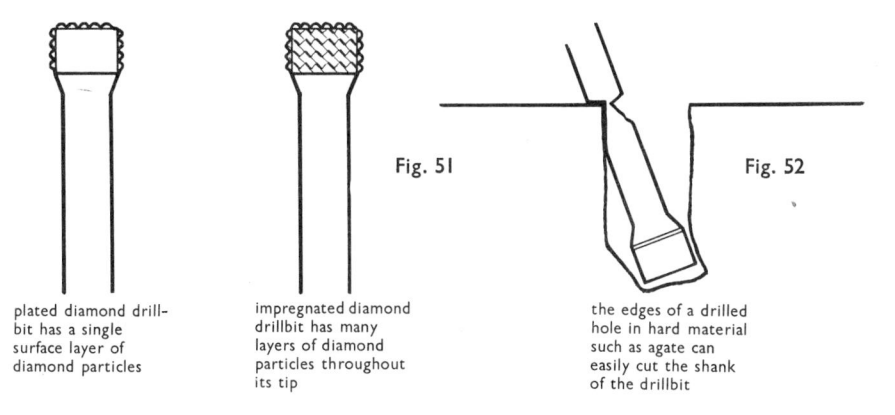

Fig. 51

Fig. 52

plated diamond drill-bit has a single surface layer of diamond particles

impregnated diamond drillbit has many layers of diamond particles throughout its tip

the edges of a drilled hole in hard material such as agate can easily cut the shank of the drillbit

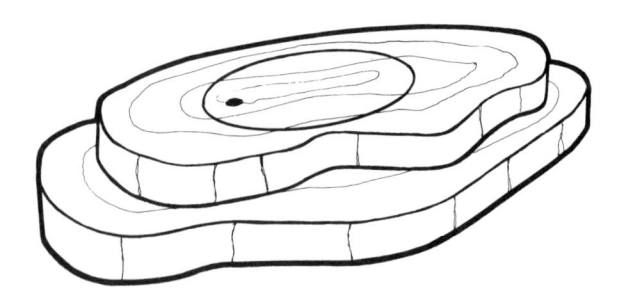

Fig. 53 Marked workpiece temporarily glued to a piece of waste slab

and then temporarily glue the preform to a similarly sized piece of waste slab. This is necessary in order to prevent fractures around the drilled hole as the bit breaks through the back of the workpiece.

You will now need a small, flat-bottomed plastic or glass container into which the prepared stone can be placed. (Plastic tops from aerosol spray cans are ideal.) Put the workpiece into this container and pour in clean water until the top of the stone is covered to a depth of approximately $\frac{1}{8}$ in. After providing the correct power supply, mounting the drill in the stand, and fixing the drillbit in the chuck according to the manufacturer's instructions, the plastic container should be placed on the stand and the drillbit aligned with the point on the stone where you wish to drill the hole.

Fig. 54 A plastic water container holding workpiece is positioned beneath the drillbit

Drilling is carried out with a series of very short runs by the bit. Bring the drill into contact with the stone for 2 or

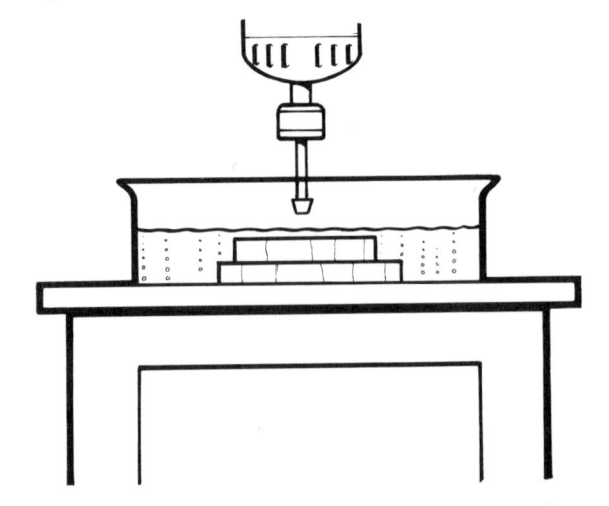

3 seconds and then withdraw the bit so that water can reach the bottom of the hole to reduce the temperature and wash out the cuttings. As the hole deepens, the drilling time should be reduced to 1 or 2 seconds while the length of time for which the bit is withdrawn from the hole should be increased. It is a slow process, particularly when drilling very hard material such as agate; it may take up to 15 minutes to make a single hole in a slab. On no account must you attempt to speed up the process by keeping the bit in contact with the stone for long periods. You will damage the drill irreparably if you do so.

Some stones are so resistant to drilling that it becomes necessary to sharpen the diamond bit halfway through the cut. To do this remove the plastic container and drill a hole into a piece of discarded No. 220 silicon carbide grinding wheel. This will dress the face of your diamond drillbit and restore it to peak cutting efficiency.

7 Simple faceting

A faceted gemstone has a number of flat planes, or facets, cut symmetrically across its surface, and when these are polished, rays of light which fall upon them are reflected and refracted to enhance the fire and brilliance of the gem. The professional facet cutter who works with diamonds, sapphires and other precious gems possesses a considerable knowledge of physics and mathematics; he spends many years perfecting the techniques of his craft to produce gems of great beauty. Often he will study a gemstone for several days before deciding to facet it in a particular way so that its hidden beauty may be revealed to the best advantage. He is, indeed, a Master Craftsman.

How then can you, a newcomer to amateur lapidary, hope to facet your semi-precious stones successfully? In fact, so long as you are prepared to accept that the simple faceting we are about to attempt with some inexpensive attachments used on one of the machines already described in this book is somewhat removed from the world of the professional facet cutter, you can certainly emulate his skills and produce quite delightful faceted semi-precious stones. They may lack the technical brilliance of the gems cut from precious stones, but they will give you hours of pleasure in the making and endless satisfaction when you display them to the admiration of relatives and friends. Later, as your lapidary skills develop, you may decide to purchase a precision faceting machine which, with long practice, will enable you to develop professional skills.

Meanwhile, we will return to the cast-iron lapping machine discussed in Chapter 3. As you know, this machine is used to produce an absolutely flat surface on a slab with the aid of loose silicon carbide grits. If you were to take a beach pebble and work it across the flat lap using No. 80 silicon carbide grit, you would grind a flat on the oval pebble and this flat would, in fact, be a facet. If you then turned the pebble slightly between your fingers and proceeded to grind a second flat adjacent to the first a faceted stone would begin to take shape. If additional flats were produced around the first one you would end up with a crudely faceted stone.

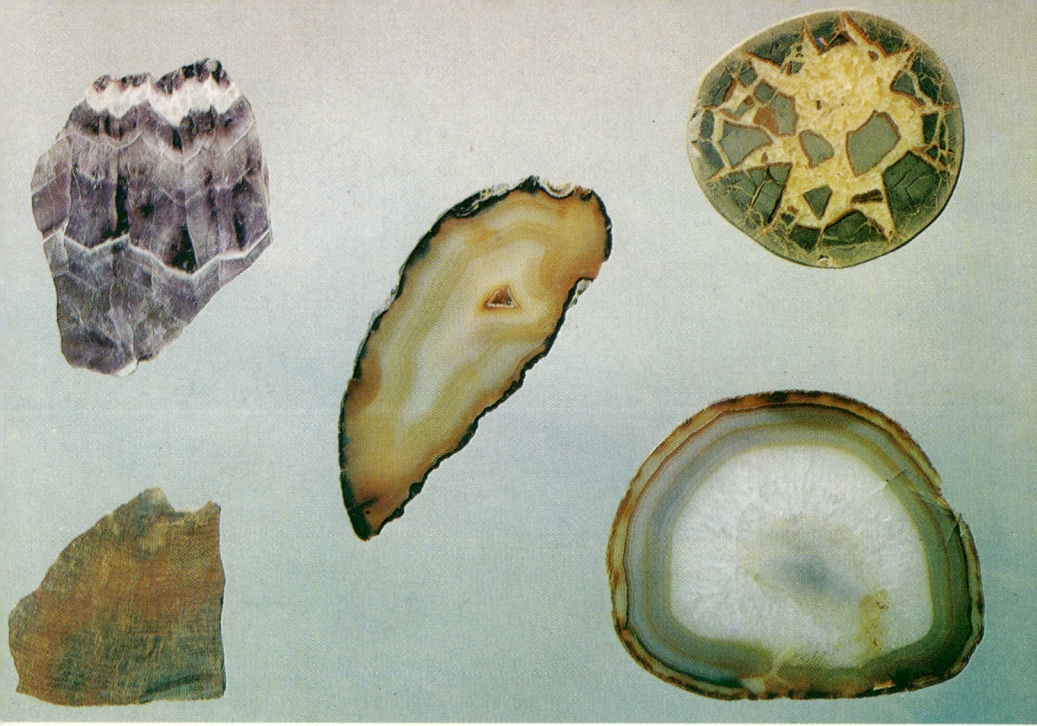

Plate 4 Some beautiful slabs ready-cut by suppliers from imported rocks

Phantom amethyst

Brazilian agate

Septarian nodule

Petrified wood

Brazilian agate

Plate 5 Delightful examples of faceted stones

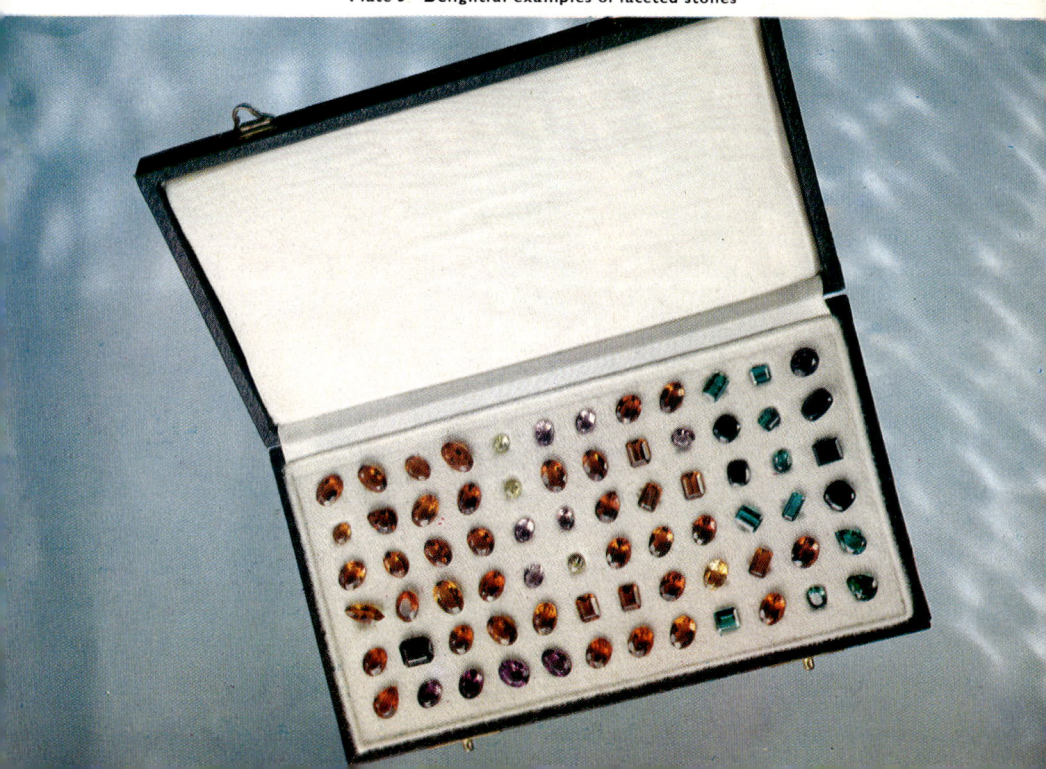

Plate 6   A selection of cabochons

Plate 7   Some jewellery which can be made with cabochons

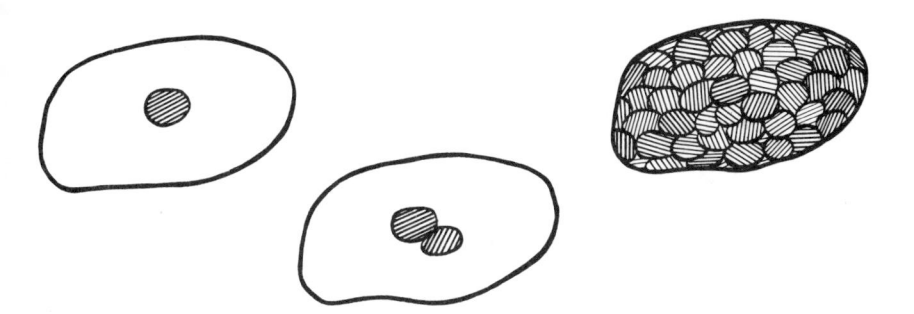

The finished stone would look crude only because the facets were formed with the stone held between your fingers; you would be unable to position the stone accurately on the lap so that facets were formed symmetrically around its surface. In order to position the stone accurately on the lap you require a faceting attachment.

This consists of a vertical metal rod mounted at the side

Fig. 55 A crudely faceted pebble

Fig. 56 Simple faceting attachments for an 8-inch lap

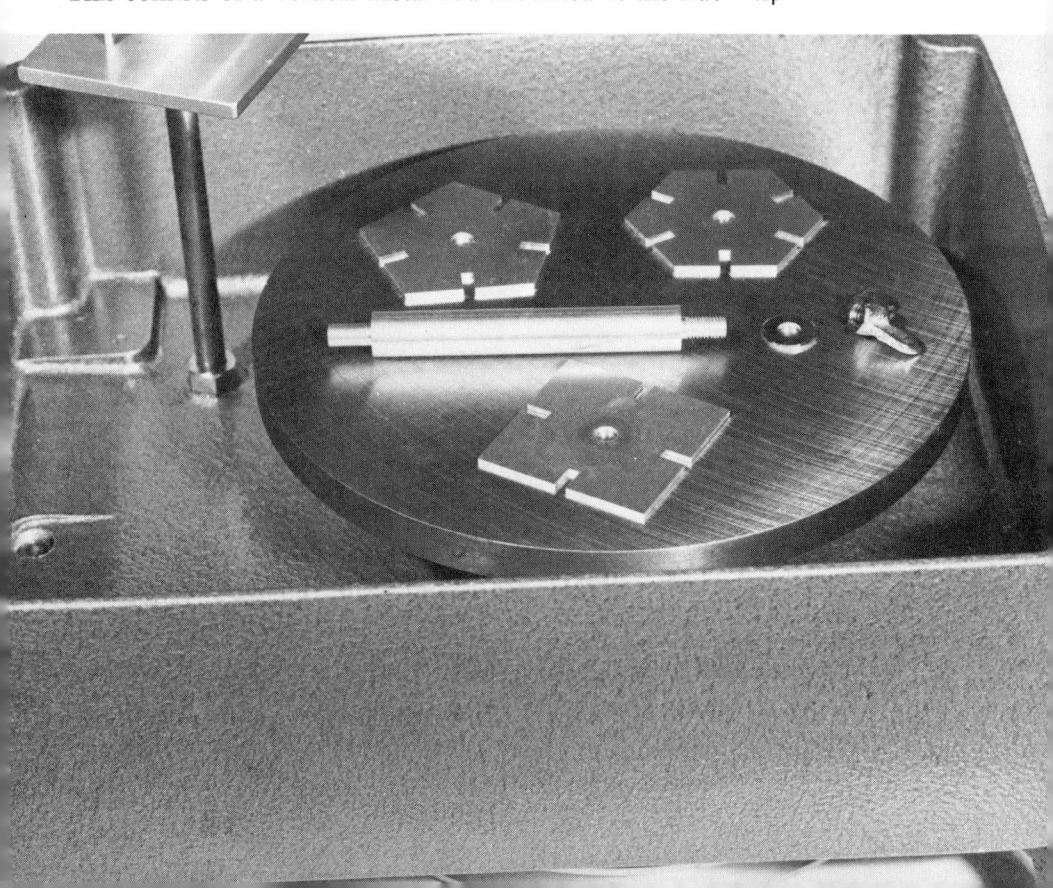

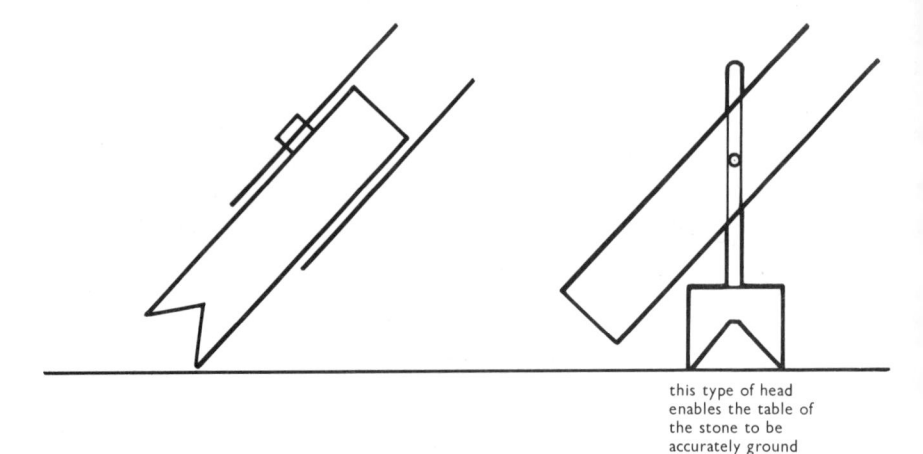

this type of head enables the table of the stone to be accurately ground

Fig. 57 Dopstick heads

of the lap tank on which a flat worktable can be raised or lowered and locked at any height. On this worktable a metal former, or template, of symmetrical shape is rested. It has a central hole through which a metal dop stick of sufficient length to reach the flat lap can be screwed.

The dop stick is rather special. It has several removable heads to take stones of different sizes, and on some units a head can be attached at an angle of 45° so that the flat top, or table, of the gem can be ground. On other units this table is formed with the dop stick held in a free-hand position. Some of the dop stick heads are partly hollowed or recessed to enable the preformed stone to be dopped

Fig. 58 Grinding a rough preform

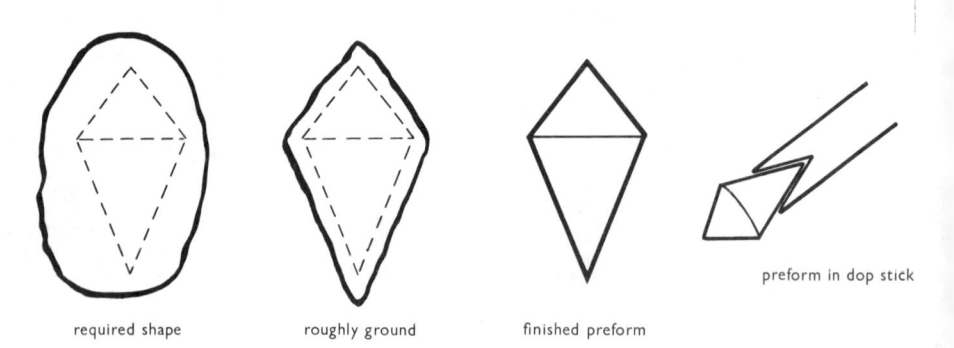

required shape   roughly ground   finished preform   preform in dop stick

squarely and accurately, and also to provide better adhesion between stone and dop stick.

Preforming the stone

You can, as we have seen, facet a baroque pebble by holding it in your hand. You can also facet slabs and cabochons in the same way to produce interesting lozenge-shaped stones. But best results are achieved if you preform a rough stone so that it can be held in one of the recessed dop stick heads in order to produce geometrically accurate facets.

The shape required is rather like an old-fashioned spinning top or two pyramids—one about half the height of the other—joined at their bases. This can be roughly formed on your coarse grinding wheel so that the apex of the largest pyramid fits into one of the recessed heads. It must then be carefully dopped as outlined in Chapter 5, care being taken to ensure that the stone sits squarely and securely in the recessed dop.

Faceting or forming the stone

The first task is to produce the flat top, or table, of the faceted gem. Prepare the lap as for grinding a flat slab, using a paste of water and No. 220 silicon carbide grit, and grind the table by holding the dop stick perpendicular to the lap.

When a suitable table has been ground lift the stone from the lap and switch off the machine. Now select one of your templates and secure this to the top of the dop stick. Rest

Fig. 59 Symmetrical facets

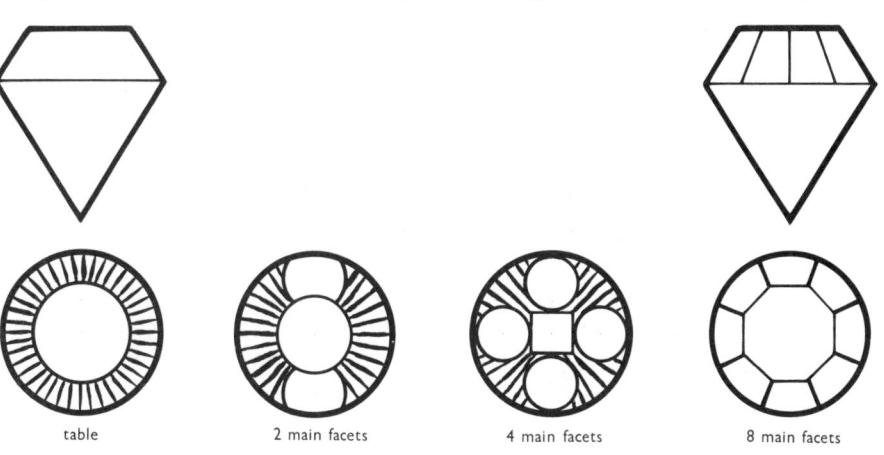

table   2 main facets   4 main facets   8 main facets

the template on the worktable so that the side of your stone is in contact with the stationary cast-iron lap and move the worktable up or down on the vertical rod until the stone is at the angle required on the lap. When you have decided on the angle at which you will cut your facets, secure the worktable at the selected height and lift the dopped stone from the lap *before* you switch on the motor once again. Now bring the dop stick gently into contact with the lap so that the stone is ground *in the direction of rotation.*

When a facet has been formed lift the dop and rotate the template on the worktable to the next flat. Bring the stone into contact with the lap once again and grind the next facet, continuing in this way until facets have been formed symmetrically around the table.

The next step is to repeat the entire process, including the grinding of the table, using No. 400 grit. Do not move the worktable on the vertical rod, otherwise you will have difficulty in placing the stone on the lap at the same angle used during the previous grinding stage. The polishing stage, using cerium oxide, follows the fine grind.

With the grinding and polishing of the table and main facets completed, the stone must be removed from its dop stick and re-dopped on a flat-ended dop head using the table as the base of the stone. The faceting of the lower portion, or pavilion, of the stone is then carried out as described above.

We have dealt with the simple faceting of semi-precious stones using a cast-iron lapping machine, but it should be noted that similar faceting attachments are also available for use with the horizontal combination unit described in Chapter 5. Copper laps impregnated with diamond particles are also available for use on a number of horizontal machines, though they are more likely to be used with an advanced faceting unit.

Manufactured fittings for faceted gemstones are not readily available, but I feel sure this will not deter you from producing faceted stones which can look really beautiful when simply displayed against a background of rich velvet. If you wish to use the stones in pad or cabochon fittings you can grind a flat on the lower portion of the stone so that it fits neatly into the mount.

Fig. 60 A reasonably priced, advanced faceting machine

Fig. 61 Faceting terms

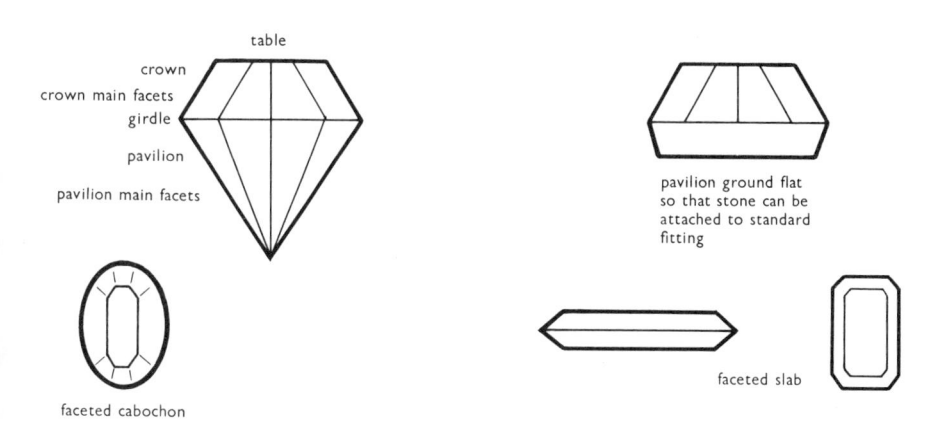

table
crown
crown main facets
girdle
pavilion
pavilion main facets

pavilion ground flat so that stone can be attached to standard fitting

faceted cabochon

faceted slab

81

8 Gem collecting

Having whetted your appetites with the title of this chapter, let me now say a few words to those readers who imagine that after reading the next few pages they will no longer need to visit their local rock shops to buy rough material to cut and grind on their machines. The specimens you *may* find by following the rules set out below are most unlikely to compare with the excellent rough gems on sale in rock shops unless you happen to live in North America or Australia—countries renowned for their spectacular gems. Such readers are to be envied. The basic geological rules set out here apply no matter where they are used, and all overseas readers will benefit from learning them.

British readers may find consolation in the fact that diamonds, sapphires, gold and giant-size semi-precious crystals *have* been found in Britain; and that within these islands almost every known geological formation, rare mineral and precious gem can be found. This chapter is written for those adventurous souls prepared to risk disappointment, enjoy the scenery, and perhaps take home a few specimens for a collecting cabinet. I hope that some of you will take home gemstones worthy of faceting, or at least of cabochon cutting, but you must remember that the best gemstones in Britain are to be found in the High Street where your local lapidary dealer has his premises.

There is nothing difficult about finding semi-precious stones in Britain. Spend an off-season weekend at any seaside resort in Scotland, Cornwall or the east coast of England and wander, eyes down, along the deserted shingle beaches. Keep at it throughout Saturday and Sunday, your mind as well as your eyes on the pebbles beneath your feet, and pick up every brightly coloured or shining specimens you see. By late Sunday afternoon a pound or two of attractive pebbles should be in your collecting bag—and some of them will almost certainly be amethyst, cairngorm, citrine, agate, amber, cornelian or jet.

That's how easy it is when you know where to look, and you are prepared to be patient and to use your powers of observation. It is a formula for success which works equally well if you apply it to a hunt for semi-precious gems on the high, wild moors, hills and mountains we are about to discuss. You may not find all the specimens a trained geologist would locate if he covered the same stretches of countryside; and I am not suggesting that a knowledge of geology is quite unnecessary in order to become a successful rockhound. A little knowledge is certainly *not* a bad thing when it comes to hunting semi-precious rocks and minerals. The few geological clues set out here are very likely to guide you to at least some of the crystal specimens and gems which lie hidden in many areas of Britain; and they are unconditionally guaranteed to guide you to some of the most spectacular scenery within these islands. Shortcomings in geological expertise can be more than made up by improving your powers of observation, and by possessing the patience to keep looking when the less determined have given up and gone home empty-handed.

The rules for success

1 *Keep out of danger.* Heathery moors, magnificent mountains and craggy rock faces far from the hustle and bustle of city life have given delight, excitement and the pleasures of solitude to millions of people. In summertime they are the adventure playgrounds of the great outdoors where your rockhounding excursions will be as safe as a day trip to Margate or Blackpool. Be warned, however, that in winter such places change their characters as dramatically as Doctor Jekyll changed to Mister Hyde.

An acquaintance of mine who ventured into the wilds of Sutherland in mid winter on a gold-prospecting expedition lost his tent and sleeping bag when a mountain stream suddenly changed course. He spent several days in hospital recovering from frostbite. Another, caught in a November snowstorm on the North Yorkshire Moors, where he was hunting freshwater pearls, sprained an ankle and lost most of his equipment when he fell into a moorland stream which had been blanketed by a snowdrift. He was saved from severe exposure only by his good fortune in stumbling upon a lonely farmhouse.

Both of these men were experienced treasure hunters who had spent many winters in mountainous regions and they had taught themselves the rules of survival when Nature turns nasty. Yet even they came very close to losing their lives. The message is absolutely clear: confine your rock-hounding to the months of May, June, July and August.

Long abandoned mine workings are familiar sites in the regions you will visit. You are certain to be fascinated by the old equipment and derelict buildings often found near them where the ghosts of a long-dead prosperity still seem to linger. Some make delightful settings for picnics on family outings, and there are excellent prospects of finding exciting gem material in the overgrown spoil heaps which will surround the site. Search them by all means; but *please* do not enter the abandoned mine shaft no matter how safe it appears when viewed from the surface. The chances of finding gem specimens in the old workings are poor: most of the worthwhile material will have long ago been thrown on to the spoil heap by the miners who followed the mineral lode. The chances of a fall, however, are extremely high if you venture into the shaft. Again, the message is clear: stick to the spoil heaps where the best finds await you.

Working mines and quarries can also be dangerous places, especially those where explosives are used. Blasting often weakens walls and falls of rock can occur. Keep away unless you have obtained permission to search spoil heaps from a responsible person in charge of operations.

2 *Carry the right equipment.* The absolute essential is a geological hammer. Gem crystals are often called 'flowers of the rocks'—but you cannot pluck them with your bare hands. You must have the correct tool for the job. There are two basic types of hammer. The first has a pointed tip on one side of the hammer head and is known as a *pick head*; the other has a flat edge instead of a point and is known as a *chisel head*.

If you wish to keep the amount of equipment you have to carry to an absolute minimum the chisel head is probably best. On the other hand, there are some excellent small chisels available which are ideal for the often delicate job of extracting crystals from rock. Small chisels from your own

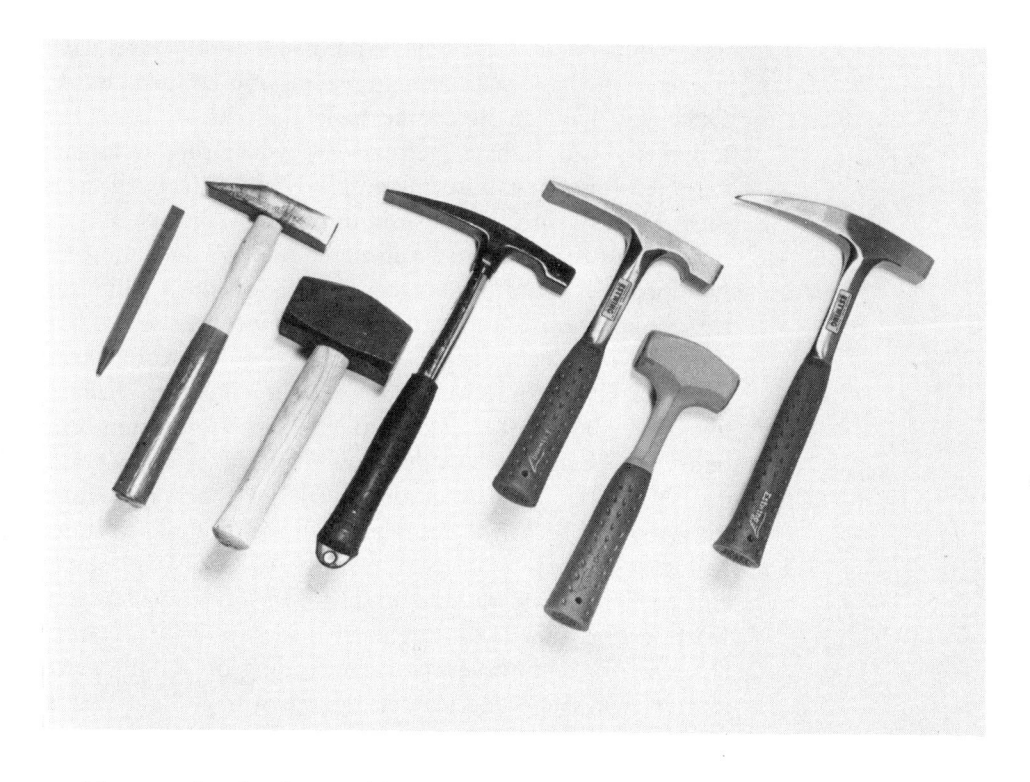

Fig. 62 Rockhounding tools, available from many rock shops

tool box might also be suitable, in which case it is better to buy the pick head because it will provide you with an extra tool on the other side of the head.

A rucksack is next in order of importance. Gem-collecting locations cannot be reached by car, though you will be able to drive to within reasonable walking distance of many sites. Eventually, however, you will have to rely on your legs to carry you and your equipment over broken ground. You will also have a fair load in the way of collected specimens to carry back, and for this job a good quality rucksack is needed. The unframed types are generally lighter and less expensive, and they provide adequate storage space for everything needed on a one-day outing, with plenty of room to spare for your finds.

A one-inch Ordnance Survey map of the area you plan to visit and a reliable compass are also most important. Both are quite useless unless you know how to read them. Do not venture far into wild countryside until you have mastered the basic skills of map reading and compass work. Once you have mastered the basic skills, trust them. Far too many people have become lost when caught in unexpected mists or rainstorms simply because they relied on their 'sense of direction' instead of on their compasses.

Clothing for a day to be spent on high ground must be windproof yet comfortable to wear. Nylon shirts and jeans may be ideal for a stroll around a nearby tourist town, but they are useless and can be dangerous on hilltops where they quickly become wet and cold if the weather changes unexpectedly. Instead, select woollen shirts, loose-fitting and lightweight sweaters, woollen trousers or slacks, and a good quality anorak. A pair of stout walking shoes and fairly thick woollen socks will complete your rockhounding outfit.

'Luxury' items such as a thermos of hot soup, some sandwiches, a camera, and even a pair of binoculars are worth taking on a trip lasting more than two or three hours. Do remember, however, that overloading on the outward journey will result in a very tiring return trip. Plastic bags, a multi-bladed penknife, and perhaps some soft tissue paper to wrap any delicate specimens you find can be carried in the pockets of your anorak.

3 *Know which rocks to look for.* Hunting a needle in a haystack is not the impossible task most people believe it to be. A simple solution to the problem would be to burn the haystack to the ground and go over the ashes very carefully with a metal detector. You would probably find the needle —but you would then have to face the irate farmer.

A more scientific approach would be to find out as much as possible about the person who hid the needle in the first place. How tall was he? What was the length of his arm? Did he use a ladder to reach the upper part of the stack? Such scientific detective work would then enable you to eliminate large areas of the haystack and to concentrate your search on those places most likely to hold that elusive needle.

The same scientific approach can be made when hunting

semi-precious gems. Nature hid most of her prizes in or alongside certain types of rocks. If you can identify those rocks you will be able to concentrate your search in the most likely places and greatly increase your chances of making worthwhile finds. You will not discover every gem which Nature has hidden—you will still require patience and careful observation if you are to achieve any success at all—but you will certainly shorten the odds considerably in your favour if you take the trouble to familiarize yourself with the likely hiding places of many gems.

Igneous rocks

The rocks which hold the widest variety of gems and therefore interest us most are known as *igneous* rocks. They were formed many millions of years ago when red-hot molten substances which geologists call *magmas* rose upwards from deep within the bowels of the earth. Sometimes these molten magmas reached the surface as *lavas* which poured forth from volcanoes or from cracks within the earth's crust. Rocks formed from these lavas are known as *volcanic* or *extrusive* rocks.

Some molten magmas did not reach the surface, in spite of the enormous forces which pushed them upwards. Instead, they forced their way into other rocks beneath the surface where they then solidified. Igneous rocks formed in this way are known as *intrusive* or *plutonic* rocks. Millions of years later, when the overlying rocks had been worn away by the erosive action of the weather, or more recently when railway cuttings, quarries and road constructions removed their coverings, the intrusive or plutonic rocks were also exposed as outcrops on the surface.

Because they solidified underground, the intrusive rocks cooled slowly. This enabled them to develop relatively large mineral crystals which give intrusive rocks a typical coarse grained texture.

Granite is the best known example of the intrusive, coarse-grained rocks. If you look at a piece of granite closely you will see that it is composed of a jumbled mass of small crystals varying in size from $\frac{1}{16}$ in. to $\frac{1}{2}$ in.; and that it has a characteristic sparkle which is caused by tiny particles of mica between the crystals. Granite is typically light in colour, and may be white, grey, pink or yellowish brown. The size of its crystal grains is determined by how slowly the magma cooled beneath the earth's crust. In some granites known as *pegmatites* (*see* p. 94), which cooled very slowly, the crystals can measure many feet across; in others which cooled near the surface and therefore much quicker the crystals are quite small. But the common feature of all granites is their hardness which makes them ideal building and road-making materials. They occur widely in Britain, particularly in Cornwall, The Lake District, Caernarvonshire and Scotland.

Porphyry is a variety of granite in which bands of larger crystals stand out clearly. The Shap granite of Westmorland is a good example. It displays quite large crystals of pink feldspar.

Gabbro is a heavy, dark-coloured, coarse-grained rock which contains a green mineral known as olivine. The crystals in gabbro are usually dark green, grey or black. It is found mainly in Cornwall, Pembrokeshire, The Lake District and Scotland.

Syenite is a coarse-grained rock resembling granite, but darker in colour, and usually of a grey or reddish hue. It is found mainly in Caernarvonshire and Ireland.

Diorite is another rock resembling granite. It may be dark grey in colour, but often displays a green and white mottled effect to which it owes its commoner name of greenstone. It is found in Pembrokeshire.

The five rocks listed above—granite, porphyry, gabbro, syenite and diorite—are all coarse-grained intrusive rocks, and many of the gemstones we are seeking will be found in or near them. The fine-grained extrusive rocks contain fewer semi-precious specimens. Nevertheless, they are most worthy of our attention:

Basalt is the best known of the fine-grained extrusives. It is a heavy, compact rock which was formed when floods of lava poured from numerous cracks in the earth's crust and flowed over the surface before hardening. When some of these basalt lava flows cooled the rocks contracted and split into columnar structures which can be vividly seen in The Giant's Causeway on the coast of Northern Ireland. Some basalts contain numerous open spaces or pores which were caused when gas and steam bubbled out of the cooling lava. This porous basalt is known as *scoria*, and its mineral-filled pores often contain fine crystals.

Dolerite is very similar to basalt in its mineralogical make-up and appearance. Indeed, it is almost impossible to distinguish between the two when they are seen as small specimens in a geological cabinet, but dolerite is found under different conditions. When the molten lava solidified as a sheet or sill beneath a very thin covering of other rocks the result is dolerite. It is, therefore, an intrusive rock; but it cooled so near the surface that it is extremely fine-grained. The Great Whin Sill which runs across the north of England, and on which part of Hadrian's Wall stands, is the largest mass of dolerite in Britain.

Andesite is a fine-grained extrusive rock which is much lighter in colour than basalt, but which is also occasionally found in columns similar to those formed by basalt.

There *are* other igneous rocks to be found in Britain, but if you concentrate your search on the eight we have discussed your chances of locating gemstones will be excellent.

Summary of rocks to look for

Rock	Appearance	Typically seen in
Granite	Coarse-grained; visible crystals; sparkle; light colours—white, grey, pink, yellowish brown	Cornwall, The Lake District, Caernarvonshire, Scotland
Porphyry	As granite, with bands of larger crystals	Westmorland
Gabbro	Coarse-grained; dark green, grey or black	Cornwall, Pembrokeshire, The Lake District, Scotland
Syenite	As granite, but darker in colour; usually grey or reddish hue	Caernarvonshire, Northern Ireland
Diorite	As granite; sometimes dark grey; often mottled green and white	Pembrokeshire
Basalt	Fine-grained; black, dark grey, dark green, dark brown; sometimes seen as columns; sometimes seen as porous scoria	Northern Ireland, Scotland

Dolerite	As basalt, but occurs in sills	Northern England
Andesite	Fine-grained; lighter in colour than basalt, but sometimes seen as columns	Cumberland

4 *Know which rock formations to seek.* At your local lapidary shop you will find many guidebooks for rockhounds which provide long lists of exact locations, mines and quarries recommended for specimens of this or that gemstone. I recommend them to those less adventurous readers prepared to look no further than spots where thousands of rockhounds have looked already. The sites *are* excellent, but they have been very thoroughly searched. Still, you could be lucky!

A far better method of hunting gemstones is to search those areas well off the beaten tracks. It is, of course, more difficult than simply heading for a well-publicized location, but if you teach yourself to recognize the clues which Nature provides, your chances of good finds will be much higher. Just as there are certain igneous rocks you must look out for, so there are certain igneous rock formations you must find if you are to track down those elusive 'crystal flowers'.

Granite outcrops and bosses are the most important of these formations. As we have seen, granite solidified as an intrusive rock beneath the surface of the earth. When the molten magma thrust upwards it often forced the overlying rocks into a huge blister and flowed into the dome thus created. Beneath this protective umbrella the magma was able to cool slowly to form coarse-grained granite which was only exposed when the softer overlying rocks were worn away by weathering. The result is a granite outcrop or boss—hundreds of which are to be found in the wilder regions of Britain. (*See* Fig. 63).

Dykes are masses of igneous rock formed when molten magma was forced upwards between the joints and cracks in the overlying rocks. After the softer material surrounding them has been worn away, the igneous dykes remain as vertical walls of solidified magma which cut across the layers or beds of other rocks. Dykes are widespread in

(a)

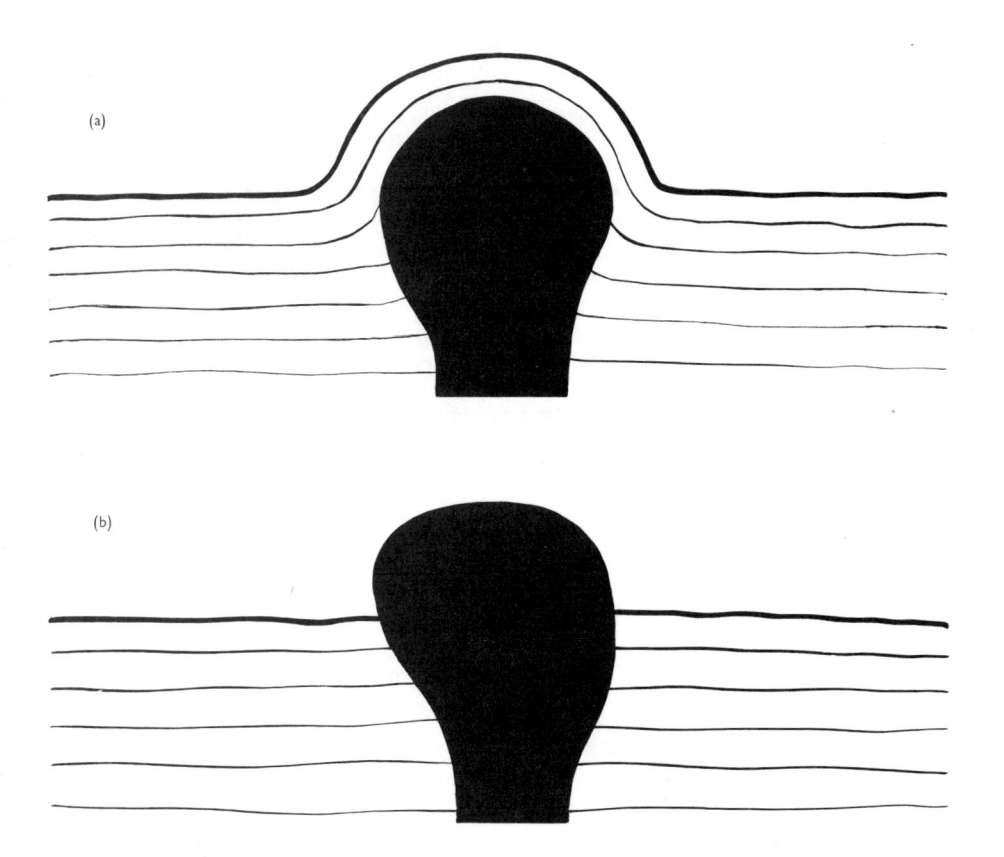

(b)

igneous regions, and in some places—such as the Isle of Arran—they occur in swarms. On the island of Mull they form rings around large igneous masses (see Fig. 64).

Volcanic necks are formed in a similar way. Much of the lava in a volcano is trapped inside the crater. When the volcano dies the lava in the neck hardens to a solid plug which in time weathers to a steep sided hill. A number of these volcanic necks are to be found in Lowland Scotland, notably Arthur's Seat in Edinburgh, and North Berwick Law in East Lothian (see Fig. 64).

Sills are formed when molten magma spreads as a horizontal sheet between beds or layers of rock close to the surface. They differ from dykes in that they are parallel to the surrounding beds while dykes are vertical formations. As we have already seen, sills are usually composed of dolerite,

Fig. 63(a) Intrusive magma pushes overlying rocks upwards before it solidifies and (b) when softer overlying rocks are eroded by weathering, the granite is exposed as an outcrop or boss

volcanic neck vertical dyke horizontal sill—exposed when overlying rocks are eroded by weathering

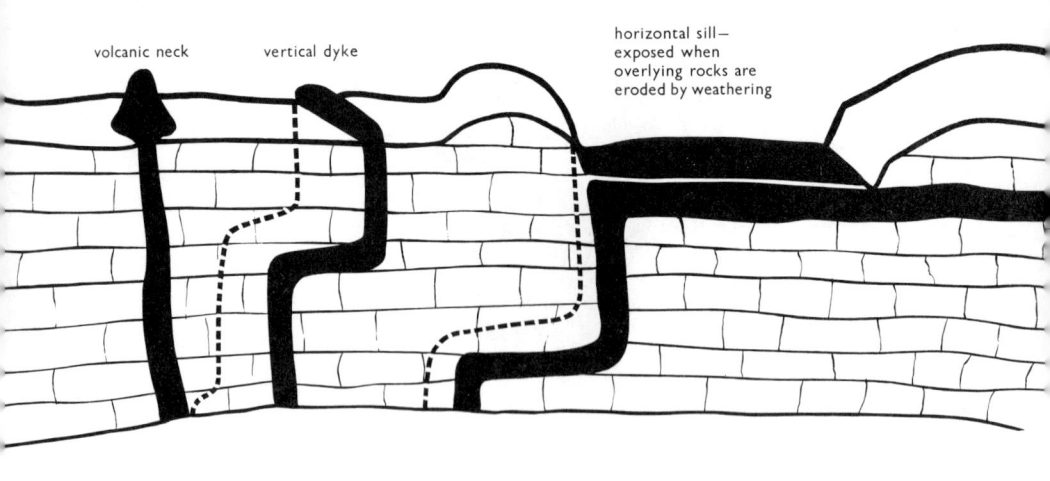

Fig. 64 and the Great Whin Sill is the best known example in Britain. Remember that sills were formed beneath the earth and exposed by erosion (*see* Fig. 64).

Lava flows can resemble sills in that they sometimes appear as layers between stratified rocks, in spite of the fact that they originally flowed over the surface of the earth. Formed on the surface, they may have been buried later by other rocks and then exposed again by weathering. Their surfaces are sometimes slaggy and cinder-like; or they can have a porous structure caused by bubbles of gas and steam in the original magma; or they can display the typical columnar jointing of basalt. In various parts of Britain, notably North Wales, there are pillow lavas which were formed when volcanic eruptions occurred underwater. As the boiling lava met the cold water its surfaces hardened into pillow-like heaps. Lava flows are common in the igneous regions of Northern Ireland and Scotland (*see* Fig. 65).

5 *Know where the gemstones are found.* So far we have established that the gemstones we are seeking are associated with igneous rocks, including intrusive granites, extrusive basalts and others; and that these rocks are found as outcrops, dykes, sills and lava flows which occur mainly in the mountainous and moorland regions of Britain. Your success at locating

the elusive crystals and veins of semi-precious material which they contain depends, from this point onwards, on how much patience you have and on how well you develop your powers of observation. Even so, we can narrow the search area just a little more by concentrating our efforts on those places within the rock formations where crystals and veins are most likely to be discovered.

Let us assume that you have located an interesting igneous outcrop on some lonely stretch of moorland. This mass of rock might cover anything from a few square yards to many square miles; while the entire outcrop which is visible will only be the exposed area of a far greater mass of solidified magma. You must bear in mind that the igneous rock does not end abruptly where it dips and disappears beneath the surrounding countryside.

We have already seen that igneous rocks are composed of a jumbled mass of tightly cemented crystals—some large, others so small they are invisible to the naked eye. Their size depends on the depth at which the magma cooled, and on how slowly the cooling took place. During this cooling period the gases and steam within the mass escaped, and as they did so they formed bubbles which the hardening magma was unable to close over. The resulting cavity is known as a *druse* and large crystals will often have developed on its walls. Druses can be anything from a few inches to several yards across and they can occur anywhere in the outcrop.

Fig. 65 Typical columnar jointing seen in some basalt lavas

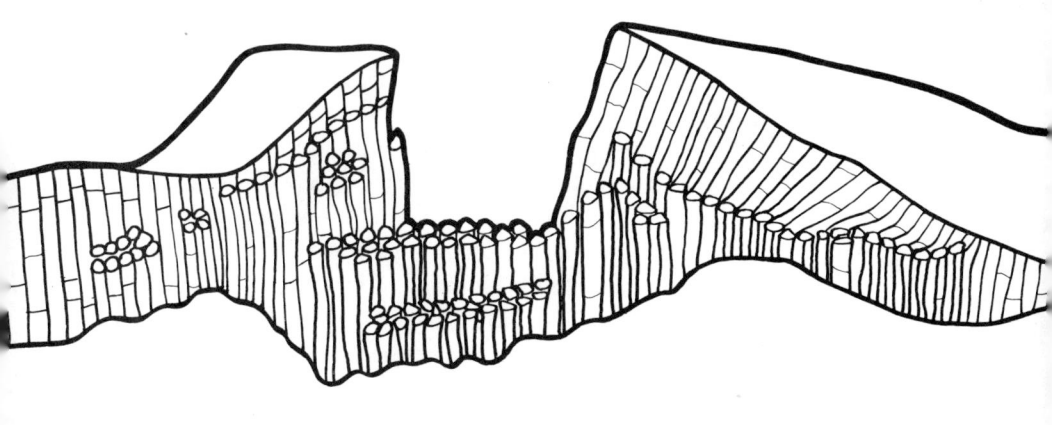

If you find one, use your hammer and chisels very carefully when extracting specimens. Do not attempt to break off single crystals but cut out pieces of the parent rock with crystals attached. This will not only save the crystals from damage, but will also provide you with a much more interesting specimen to display.

Veins are often associated with druses and you should always follow interesting veins across the face of the rock in the hope of finding a druse or a spot where erosion has loosened the material in the veins. Such veins often give the surface of the rock a maggoty appearance.

Pegmatites also occur as veins within the body of the outcrop. They are composed of very large crystals which are often several inches across. Pegmatite veins can also contain druses where extremely large crystals will often have grown.

When the red hot magma thrust its way towards the surface before cooling it often brought with it the molten ores of valuable metals such as tin, lead, silver and gold. When the ores cooled they formed *lodes*, and it is these which miners seek when they sink shafts into the rock. Lodes are always bordered by what are known as *gangue minerals* which include quartz, tourmaline, topaz, fluorite and many more of the semi-precious gemstones you are hoping to find. Remembering that the miner is after the ores in the lode, it will be obvious that if your particular outcrop has a disused mine on or near it, the *spoil heap* is the 'hot spot' you should head for because that is where the miner will have thrown the gangue, or waste.

The best spoil heaps are those much overgrown with weeds; they are better still if they are well off the beaten track. You could be the first gem hunter to pick them over since the long departed miners dumped them. Locate the most inaccessible part of the heap—perhaps hidden under bushes—and dig in, keeping your eyes peeled for the attractive colour, sparkle or shape of crystals.

You may, of course, find very small lodes which have not been worked by miners because the ores occur in only tiny, uneconomical quantities. Many attractive specimens can be chiselled out of these minor lodes, where you should also look out for cavities in the gangue, similar to the druses mentioned above, where beautiful crystals can develop.

The perimeters of igneous outcrops are also very likely to contain gemstones. The tremendous heat from the magma baked and changed the surrounding rocks which it touched—a process which geologists call *contact metamorphism*. This baked area around the igneous rock is known as the *aureole* or *halo* and it can measure anything from a few inches to a mile or more in width, depending on the size of the igneous mass and the heat which the molten magma generated. The surrounding rocks are changed in character and often they have been melted and have resolidified to produce entirely new minerals and sometimes large and interesting crystals (*see* Fig. 66).

One of the ways in which a lava flow differs from a sill is in the nature of its baked zone. Contact metamorphism will have occurred above and below a sill because it was formed as a layer *between* the surrounding rocks. A lava flow, on the other hand, will have altered only those rocks which lie immediately beneath it because it originally flowed across the *surface* of the earth. In lava flows the likely places to find gem material—in addition to the baked zone—are the cavities formed when gas and steam bubbled out of the molten material. Because the lava was flowing when they

Fig. 66

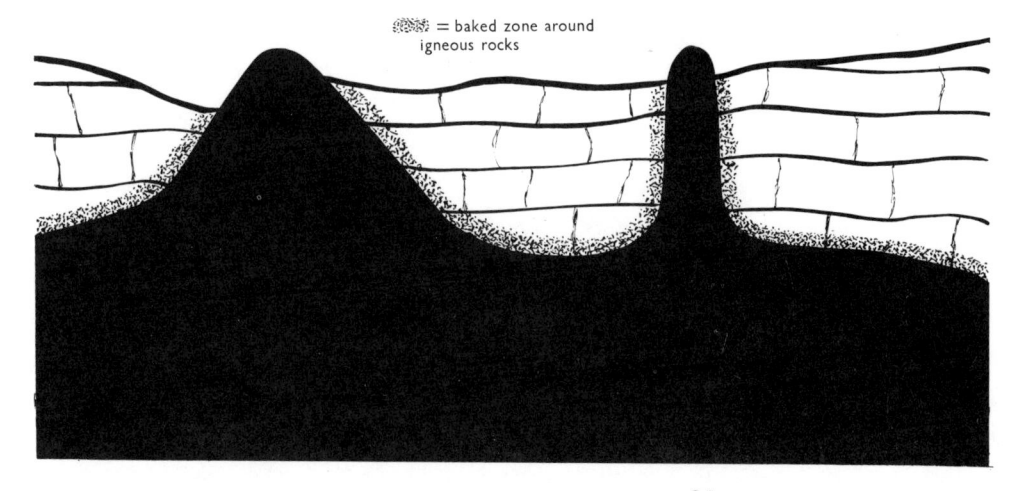

= baked zone around igneous rocks

were formed, these cavities are often stretched or almond-shaped. They often contain agate or chalcedony, and they are known to geologists as *amygdales*.

If the area you are searching is close to a *stream*—a very common occurrence in mountainous regions—the stream bed is well worth searching for gem material in the shape of fragments torn from the rocks by the erosive power of the rushing water. Readers of my book, *Bottle Collecting*, will find the glass-bottomed buckets and plastic tubes described in that book ideal when searching mountain streams for semi-precious gems.

Finally, you must always be on the look out for *quarries*, *railway cuttings* and *road works* in any area close to igneous rock formations. Inaccessible veins, lodes and druses are often exposed when cuttings are made for roads or railways; while in quarries, which are often found in igneous regions because such rocks are used for road-making, new material is constantly being exposed. It is essential that permission to search such places—particularly working quarries—is obtained *before* you start your search. A polite request will only rarely meet with a refusal.

Summary of likely gemstone haunts in igneous rocks

Druses	Cavities caused by gases or steam in cooling magma of intrusive rocks.
Veins	Bands of crystals running across the face of the outcrop.
Pegmatites	Igneous rock made up of very large crystals; contains druses and veins.
Lodes	Bodies of ore.
Gangue	The material surrounding a lode; often contains excellent gemstones.
Spoil heap	The spot near a mine where the gangue has been dumped.
Aureole	The baked area immediately surrounding an igneous body of rock.
Amygdales	Cavities formed by gases or steam in extrusive lava flows.
Stream beds	Wherever they cut through igneous rocks.
Quarries and cuttings	In igneous regions.

Further study

This very brief look we have taken at igneous rocks and their modes of occurrence should guide you to some interesting finds. I hope that it will also stimulate a lasting interest in geology, and that you will go on from this very sketchy introduction to a scientific study of the subject. If you do, many more exciting gems await you. I have confined the 'geology' in this chapter to igneous rocks because they are fairly easy to find, and because they will introduce you to some beautiful scenery. Please do not imagine that I have exhausted the subject of gemstone locations. Nothing could be further from the truth. I have not mentioned regional metamorphism, gneiss, schists, geodes, marcasite nodules, and the many other subjects which a detailed study of geology will bring to your attention. With greater knowledge you will be able to spread your gem-hunting net even wider and greatly improve your chances of excellent finds. The more you know, the better will be your finds; the better your finds, the more you will want to know.

The gemstones you might find

Positive identification of your gemstones is not terribly important during your early days as a rockhound. Concentrate on finding them, noting their locations on your maps, and, whenever possible, extracting your specimens attached to samples of the surrounding rock. If you then take your finds to a rock shop, local museum or lapidary club you are sure to find someone able to tell you exactly what you have found.

Many rock shops have expert staff who are always delighted to help beginners identify their finds. At some shops, particularly those close to the area you have been searching, you will be able to buy small samples of local gemstones. They are usually attractively boxed, have neat identification labels attached, are quite modestly priced, and well worth buying if you intend to do most of your gem hunting in that particular area.

You will find large specimens of local rocks and minerals on display in many museums, and an afternoon spent browsing in a museum is time well spent. My first find as a rockhound was a small cluster of cubic crystals with a violet tint which I picked up on the spoil heap of an abandoned mine in County Durham. At the time I had no idea what I had found. The crystals were beautiful and I had found them; that was all that mattered. Months later, while browsing in Middlesbrough Museum, I spotted an identical specimen in a display cabinet and eagerly read the printed card beneath. To my delight I learned that I had in fact found a cluster of fluorite crystals. You may find it easier to wait until you find something you cannot identify and then take it to a museum in the hope of spotting a similar specimen rather than read up and memorize facts about gems you may never find before you start looking. In this way you will add to your knowledge slowly but surely.

Joining a local lapidary club is a good idea even if you do not intend to cut and polish gemstones. You will meet many other enthusiasts who will be able to answer any questions you have about rocks, minerals and gemstones. Every member started as an absolute beginner like you and you will find them very sympathetic listeners. Many clubs organize rockhounding excursions to a wide variety of collecting areas, and by joining in you will add to your knowledge and to your collection.

The following brief notes on possible finds in igneous regions will start you on the road to gemstone identification. When you make a find check the notes to see if you can decide what it is you have found. If you cannot do so, put it in your rucksack and look it up when you get home.

Agate   Formed when silica solutions filled gas and steam cavities (amygdales) in cooling lavas. When cut, reveals coloured banding caused by various minerals in the original solution. Often almond-shaped. They weather out of the surrounding rock and are often found on beaches and in mountain streams. Colours: bands including white, black, yellow and blue. Good locations: beaches of Scotland and Northern Ireland.

Amethyst   Formed when silica crystallized out of molten magma. Usually found in granite where large crystals can develop in vein cavities (druses). Colours: shades of purple common, green and others not unknown. Good locations: Cornish granites.

Andalusite   Can be found in metamorphic aureoles. Crystals are

Apatite	usually thick cubes coated with sparkling mica flakes. Colours: greyish pink, dark green, brown, yellow, red. Good locations: Durham, Cumberland. Usually found in gangues bordering ore-bearing lodes (especially tin) in granite. Also occurs in gabbro. Colours: crystals are usually green, but can be blue, brick red, yellow or colourless. Good locations: spoil heaps of abandoned tin mines in Cornwall.
Azurite	A blue carbonate of copper usually found encrusted to rocks and minerals in a 'cluster of grapes' (botryoidal) formation. Occasionally as thick, plate-like crystals in gangues bordering ore-bearing lodes (especially copper) in granite. Colour: azure blue. Good locations: spoil heaps of abandoned copper mines in north Lancashire, Cumberland, Cheshire, North Wales and Cornwall.
Beryl	Usually found as veins in granite where large crystals might develop in druses. Crystals are usually pencil-like (hexagonal). Colours: green, blue, yellow. Good locations: Cairngorm Mountains, Mourne Mountains, Devon, Cornwall, Arran.
Cairngorm	As amethyst. Colour: smoky brown. Good locations: Cairngorm Mountains.
Calcite	Usually found in gangues bordering ore bearing lodes. Crystals range widely in shape. Will effervesce when a small drop of vinegar is placed on the specimen. Colours: white, colourless, often with tints on crystal tips. Good locations: Cornwall, Merionethshire, north Yorkshire.
Cassiterite	Tin oxide; found in gangues bordering ore-bearing lodes (especially tin) in granite. Often found in association with apatite. Crystals range widely in shape. Colours: reddish brown to black. Good locations: spoil heaps of abandoned tin mines in Cornwall.
Chalcedony	As agate. Colours: greyish blue. Good locations: Cumberland, Perthshire.
Citrine	As amethyst. Colours: shades of yellow. Good locations: Cornwall.
Cornelian	As agate. Colours: red. Good locations: Cumberland, Arran.
Epidote	Found widely in igneous formations, but good specimens uncommon. Crystals are elongated pencil shapes,

	easily confused with tourmaline. Colours: a wide range including dark green, bluish green, brown, yellow. Good locations: Cornwall, Merionethshire.
Fluorite	Found widely in igneous formations, but best locations are gangues bordering ore-bearing lodes (especially lead, zinc and copper); and in metamorphic aureoles. The crystals are usually cubes. Colours: a wide range including violet, green, yellow and blue. Good locations: Durham, Cumberland, Derbyshire.
Garnet	Can be found in metamorphic aureoles and granite outcrops. Crystals are usually multi-sided and are found singly embedded in the parent rock. Colours: although red is best known colour, garnets are often brown, green or yellow. Good locations: Northern Scotland, Westmorland, Devon, Fifeshire.
Haematite	Also known as 'Kidney Ore' because it often occurs as kidney-shaped masses; usually in gangues bordering ore bearing lodes, though it is fairly widespread in igneous regions. Colours: reddish brown. Good locations: Cumberland.
Jasper	As agate. An admixture of clayey material in the silica solution produces jasper. Colours: red, green and variations of red and green. When the green variety is spotted with red dots it is known as bloodstone. Good locations: Most beaches of Scotland, Northern Ireland and North Wales.
Labradorite	Can be found in basalts. It often shimmers with a play of colours not unlike opal. Colours: various, including green, pale blue, yellow. Good locations: Antrim, Derbyshire.
Malachite	As azurite, but a green carbonate of copper. Colours: light to a blackish green. Good locations: spoil heaps of abandoned copper mines in Cumberland, Cheshire, Lanarkshire, Cornwall, North Wales, Durham and Derbyshire.
Natrolite	Found in basalts as pyramid-topped, elongated cubes. Colours: white, yellow, or pink, with a satin sheen. Good locations: Northern Ireland, Staffordshire, Renfrewshire.
Olivine	Usually found in basalts and volcanic necks. Colours: olive green, bright green, brown. Good locations: Derbyshire, West Lothian, Antrim.
Opal	Opal is a mixture of silica and water and is commonly found in basalts and lavas where it occurs in amygdales. Colours: a milky sheen with a play of rainbow colours.

Prehnite	Good locations: Antrim, Tyrone, Argyllshire, Devon. Found in basalt and in lava amygdales, often in 'cluster of grapes' (botryoidal) formations; occasionally as flat, tablet-like crystals. Colours: green, yellow, white. Good locations: Northern Ireland, Ayrshire, Skye.
Rhodonite	A silicate of manganese found in gangues bordering ore-bearing lodes (especially lead and zinc) in granite. Usually occurs in tight veins, Crystals are rare. Colours: pink and red with a pearly lustre and, often, with wavy banding of lighter and darker shades. Good locations: Devon, Cornwall, Lanarkshire.
Sphene	Found as wedge-shaped and tabular crystals in granite and diorite. Colours: yellow, green, brown, black—all with characteristic lustre and fire. Good locations: Pembrokeshire, Morayshire.
Spinel	Can be found in metamorphic aureoles around intrusive igneous rocks. Colours: blue, red, brown. Good locations: Sutherland, Antrim.
Topaz	Found in granite, and as a gangue mineral in ore-bearing lodes (especially tin). Crystals have a multisided, flat-topped pyramid shape. Good locations: Cairngorm Mountains, Cornwall, Lewis.
Tourmaline	Found in granite and in metamorphic aureoles. Crystals are usually long prisms showing lengthwise grooves. Colours: glassy black, brown, dark green, dark blue, red. Good locations: Cornwall, Devon, Sutherland, Perthshire.
Zircon	Found in granite. Colours: red, colourless, green, pale yellow—all with characteristic lustre and fire. Good locations: Sutherland, Argyllshire, Fifeshire.

Fig. 67 The Cairngorm mountains, Scotland, where many rocks and gems can be found

9 Buying stones and fittings

Rough rock is the raw material of lapidary. Without adequate and inexpensive supplies the hobby would be beyond the reach of the vast majority of people unable to visit those exotic lands where semi-precious stones are commonplace. The agate nodule you casually cast your eyes over when browsing through the stocks at your local rock shop may not look very special, yet it was probably hacked out of its parent rock by a dusky labourer toiling in a mine somewhere in South America. On its journey to the rock shop in your High Street it was probably carried over narrow mountain roads, jungle tracks and deep oceans; it passed through loading bays, railway sidings, distribution depots and wholesale warehouses; its size, colour and weight were recorded with those of other specimens by mine foremen, shipping agents, sea captains, port officials, merchants, exporters, importers, wholesalers and finally by your rock shop manager in his mail order catalogue. Thus a substantial industry has grown up to meet the raw material demands of amateur lapidaries.

If you own a slab saw you can reduce the costs of your rough rock quite considerably by buying large, unslabbed pieces. One of the many benefits of joining your local lapidary club is that you will probably be able to use an even larger saw owned by the club to cut pieces too bulky for your equipment. You may also find that the club places large orders with rock importers on behalf of all members who benefit from a wholesale discount.

Those who prefer to enjoy the hobby in solitude need not despair. There are a number of ways in which you can track down excellent bargains when buying your stocks. The first is to buy from a dealer who handles good quality material. Rough rock is graded into first and second qualities and though second quality material often sounds like a bargain I advise you to buy only top grade material if you wish to avoid disappointing results.

When making your purchases by mail order it is a good plan to write to several suppliers and compare catalogues and price lists. The least expensive rock is unlikely to be the best, but there are quite wide price variations between dealers. Initially you should buy very small quantities from a number of dealers and compare the qualities of each consignment. Once you have found a dealer whose material is good you should stick to him. Such loyalty is beneficial to both parties; with regular customers the dealer can place larger orders with his suppliers and pass on to you some of the saving *and* some of the better quality material he obtains by doing this. In addition he will probably keep you informed about any small lots of special material he obtains which do not appear in his regular catalogue.

The range of material you can buy from mail order rock and mineral dealers is sufficiently wide to keep you cutting, grinding, and polishing for a lifetime. The list given below was compiled from the catalogues of a dozen British suppliers and it is by no means exhaustive. Only those rocks which appeared in at least three catalogues have been included and most dealers you approach will have an even wider selection. The descriptions of the fifty-odd specimens listed here were also taken from dealers' catalogues and they show that almost half of the rocks listed are available from at least two world sources—another reason why you should shop around before buying large quantities.

Selection of imported rough rock available from British dealers

Agate	Brazilian beans in red, blue and white; Australian nodules with green and red banding; South African stalactite; Brazilian nodules with cornelian; Botswana pink; Brazilian nodules with brown, blue and grey banding; Indian zebra with white and black banding; South African water-worn pebbles; Mexican tree with black and white markings; Indian tree with green and white markings; Mexican crazy lace; Moroccan banded white and grey; Indian black; African plume with yellow and green banding; South African blue lace; Indian moss.
Amber	East German pale yellow.
Amethyst	South African phantom with white and purple zig-zag banding; Mexican deep purple; Brazilian purple; Russian pale.
Amazonite	American pale turquoise; Canadian blue green; Norwegian pale blue; South African green with white and brown streaks.
Apatite	Mexican lemon.

Aquamarine	Mexican sea blue.
Aragonite	South African pale yellow with white banding.
Aventurine	Brazilian deep green; Indian blue.
Azurite	Congolese deep blue.
Bloodstone	Indian dark green well spotted with red; Indian mottled green, red and purple.
Cairngorm	Brazilian deep brown.
Chalcedony	Brazilian in two shades of green.
Chrysoprase	American bright green; Brazilian pale; Australian deep green nodules.
Citrine	Brazilian pale yellow.
Coral	Australian black; Mediterranean red.
Cornelian	Indian orange; South American red.
Cricolite	Mexican with grey, blue and green swirls.
Epidote	North American apple green.
Fossil wood	Canadian grey, brown, pink and red; American rainbow; Australian chinchilla.
Garnet	Indian almandine in deep burgundy; South African grossular in yellow; Tanzanian almandine in dark red; Rhodesian pyrope in crimson; Russian andradite in green.
Hickorite	Mexican with red, yellow, brown and purple bands, North American light tan and brick red.
Jasper	Indian red; Indian brown and green; South African deep red; Australian cream and orange.
Kunzite	North American pink.
Kyanite	North American deep aquamarine.
Labradorite	North American green, yellow, blue and red.
Lapis lazuli	Russian ultramarine; South African blue streaked with white; Afghanistan royal blue.
Malachite	Congolese deep green; Russian pale blue.
Marble	Argentinian onyx; Peruvian onyx; Connemara green and white; Iona in shades of green.
Moonstone	Indian white.
Nephrite jade	Canadian deep green.
Obsidian	American snowflake; American black sheen.
Olivine	North American deep green.
Opal	Italian white; Australian fire.
Opalite	Australian with yellow fern patterns.
Peridote	North American deep green.
Petalite	African pink.
Prehnite	Australian green and yellow.
Pyrite	Spanish golden.
Rhodochrosite	Argentinian pale satin pink.
Rhodonite	Argentinian deep red and black; Australian pink and black.

Ribbonstone	Australian with multi-coloured stripes.
Rose quartz	Brazilian cloudy pink; South African pink.
Rutilated quartz	Brazilian clear with golden needles.
Serpentine	Mexican lemon green; Norwegian deep green; Botswana lime green.
Sodalite	South African dark blue; Indian deep blue.
Spodumene	North American light green.
Sunstone	Norwegian pink and orange; Indian golden.
Tiger eye	South African yellow; South African red; South African blue.
Thulite	Norwegian pink and green.
Topaz	Brazilian yellow; Brazilian blue; Nigerian water-worn pebbles in light blue and brown.
Tourmaline	Brazilian dark green; Brazilian red; Brazilian green and blue.
Verdite	South African pale green
Wollestonite	Mexican pale yellow.
Zircon	Australian clear, orange and red.

Fittings

The range of fittings available to the home jewellery-maker compares very favourably with the range of rough rock. You should have no difficulty in locating your particular requirements if you shop around and study the catalogues of as many suppliers as possible. No two dealers offer identical fittings and you may find that you have to buy from several suppliers in order to obtain those you need. Placing several small orders in this way can be uneconomical; if possible you should order supplies to last several months at one time as this will mean that you qualify for the small discount usually given on bulk orders. You may find that your local lapidary club has bulk buying arrangements with several suppliers.

Fittings are made in a number of metals and finishes—stainless steel, Sterling silver, 9 carat gold, copper, silver- and gold-plated, and yellow or white metal. To avoid delays in dealing with your order you should always check that the catalogue from which you are ordering lists a particular fitting in the metal or finish you require, and make sure that you state your exact requirements on the order sheet. Most suppliers offer a return post service for mail order customers, but delays are inevitable if vital information is missing from the order.

Rings	Most have adjustable shanks (open or split), though the more expensive silver and gold varieties are available with solid shanks. Dealers selling rings with solid shanks usually supply a ring size card free of charge. Rings for cabochons will always have cabochon sizes clearly stated in the catalogue. Plain, lace and claw settings are made.
Ear fittings	Available as clips, screws and wires. Always sold in pairs. Some have a flat plate to take a calibrated cabochon.
Brooches	A wide variety available including fobs, bars, leaves, circles, rings and button-backs. Some have safety catches. Often available in copper and stainless steel.
Bracelets	Available with flat pads, cabochon fittings or as a simple chain to which charms can be attached.
Key rings	Available with mesh or snake chain. Some have safety catches.
Cuff links	Usually of the spring lever type. Available with flat pads or cabochon fittings. Always sold in pairs.
Tie fittings	These include crocodile clips, tie tacks and pins.
Chain	Available in many thicknesses and styles. It is more economical to buy chain by the yard and fit your own bolt rings which can be bought separately when making pendants and necklaces.
Cast mounts	These are sold in a wide range of designs including flower sprays, human figures, animals, crosses and geometric shapes. A range of Celtic designs is also available in an antique silver finish.
Fittings for polished slabs and specimens	Ballpoint pens with holders which are screwed or cemented to the slab; perpetual calendars; metal stands for polished specimens.

Many dealers also sell packaging material for finished jewellery. These include hinged-lid boxes for rings, ear fittings and cufflinks, plastic boxes for brooches and leather-covered boxes for bracelets and pendants.

10 Rock shops and lapidary clubs

The following list of shops, clubs and other addresses of interest to lapidary enthusiasts is as comprehensive as was possible at the time of writing. Rock shops are now opening in most towns in Britain and lapidary and rockhounding clubs are being formed almost as quickly whenever a dozen or so enthusiasts get together. An excellent source of information about new shops and clubs is *Gems*, the monthly British Lapidary Magazine (see address on p. 111) which you should read regularly for up-to-date information on lapidary activities in your area.

It would be difficult to give complete details about the range of machinery, gemstones and fittings offered by every rock shop on this list, but if you write to the addresses given and enclose a stamped addressed envelope you will receive comprehensive catalogues which will enable you to order your requirements by mail. Many of the shops are exciting places to visit, where you will be able to see the machines covered in this book and obtain friendly advice on any aspect of lapidary. To give you an idea of what you can expect on your first visit to a rock shop here are brief descriptions of four establishments I visited recently. A similar range of machines, rough rock, fittings, books and other accessories should be available at the shop of your choice.

Gemrocks Ltd. An 'Aladdin's Cave' situated in the centre of London. Enormous range of British, American and Australian machines including trim saws, slab saws, laps, grinders and combination units. A beautiful display of polished slabs always on show; wide range of rough rock, books and fittings.

M. L. Beach Ltd. A fascinating shop which, to quote from their literature, specializes in 'unusual leisure items for thinking people'. The company manufactures a range of lapidary equipment and 'Beach' tumblers and horizontal combination units have a world-wide reputation. Browsers are more than welcome and the variety of rough rock should keep you happy all day.

Kernowcraft Ltd. If you are on holiday in Cornwall this

shop is a perfect place to spend a rainy afternoon. British and Australian machines are stocked and there is a good selection of polished slabs, rough rock, books and fittings.
Ammonite Ltd. Worth a visit whenever you are in South Wales. A wide range of imported machines including large slab saws, trim saws, combination units, faceting machines and tumblers. Fittings, tools and books are also stocked. There is an interesting display of collector's specimens and Ammonite's well-known range of fossil replicates. School parties are especially welcome.

Other suppliers

C. Kilpatrick, 27 Colsea Road, Cove Bay, Aberdeen
Wee Gem Shop, 18 Cathcart Street, Ayr
Marbleshop, Portsoy, Banff
Love-Rocks, 56/58 North Street, Bedminster, Bristol
Natural Gems Ltd, Kingsbury Square, Aylesbury, Buckinghamshire
Worldwide Mineralogical Co., Great Shelford, Cambridge
Trilobite, 11 Chester Road, Northwich, Cheshire

Fig. 68 The interior of a lapidary shop

Gemtree, 8 Dingle Bank, Sandbach, Cheshire
Norgems, 4 Front Street, Sandbach, Cheshire
Towan Lapidary Centre, 33a Bank Street, Newquay, Cornwall
Key Minerals, Brienz, Hendra Road, St. Dennis, St. Austell, Cornwall
The Gem Rock and Lapidary Centre, 41 Fore Street, St. Just, Penzance, Cornwall
Kernowcraft Rocks & Gems Ltd, 44 Lemon Street, Truro, Cornwall
Tor Minerals, 2 The Orchard, Trevanson, Wadebridge, Cornwall
Lakeland Rock Shop, Packhorse Yard, Main Street, Keswick, Cumberland
Gemma, 494 Nottingham Road, Chaddesden, Derby
Cornerstones, 2 North Parade, Matlock Bath, Derby
Tideswell Dale Rockshop, Tideswell, Derby
Tudor Amethyst, 24 West Street, Exeter, Devon
Gallery Gems, 31 Fore Street, Kingsbridge, Devon
Rockhaven Gem Company, 125a Clephington Road, Dundee
H. & T. Gems, 31 Rosebury Road, Hartlepool, Co. Durham
Rockhound, Greenacres, Church Road, Black Notley, Braintree, Essex
D. M. Naylor, 1 The Knoll, Corwn Hill, Rayleigh, Essex
Fife Stone Craft, 3 Edison House, Fullerton Road, Glenrothes, Fife
Little Rocks, 36 Oakwood Avenue, Cardiff, Glamorgan
Ammonite Ltd, Llandow, Cowbridge, Glamorgan, CF7 7PB.
Harrisons, 174 Woodlands Road, Glasgow, C.3
Scotrocks Partners, 48 Park Road, Glasgow, C.4
Rocks and Minerals, 4 Moorcourt Drive, Cheltenham, Gloucester
R. Lane, 'The Haven', Danes Road, Awbridge, Romsey, Hampshire
Jacinth Gems, 10 Highfield Crescent, Southampton, Hampshire
Solent Lapidary, 145 Highland Road, Southsea, Hampshire
International Crafts, P.O. Box 73, Hemel Hempstead, Hertfordshire
Keystones, 1 Local Board Road, Watford, Hertfordshire
Quercus Gems, Lindisfarne House, Rucklers Lane, King's Langley, Hertfordshire
J. Simble & Sons, 76 Queens Road, Watford, Hertfordshire
Gemset of Broadstairs Ltd, 31 Albion Street, Broadstairs, Kent
Opie Gems, 13 Gilbert Close, Hempstead, Gillingham, Kent
The Craft Centre, Chart Sutton, Maidstone, Kent
Tumble Kraft, 10 High Street, Rochester, Kent

G. & B. Butler, 18b The Pantiles, Tunbridge Wells, Kent
Galloway Gems, 26 Oakwell Road, Castle Douglas, Kircudbrightshire
The Jam Pot, Slaidburn, Clitheroe, Lancashire
Crystal Tips Lapidary, 25a Linaker Street, Southport, Lancashire
Rose Gems, 637 Lord Street, Southport, Lancashire
Aintree Rockshop, 11a Lynwood Road, Liverpool L93 AE
W. A. Bolton, 19 Lynwood Road, Liverpool, 9
Craftorama, 14 Endell Street, London, W.C.2
Gemlines, 10 Victoria Crescent, London, S.W.19
Gemrocks Limited, 7 Brunswick Shopping Centre, London, W.C.1
Hirsch Jacobson, 91 Marylebone High Street, London, W.1
Gemrocks Ltd, 20/30 Holborn, London, E.C.1
Howard Minerals Ltd, 27 Heddon Street, London, W.1.
Mineral Imports, 72 Netheravon Road, London, W4 2NB
Pebblegem, 88a Wallis Road, London, E9 5LN
Whithear Lapidary Co, 35 Ballards Lane, London, N.3.
Pebblegem, 71 St. Marks Road, Bush Hill Park, Enfield, Middlesex
M. L. Beach (Products) Ltd, 41 Church Street, Twickenham, Middlesex
Timgems, The Old Shop, Ludham, Great Yarmouth, Norfolk
J. L. Newbigin, 13 Narrowgate, Alnwick, Northumberland
The Rockhound Shop, Newbiggin, Northumberland
C. & N. Mineral Supplies, Adelphi Chambers, Shakespeare Street, Newcastle-on-Tyne, Northumberland
Rough & Tumble Ltd, 3 Tyne Street, North Shields, Northumberland.
Portbeag Pebblecraft, Albany Street, Oban
PMR Lapidary Equipment, Pitlochry, Perthshire
Stones & Settings, 54 Main Street, Prestwick
Opie Gems, 57 East Street, Ilminster, Somerset
Marcross Gems, 13 Market Place, Shepton Mallet, Somerset
Caverswall Minerals, The Dams, Caverswall, Stoke-on-Trent, Staffordshire
Gemlode, 35 Bolton Road, Chessington, Surrey
Westcott Antiques, 2 The Green, Westcott, Dorking, Surrey
Baines Orr Ltd, 1–5 Garlands Road, Redhill, Surrey
Fidra Stone Shop, 47 Meeting House Lane, Brighton, Sussex
Geobright, 28 Queens Road, Brighton, Sussex
The Stone Corner, 21 High Street, Hastings, Sussex
Hillside Gems, Wylde Green, Sutton Coldfield, Warwickshire

Merritt, Eastleigh Road, Devizes, Wiltshire
Avon Gems, Strathavon, Boon Street, Eckington, Pershore, Worcestershire
A. & D. Hughes Ltd, Popes Lane, Oldbury, Warley, Worcestershire
Mineralcraft (North), 192 Barnsley Road, Cudworth, Barnsley, Yorkshire
Gemstones, 44 Walmsley Street, Hull, Yorkshire
Lyonesse Gems, 110 Emily Street, Keighley, Yorkshire
A. Massie & Son, 158 Burgoyne Road, Sheffield, 6, Yorkshire
Glenjoy Lapidary Supplies, 19–20 Sun Lane, Wakefield, Yorkshire

Magazines

Gems, 29 Ludgate Hill, London, E.C.4
Rockhound, 24–9 Trellick Tower, 5 Golborne Road, London, W.10
Lapidary Journal, P.O. Box 80937–E, San Diego, California, 92138, U.S.A.

Clubs

Bath Lapidary Society, 10 Pulteney Street, Bath
Mid-Cornwall Rocks and Minerals Club, 91 Queens Crescent, Bodmin, Cornwall
Bristol Lapidary Society, 10 Grove Park, Redland, Bristol
Cambridge Lapidary Club, 93 Queen Edith's Way, Cambridge
Cardiff Lapidary Society, 36 Oakwood Avenue, Cardiff
North West Lapidary Society, 79 Dean Drive, Wilmslow, Cheshire
Whitehaven Lapidary Society, 110 Tomlin Avenue, Mirehouse, Whitehaven, *Cumberland*
Peak District Rock & Mineral Society, Youth Centre, Tideswell, Derby
Plymouth Mineral and Mining Club, 36 Ponsonby Road, Milehouse, Plymouth, Devon
Dorset Mineral Club, 70 Manor Road, Dorchester, Dorset
Irish Lapidary Society, Grafton Court, Grafton Street, Dublin, 2
Stanley Rockhound Club, 24 Cecil Street, East Stanley, Co. Durham
Scottish Mineral & Lapidary Club, 22b St. Giles Street, Edinburgh, 1
Essex Rock & Mineral Society, 176 Wanstead Park Road, Ilford, Essex
Exeter Gem and Mineral Society, High Barn, Kenton, Exeter
West of Scotland Mineral & Lapidary Society, 82 Dumbreck Road, Glasgow, S.1.

Cheltenham Mineral Society, 2 Westcote Road, Tuffley, Gloucester
New Forest Lapidary Society, 30 Denham Drive, Highcliff, Christchurch, Hampshire
Wessex Lapidary Society, 1 Avenue Road, Winchester, Hampshire
Thanet Mineral Society, 5 Maisons Rise, Broadstairs, Kent
Warrington Lapidary Society, 28 Thelwall New Road, Thelwall, Warrington, Lancashire
Leeds Lapidary Society, 2 Earslwood Avenue, Leeds LS8 2BR
Amateur Geological Society, Hampstead Garden Suburb Institute, Central Square, London, N.W.11
Dartford Lapidary Society, 45a Elmdene Road, London, S.E.18
Pentland Lapidary Society, 12 Kirkgate, Currie, Midlothian
Northumbrian Lapidary Teachers Association, 17 Westhill, Kirkhall, Morpeth, Northumberland
Norfolk Lapidary Society, St. Mary's, New Buckenham, Norwich
Borders Lapidary Club, 47 Albert Place, Galashiels, Selkirkshire
Southampton Lapidary Society, 52 Kinross Road, Totton, Southampton
North Surrey Lapidary Society, 28 The Causeway, Carshalton, Surrey
West Surrey Lapidary Society, 10 Whitemore Green, Hale, Farnham, Surrey
Sutherland Rockhounds, Lonemore, Dornoch, Sutherland
Golspie Lapidary Club, The Wee Shop, Golspie, Sutherland
Teesside Lapidary Society, 65 Staindrop Drive, Acklam, Middlesbrough, Teesside
West Midlands Lapidary Society, 148 Foleshill Road, Coventry, Warwickshire
Danum Lapidary Society, 39 St. Augustines Road, Bessacarr, Doncaster, Yorkshire
Harrogate Lapidary Society, 71 Wetherby Road, Harrogate, Yorkshire
Huddersfield Mineralogical Society, 25 Branch Street, Paddock, Huddersfield, Yorkshire
Kingston Lapidary Society, 219 Summergangs Road, Hull, Yorkshire
Sheffield Amateur Geological Society, 5 Hutcliffe Wood Road, Sheffield, Yorkshire

In the following pages I have given some likely gemstone haunts in the British Isles. No rockhounding maps have been included for those areas (eastern and south-eastern England) which are not rich in precious or semi-precious stones.

Maps showing the location of rocks and gems in Britain

SOMERSET

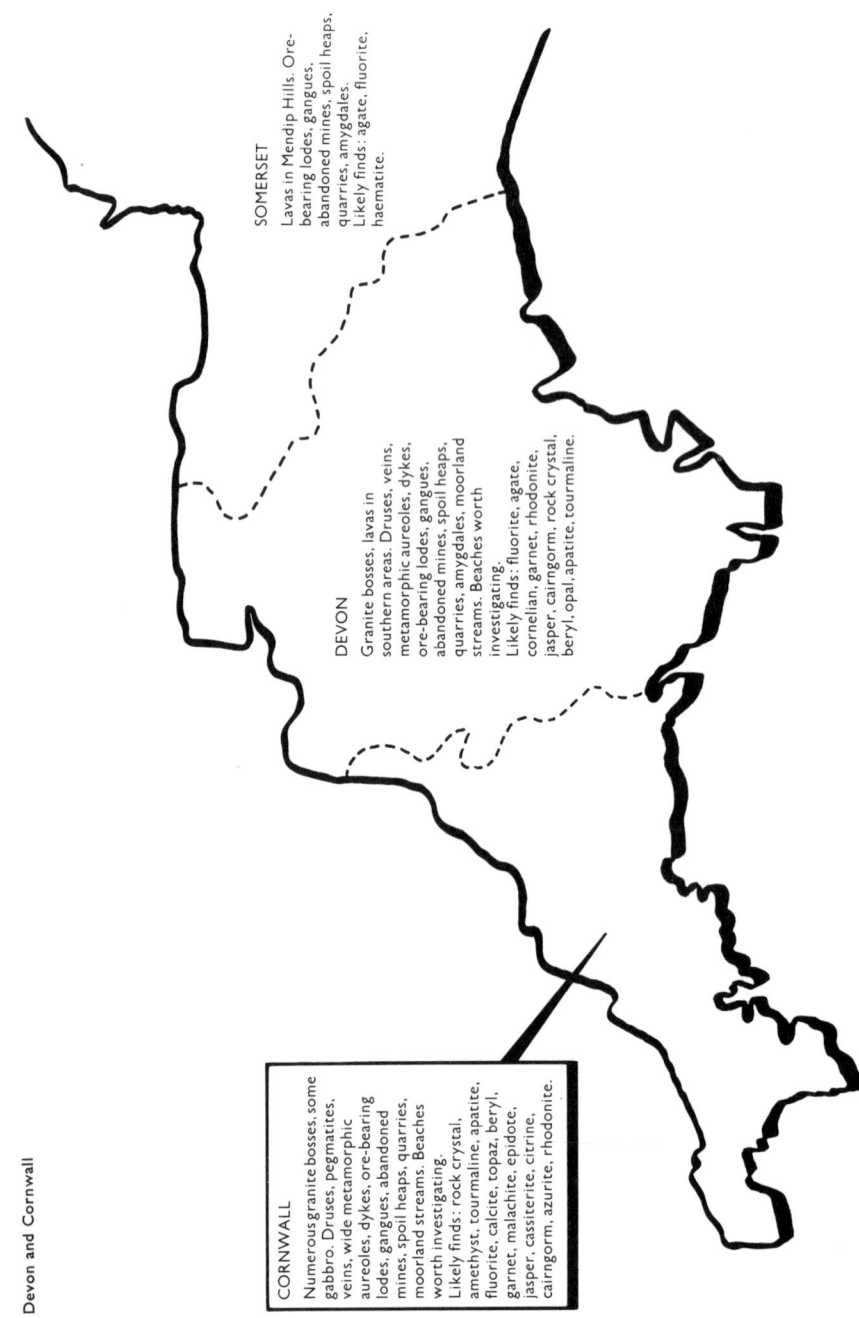

Lavas in Mendip Hills. Ore-bearing lodes, gangues, abandoned mines, spoil heaps, quarries, amygdales.
Likely finds: agate, fluorite, haematite.

DEVON

Granite bosses, lavas in southern areas. Druses, veins, metamorphic aureoles, dykes, ore-bearing lodes, gangues, abandoned mines, spoil heaps, quarries, amygdales, moorland streams. Beaches worth investigating.
Likely finds: fluorite, agate, cornelian, garnet, rhodonite, jasper, cairngorm, rock crystal, beryl, opal, apatite, tourmaline.

CORNWALL

Numerous granite bosses, some gabbro. Druses, pegmatites, veins, wide metamorphic aureoles, dykes, ore-bearing lodes, gangues, abandoned mines, spoil heaps, quarries, moorland streams. Beaches worth investigating.
Likely finds: rock crystal, amethyst, tourmaline, apatite, fluorite, calcite, topaz, beryl, garnet, malachite, epidote, jasper, cassiterite, citrine, cairngorm, azurite, rhodonite.

Devon and Cornwall

Wales

ANGLESEY
Lavas.
Likely finds: jasper, chalcedony, agate.
Beaches worth investigating.

DENBIGHSHIRE
Lavas, intrusive formations. Veins, druses, dykes, amygdales, ore-bearing lodes, abandoned mines, spoil heaps, quarries.
Likely finds: malachite, chalcedony, agate, fluorite, rock crystal.

FLINTSHIRE
Intrusive formations.
Likely finds: fluorite, malachite.

CAERNARVONSHIRE
Syenite, granite. Veins, dykes, ore-bearing lodes, gangues, abandoned mines, spoil heaps, mountain streams.
Likely finds: amethyst, rock crystal, malachite, azurite.

MERIONETHSHIRE
Intrusive formations, lavas. Veins, druses, dykes, amygdales, ore-bearing lodes, gangues, abandoned mines, spoil heaps, mountain streams.

MONTGOMERYSHIRE
Lavas, intrusive formations. Dykes, veins, druses, ore-bearing lodes, gangues, abandoned mines, spoil heaps, amygdales.
Likely finds: malachite, fluorite, agate.

CARDIGANSHIRE
Lavas. Amygdales, moorland streams. Beaches worth investigating.
Likely finds: agate, jasper.

RADNORSHIRE
Lavas. Amygdales, quarries.
Likely finds: agate.

PEMBROKESHIRE
Diorite, lavas, gabbro. Dykes, druses, veins, amygdales, moorland streams. Beaches worth investigating.
Likely finds: sphene, apatite, jasper, agate, haematite.

CARMARTHENSHIRE
Intrusive formations. Veins, druses, ore-bearing lodes, gangues, abandoned mines, spoil heaps, moorland streams.
Likely finds: cairngorm, amethyst, rock crystal, haematite.

Northern England

CUMBERLAND
Lavas, granite, andesite. Metamorphic aureoles, veins, druses, dykes, ore-bearing lodes, gangues, abandoned mines, spoil heaps, mountain streams, quarries, amygdales. Beaches worth investigating.
Likely finds: agate, cornelian, jasper, chalcedony, cairngorm, rock crystal, tourmaline, andalusite, malachite, apatite, fluorite, haematite, azurite, calcite.

NORTHUMBERLAND
Granite, lavas, dolerite. Dykes, sills, veins, druses, amygdales, ore-bearing lodes, abandoned mines, spoil heaps, quarries, moorland streams.
Likely finds: rock crystal, fluorite, amethyst, agate.

DURHAM
Dolerite. Sills, metamorphic aureoles, dykes, veins, ore-bearing lodes, abandoned mines, spoil heaps, quarries, moorland streams.
Likely finds: fluorite, rock crystal, andalusite, garnet, malachite.

WESTMORLAND
Granite, porphyry, pegmatites. Veins, druses, metamorphic aureoles, ore-bearing lodes, gangues, abandoned mines, spoil heaps, mountain streams, quarries.
Likely finds: garnet, cairngorm, fluorite.

YORKSHIRE
Intrusive formations in north. Veins, druses, ore-bearing lodes, gangues, abandoned mines, spoil heaps, moorland streams.
Likely finds: fluorite, calcite.

DERBYSHIRE
Intrusive formations, lavas, basalt. Druses, veins, ore-bearing lodes, abandoned mines, spoil heaps, quarries, moorland streams, amygdales.
Likely finds: fluorite, rock crystal, amethyst, cairngorm, chalcedony, agate, olivine, malachite, haematite, opal, labradorite.

LANCASHIRE
Gabbro and granite in north. Veins, druses, ore-bearing lodes, gangues, abandoned mines, spoil heaps, quarries, moorland streams.
Likely finds: rock crystal, fluorite, haematite.

CHESHIRE
Intrusive formations. Veins, druses, ore-bearing lodes, gangues, abandoned mines, spoil heaps.
Likely finds: malachite, azurite.

SHROPSHIRE
Intrusive formations. Veins, druses, ore-bearing lodes, gangues, abandoned mines, spoil heaps, quarries.
Likely finds: rock crystal, fluorite, malachite.

STAFFORDSHIRE
Basalt. Dykes, veins, druses.
Likely finds: olivine, natrolite.

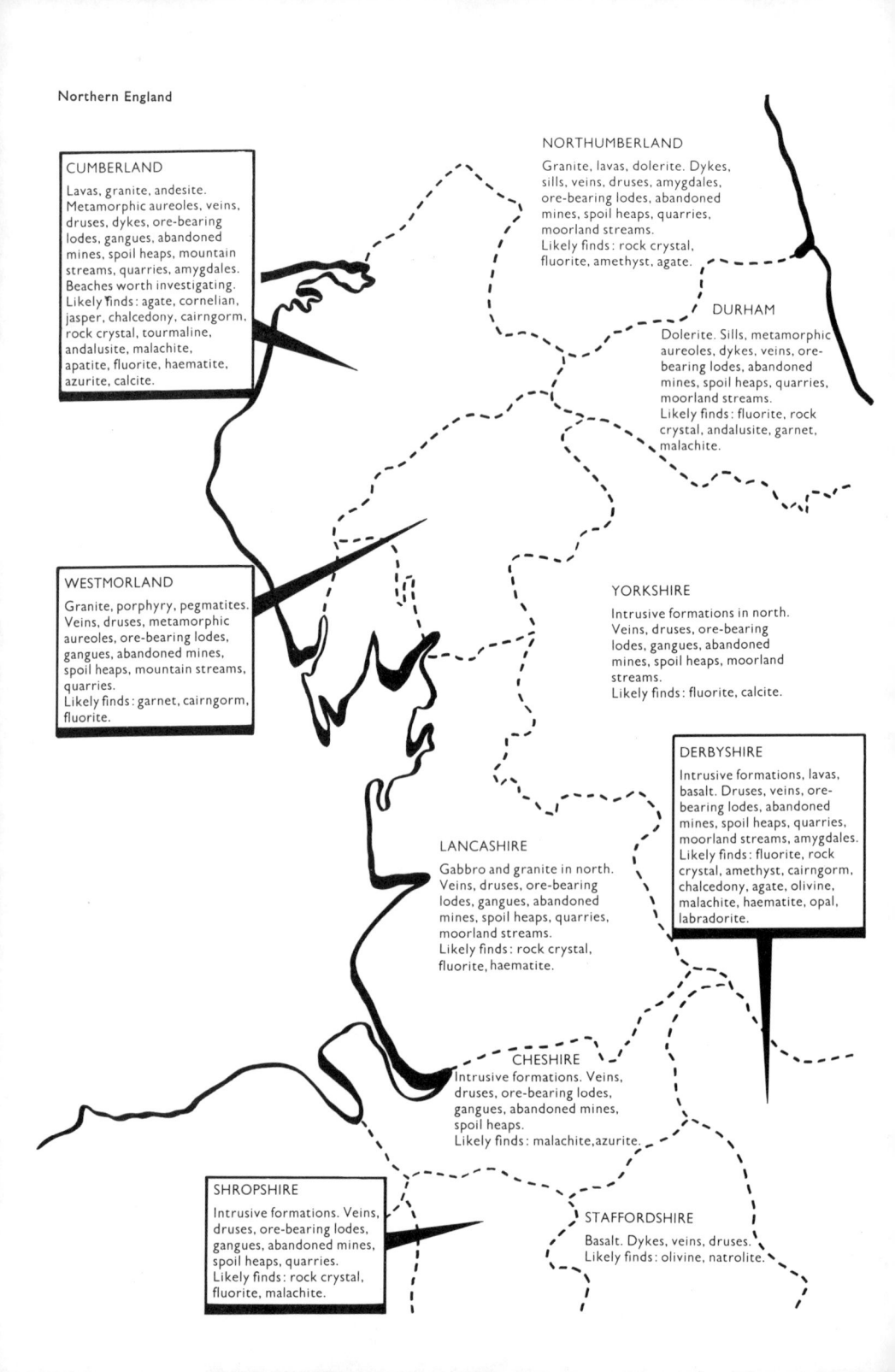

Southern Scotland

RENFREWSHIRE
Basalt, lavas, porphyry. Veins, druses, amygdales, quarries.
Likely finds: natroline, prehnite, agate, cairngorm, amethyst, fluorite.

EAST LOTHIAN
Lavas, volcanic necks. Amygdales.
Likely finds: agate.

WEST LOTHIAN
Volcanic necks.
Likely finds: olivine.

BERWICKSHIRE
Lavas. Amygdales.
Likely finds: agate.

ROXBURGHSHIRE
Lavas. Amygdales.
Likely finds: agate.

MIDLOTHIAN
Lavas, volcanic necks. Amygdales.
Likely finds: agate.

PEEBLESSHIRE
Lavas. Amygdales.
Likely finds: agate.

SELKIRKSHIRE
Lavas. Amygdales.
Likely finds: agate.

LANARKSHIRE
Intrusive formations, lavas. Veins, druses, amygdales, ore-bearing lodes, abandoned mines, spoil heaps.
Likely finds: fluorite, malachite, azurite, agate, rhodonite.

DUMFRIESSHIRE
Lavas. Amygdales.
Likely finds: jasper, agate.

AYRSHIRE
Granite, lavas. Veins, druses, dykes, amygdales.
Likely finds: prehnite, agate, fluorite, opal.

KIRKCUDBRIGHTSHIRE
Granite, lavas. Veins, druses, amygdales.
Likely finds: tourmaline, amethyst, malachite, rock crystal.

ARRAN
Granite, lavas, gabbro. Dykes, veins, druses, amygdales.
Likely finds: agate, cornelian, jasper, cairngorm, beryl, garnet.

Central Scotland

SKYE
Gabbro, lavas.
Likely finds: beryl, cairngorm, agate, prehnite.

BANFFSHIRE
Granite. Veins, druses, dykes, mountain streams.
Likely finds: cairngorm, tourmaline, garnet.

ABERDEENSHIRE
Granite. Veins, druses, dykes, quarries, mountain streams.
Likely finds: cairngorm, amethyst, beryl, topaz.

KINCARDINESHIRE
Granite, lavas. Veins, druses, dykes, amygdales.
Likely finds: amethyst, tourmaline, agate.

FIFESHIRE
Granite, lavas, volcanic necks. Veins, druses, dykes, amygdales.
Likely finds: garnets, zircon, amethyst, fluorite.

ANGUS
Granite, lavas. Veins, druses, dykes, quarries, amygdales.
Likely finds: tourmaline, amethyst, agate.
Beaches worth investigating.

INVERNESS-SHIRE
Granite. Veins, druses, dykes.
Likely finds: fluorite, cairngorm, sphene, beryl.

PERTHSHIRE
Granite, lavas. Veins, druses, dykes, amygdales, quarries, mountain streams.
Likely finds: cairngorm, tourmaline, fluorite, topaz, beryl, garnets, agate, chalcedony, jasper, opal.

STIRLINGSHIRE
Basalt, lavas.
Likely finds: amethyst, natroline, agate.

ARGYLLSHIRE
Granite, lavas. Veins, druses, dykes, amygdales. Beaches worth investigating.
Likely finds: agate, chalcedony, topaz, amethyst, opal, garnets, zircon.

DUNBARTONSHIRE
Basalt.
Likely finds: fluorite, prehnite, natroline.

MULL
Basalt, lavas.
Likely finds: agate, tourmaline, epidote.

Northern Scotland

CAITHNESS
Granite.
Likely finds: cairngorm.

MORAYSHIRE
Granite. Quarries.
Likely finds: fluorite, sphene.

SUTHERLAND
Granite. Veins, druses, dykes, metamorphic aureoles.
Likely finds: olivine, fluorite, garnets, beryl, spinel, tourmaline, cairngorm, zircon.

NAIRNSHIRE
Granite.
Likely finds: cairngorm.

ROSS AND CROMARTY
Granite. Veins, druses, dykes, quarries.
Likely finds: tourmaline, garnets, zircon, fluorite, rock crystal, apatite.

LEWIS
Granite.
Likely finds: olivine, zircon, garnets, topaz, beryl.

Northern Ireland

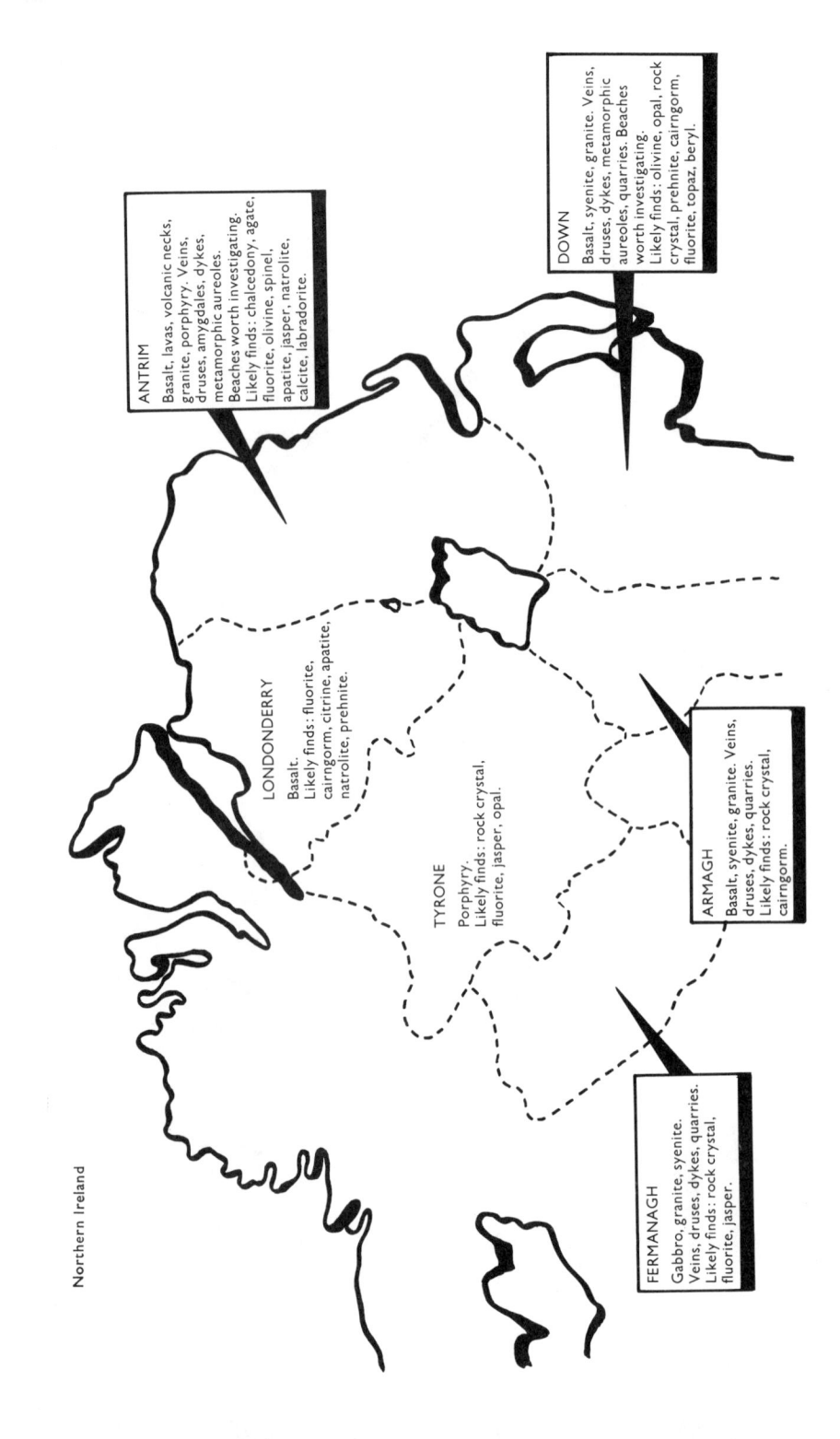

ANTRIM
Basalt, lavas, volcanic necks, granite, porphyry. Veins, druses, amygdales, dykes, metamorphic aureoles. Beaches worth investigating.
Likely finds: chalcedony, agate, fluorite, olivine, spinel, apatite, jasper, natrolite, calcite, labradorite.

DOWN
Basalt, syenite, granite. Veins, druses, dykes, metamorphic aureoles, quarries. Beaches worth investigating.
Likely finds: olivine, opal, rock crystal, prehnite, cairngorm, fluorite, topaz, beryl.

LONDONDERRY
Basalt.
Likely finds: fluorite, cairngorm, citrine, apatite, natrolite, prehnite.

TYRONE
Porphyry.
Likely finds: rock crystal, fluorite, jasper, opal.

ARMAGH
Basalt, syenite, granite. Veins, druses, dykes, quarries.
Likely finds: rock crystal, cairngorm.

FERMANAGH
Gabbro, granite, syenite. Veins, druses, dykes, quarries.
Likely finds: rock crystal, fluorite, jasper.

Index

The figures in bold refer to the colour illustrations between pp. 60 and 61 and 76 and 77.

agate 98, 103, **Pl. 3, 4**
amazonite 103, **Pl. 3**
amber 103
amethyst 98, 103, **Pl. 1, 2, 4**
amygdales 96
andalusite 98
andesite 90
apatite 99, 103
aquamarine 104
aragonite 104
aureole 95, 96
aventurine 104, **Pl. 3**
azurite 99, 104

basalt 88, 89
beryl 99
bloodstone 104, **Pl. 3**
bracelets 106, **Pl. 7**
brooches 106, **Pl. 7**
buying stones 102–5

cabochons 57, **Pl. 6, 7**
 from pebbles 58
 from slabs 66
 grinding 69
 in jewellery 70, **Pl. 7**
 machines 57–8
 polishing 69
 sanding 69
cabochon units 69
cairngorm 99, 104, **Pl. 1**
calcite 99
cassiterite 99
cast-iron laps 34
cast mounts 106
chain 106
chalcedony 99, 104
chrysoprase 104, **Pl. 3**
citrine 99, 104, **Pl. 1**
clubs 111
contact metamorphism 95
coolants 16
coral 104
cornelian 99, 104
cricolite 104
cuff links 106
cutting tables 17

diamond blades 11
 drills 71–3
 sharpening 24
diorite 88, 89
dolerite 89, 90
dopping stones 61–5
 units 62
drilling stones 71
druses 93, 96
dykes 90

ear fittings 106, **Pl. 7**
epidote 99, 104

faceting 76, **Pl. 5**
fittings 105–6
fluorite 100
fossil wood 104, **Pl. 4**

gabbro 88, 89
gangue minerals 94, 96
garnet, 100, 104
gem-collecting 82–7
glass-bottomed buckets 96
granite 87, 89
 bosses 90
 outcrops 90
grinding machines 46–52
 wheel maintenance 52
guide fences 32

haematite 100
hickorite 104
horizontal combination units 58–9

igneous rocks 87

jasper 100, 104, **Pl. 1**

key rings 106
Knoop Scale 11
kunzite 104
kyanite 104

labradorite 100, 104, **Pl. 3**
lapidary clubs 107, 110
lapis lazuli 104, **Pl. 3**
lava flows 92
lodes 94, 96

magazines 110
malachite 100, 104
maps 112–19
marble 104
Moh's Scale 11
moonstone 104, **Pl. 3**
motors 15
museums 97

natrolite 100
nephrite jade 104

olivine 100, 104
opal 100, 104
opalite 104

pebble cutting 20
pegmatites 88, 94, 96
peridote 104
petalite 104

porphyry 80, 89
preforms 46
 grinding 53
 in jewellery 56
 polishing 55
prehnite 101, 104
pulleys 14
pyrite 104

quarries 96

railway cuttings 96
rhodonite 101, 104, **Pl. 2**
ribbonstone 105
rings 106, **Pl. 7**
roadworks 96
rock hammers 85
rockhounding,
 equipment 84
 safety rules 83
rock shops 97, 107, 108
rose quartz 105, **Pl. 3**
rutilated quartz 105

serpentine 105
silicon carbide 37
sills 91
slab
 buying 36
 cutting 37
 grinding 38
 polishing 42, **Pl. 4**
 saws 26
sludge cleaning 33
sodalite 105, **Pl. 3**
sphene 101
spinel 101
splash guards 17
spodumine 101
spoil heaps 94, 96
streams 96
sunstone 105
suppliers 107–111
syenite 88, 89

tanks 16
templates 49
thulite 105
tie fittings 106
tiger eye 105, **Pl. 2**
topaz 101, 105
tourmaline 101, 105
trim saws 10

veins 94, 96
verdite 105
vices 27
volcanic necks 91

zircon 101, 105

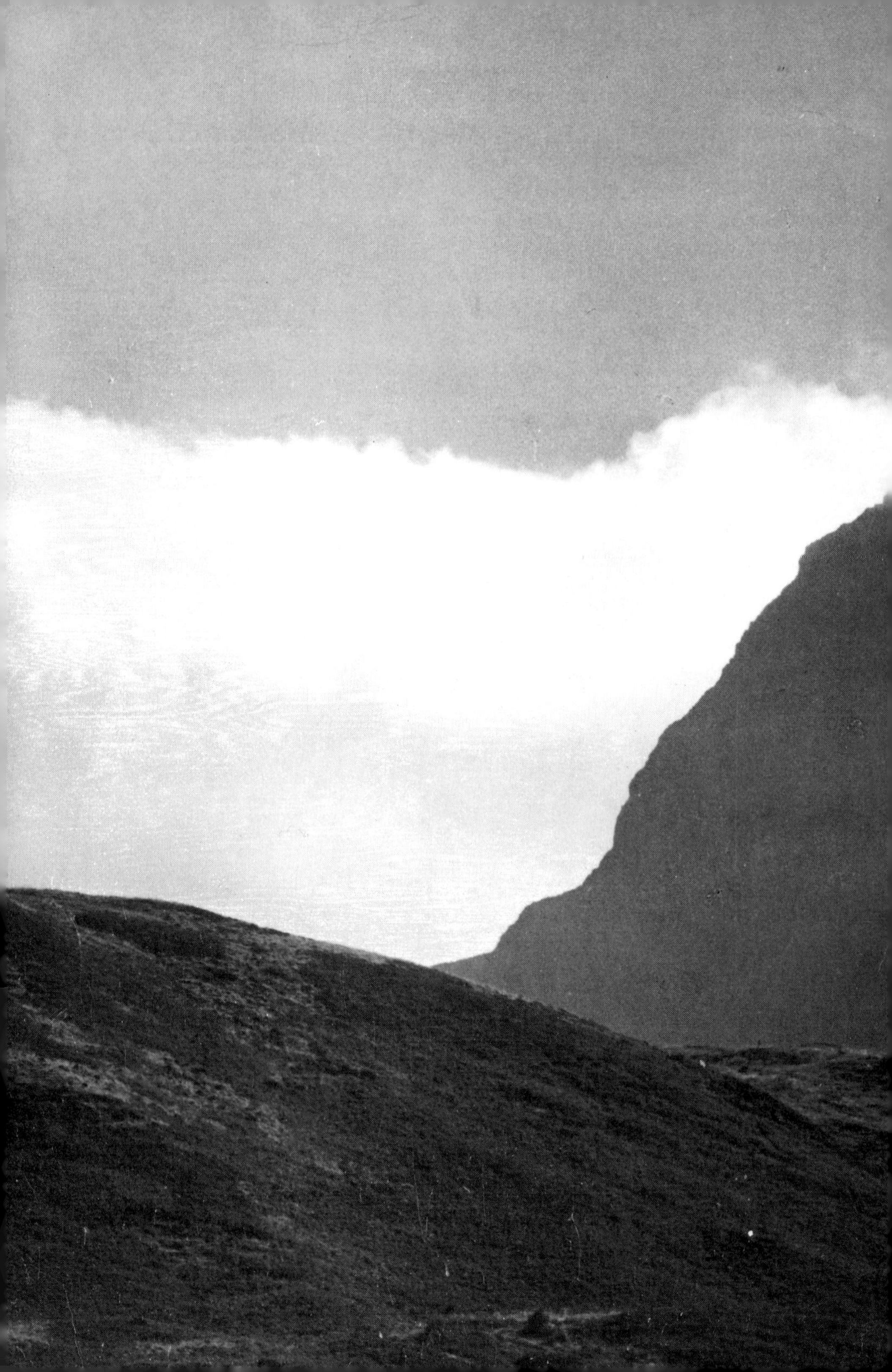